NIGHT OF THE LITANI

Oasis Center Library
317 East Call Street
Tallahassee, Florida 32301

NIGHT OF THE LITANI

Andrea Brunais

MANCORP PUBLISHING, INC.
Tampa, Florida

Copyright © 1996 by Andrea Brunais

All rights reserved.

No part of this book may be reproduced in any form or by any means without permission in writing from the publisher.

Published by Mancorp Publishing, Inc.
P.O. Box 21492, Tampa, Florida 33622

Library of Congress Cataloging-in-Publication Data

Brunais, Andrea, 1954 -
   Night of the Litani / by Andrea Brunais.
      p. cm.
   ISBN 0-931541-55-7
PS3552.R7994NS 1994
813' .54-dc20   94-13762
                                                    CIP

Manufactured in the United States of America

ISBN 0-931541-55-7

CONTENTS

1. Ann Arbor 1
2. Baraka 15
3. Beirut 41
4. 'Psychosis of Fear' 79
5. The Embassy 101
6. Wind and River 125
7. Refugees 153
8. Unexploded Territory 245
9. Holding 189
10. Garden of the Mad 205
    Epilogue 223

1

Ann Arbor

The apartment had the look of 24 hours to leave town. Candles, hurriedly lit, threw shadows on the now bare walls. Noise echoed in half-empty rooms. Camellia could smell sandalwood, the scent of Khalil.

She stood taking mental notes with the appraising eyes of a news reporter, which she was, as campus correspondent at the University of Michigan for the Ann Arbor News these last five years since graduation.

She was listening to snow riding the wind to stipple the windows, with Khalil banging things in the kitchen. Tonight he had prepared a cinnamon-pepper-scented stew, a rare thing for him to do. Now something even rarer, he was cleaning up the kitchen.

It was time to go but she was reluctant as lovers always are when they sense things are winding down. She and her Arabian knight, now a Ph.D., had been lovers for three years. He had told her nothing but she knew he was going back to Lebanon soon. And alone.

Khalil came in carrying a newly opened bottle of Chateau de Beaulieu and two wine glasses. He poured as she gestured no.

"I can't stay," she said. "My mother claims, even now, that she can't sleep until I'm inside, in bed, with the door bolted."

"She fears for your life, alone with an Arab — with me."

"Don't be silly. Sometimes I think Angela likes you better than me." She shivered as she watched him pour. Just a thing that simple — his fluid grace — made him a pleasure to watch. But nothing masked the emptiness of these rooms. The wine was tart and dry. She looked at the label on the bottle — "1970," she said. "Do you always know the good years?"

"It was the year I came to this country. ... But you are cold. Come, sit next to me. You say it warms you to hear my heart."

"I would never say anything so hopelessly romantic." She pouted. But she put her head against his chest, finding the rhythm of his heart. Reassuring it was and slow, like Pachelbel's Canon. She sighed, thinking this would probably be their last night together. Tomorrow she must convince herself she had never really loved him. It was mere fascination, she almost believed. Who could fail to be thrilled by beauty in such a man: stunning black-on-white starkness of hair and skin, lithe sculpture of fine bones?

"Did you not know...?"

(Ah, but how to forget the syntax, the result of English, endearingly stilted, superimposed on Arabic?)

"Men first see beauty," he continued. "Women are different. They hear it. The sound of a man's voice stimulates them to love."

"You, sir, sound like an expert; have you been reading *Psychology Today*?"

He stroked her dress of shirred coral silk, letting his fingers linger on her skin.

She moved away. "Talk to me," she said. "Don't deprive me of that husky voice."

"What should I say?"

"Tell me a story — about 'Leila and the Wolf.'"

He shrugged, waiting.

"Admit it," she said, finally. "You are leaving": marvelous understatement given the condition of the apartment.

For answer he kissed her, long and hard.

"Why can't you admit you're going back to Lebanon?" she demanded.

"I never admit to anything."

"God, don't begin with Lawrence of Arabia."

"Not Lawrence, that's Mary Poppins."

"That's what I get," she laughed, "for exposing you to Disney."

He kissed her again. He knew she would respond.

Damn you, she said to herself, digging her nails into his rumpled linen shirt. You're hungry for me. You *are* leaving.

****

They made love to the scent of incense and the strains of Scheherazade, the wily one postponing death. And like Scheherazade, she wished the moment could last forever. If it were too staged, too hokey, too sweet, it was right for the moment.

She rode the rhythms of the music as he rode her pliant body. Hands and mouth and music and his hardness all swirling in a concert of ecstacy. Then he convulsed, shuddered a last time and lay quite still. Soon, she knew, he would be fast asleep. He lay graceful in repose, limbs akimbo, body all lean and fluid. His musky smell overpowered the incense.

She listened to the last of the music, thinking, he's left me already. She watched the candles huddling in hot wax and the last of the wine catching sediment in the bottom of the glasses.

A garish light bulb shone on this room that only yesterday had housed an intricate water pipe, statues of Jerusalem olive wood, copper trays and embroidered Damascene.

The music ended ... a shiver of violins, a joyous melding of strings and wind, the solitary trill of the flute ... The needle scratched and lifted. The stereo shut itself off with an almost apologetic click.

****

As she was tiptoeing out the door, Khalil's voice stopped her. "Midnight already?"

"You sound surprised," she said. She buttoned her coat, refusing to bridge the distance between them.

"Camellia," he said in his most endearing tone, "It's already February."

"You see? I'm *very* late."

"My visa expires soon."

"So go, then, go back to Lebanon."

"Sah! You don't even care. Camellia —"

"Don't say it. I'm not the first American woman to fall for a ... a ... You've got your Ph.D. Now you are Dr. Majdi and you are going home. Sayonara!"

"No, You mean *Al-Wida'a*."

She didn't respond.

"Why do you think I am still in this Midwestern town when I could be in Beirut?"

"How should I know?" she answered in tears.

"Everything I want is in Lebanon — except you."

"Spare me the declarations, the Kahlil Gibran, the 'love that is cleansed by tears.' Just *go*."

"Let me finish, please. I am going to the mountains. To Lebanon ... to my soul." His face muscles tightened. "Five years," he said softly to himself. "I was careful. I avoided entanglements..."

Suddenly, he looked vulnerable and she moved to him, leaning her head on his shoulder.

He spoke softly but still with decision.

"Come with me," he begged her. "It will seem exotic, maddening but Lebanon is ... all there is to this world."

"You want me to drop everything, my mother and sister, my job and just go to Lebanon?"

"Or stay and wither, missing me."

"This is 1975, remember? Women don't trail after men. But, your invitation sounds like an afterthought. The hell of it is, I'll probably go."

"Love," he said, "is like wine. It cannot be rushed to ripeness."

"And you lie like some people tell the truth."

"That may be, but that is one of the things you love about me." He kissed her goodbye, and she ran her hands under the blanket, stroking his thigh. "You've never said you love me."

"It had not occurred to me," he said.

"To say it? Or to love me? Do you?" She pinched him hard. "Macho Arab."

"You are wrong." He sighed. "We are a race of romantics. That you will learn."

"And polygamy, do romantics believe in that, too?"

"I am not a Moslem. And even they no longer have harems."

"My mother will be relieved to hear *that*!"

"Leave Angela to me. I will tell her stories ... the 'Thousand and One Nights.'"

"Don't make it too alluring. She'll follow us to Beirut. What about *your* mother? Surely she'd rather see you free to commit yourself to someone of your religion and heritage..."

"A virgin?"

"Is that the criteria?"

"One of many. Please hand me my robe."

"Stay in bed. It's still snowing."

She opened the door to go. Snow dusted through the opening.

"Well, do you love me?" she repeated.

From under the blanket came his indolent reply: "Ask me when we get to Beirut."

As a correspondent for The News these last few years Camellia was a bridge between town and gown in Ann Arbor. Academe was the city's industry and the university in turn depended on Ann Arbor for its day-to-day existence.

Her news beat covered the chancellor's office and the offices of the deans of the various schools. She also wrote any number of feature stories about the professors and their students and the scientific and cultural activities that are the mosaic of a great school of higher learning. Critics often referred to the giant schools in the Big 10 as factories and there was much truth in the charge, but Camellia loved the atmosphere and the job.

Among the foreign students on campus were a disproportionate number of Iranians and Saudis, something she recognized but never wondered about. They were moneyed graduate students mostly and like the wealthy anywhere they continued to attract more and more of their own to the campus.

Now as she sat in the huge library munching on a Snickers bar, she studied her friend Huda, the lovely exotic Huda who had introduced her to Khalil. Would Huda, she wonder, approve of her deepening commitment to Khalil? And was

Camellia truly in love or maybe coming down with the flu?

She missed him when he was gone for more than an hour; more than a day was real, actual pain. Ridiculous, she told herself. It operated outside rationality. Take the cravings, for example. Because she loved chocolate, Camellia had trained herself to walk past the campus vending machines without seeing them. This time she indulged, an inexplicable urge to devour a Snickers.

Bracing Huda about Khalil was tough. Her friend would have loved him, too, if she had not hated him so.

Huda was a Moslem, a Palestinian; Khalil a Lebanese Christian. Each wore the distinction like a tattoo. They couldn't be discreet about it, not even in America, where tribal identities ought to be irrelevant. As for Camellia she hardly knew a Moroccan from a Mohawk. Meeting and finding instant rapport with Huda had changed all that — Huda of the husky laugh and opulent jewelry. With her serpentine 24-karat necklaces, gleaming bracelets and beveled rings, Huda was a walking advertisement for Beirut's Street of Gold.

Here on campus and in Ann Arbor near Detroit were more Arab-Americans than anywhere else in the United States. Back in their Arab world they had killed each other over the centuries, for so long no one remembered why. In Ann Arbor and huge Detroit nearby the Arabs were one people.

On the surface Khalil and Huda were compatible. They showed up at the same parties, spoke Arabic, shared friends. They even looked alike: glossy black hair, Semitic profiles, lean limbs. But their nationalities were an argument they couldn't resolve or hope to win.

"Khalil's taking me to Lebanon," she finally whispered.

"To Beirut?" Huda hissed, causing heads to turn. Huda's five gold bracelets fairly danced on her arm in disbelief. "Home?"

"Why shouldn't he take me there? He loves me. Do you think, just because I'm an American — "

"No."

"Do you think because we've lived here only 200 years to your 2,000 there, do you think I don't know what it means to Khalil — to go home?"

She knew at once she had been tactless. Huda was a Palestinian caught in a modern diaspora, moving from county to country. Who could blame her for envying Khalil?

"*You* should be going there, not me," Camellia whispered. "You and Khalil. If it weren't for your religion...."

"No — " and Huda took Camellia's hand. "Many barriers exist between Khalil and me." She uttered in Arabic what might have been a blessing. "It means..." she began.

Camellia leaned forward and kissed Huda lightly on the cheek. "Leave it like the Koran," she said, "uncorrupted by translation."

"'Love without beauty,'" Huda went on, "is like flowers without scent and fruits without seed.'"

Camellia snorted. "You can quote Kahlil Gibran all day if you like but men aren't roses and shouldn't pretend to be."

It all came rushing back at her, the memory of her father. His had been a Mount Rushmore face, all curved beak, square jaw, jutting cheekbones and piercing eyes. It was a face Camellia had inherited, except that Angela's delicacy had softened it, but not by much.

She sat there thinking first of her father and then of the man she loved. She had met Khalil at the Christmas *hafle*, six months after her father died. She hadn't been in a partying mood.

"Arabs know how to give parties," Huda pressed her, "especially at Christmas." What an understatement! The hall glittered with greenery and tinsel. Diamond-shaped meats and sticky pastries were pyramided on platters. The exotic smells were overpowering.

Camellia felt rather than heard the social vibrations: rustling gowns, clinking glasses, the hum of a hundred conversations punctuated by much laughter. The Arab-American elite of Ann Arbor drove Cadillacs and drank Chivas Regal. They moved in clouds of Tuscany and Chanel, jeweled women with olive-skinned men sporting cigars and movie-villain mustaches. Assimilated, perhaps, but quintessentially Arab, they were a warm and noisy crowd fluent in many languages and secure in the sense of belonging. Men and women shook her hand and smiled as if she were a friend.

Gregarious, radiant Huda sipped champagne and kissed friend after friend. Then she froze in mid-handshake, bracelets stilled. Camellia followed her gaze to the far side of the room. Khalil, tall and pale, stood aloof as a smooth-eared Vulcan — but far more beautiful. Yes, for a man, there was a masculine kind of beauty. At his side was a woman with orange lips, a gown revealing shifting breasts and eyelashes of black spider webs.

"Haram! Such magnificence!" Huda whispered.

"She looks like a fish wrapped in foil."

"Not her. *Him.* The Arab 'David.'"

Camellia looked again. He was tall and thin and the light seemed to be playing on his skin. Obsidian hair framed a chiseled face that could have been one of Michaelangelo's.

"He is pretty," Camellia said with indifference, "like a Paris dress — amusing but preposterous."

"For him," Huda said, still staring, "I'd forget my upbringing."

"You're forgetting Cosmo hanging on his arm."

"Fah!" Huda frowned. "Our men don't take up with women like that." She dismissed orange lips with a wave of the hand. "Let's go and speak to him."

The music sounded foreign to Camellia. Foreign, pulsating and loud. Huda said the musicians were Greek. They played with enthusiasm, rippling the melodies with grace notes, and Camellia followed the music as she pressed through the crowd. "My sister," Khalil greeted Huda. Camellia forgot all about the music.

The man's eyes were positively smoky as was his faintly Mediterranean scent, the expression arrogant as following custom he shook her hand. His eyes flashed recognition when Huda repeated Camellia's surname.

"Marshall Kessler's daughter? I am sorry. It was too sudden."

"Heart attacks are," she said with a trace of bitterness. "He died in his jogging shoes with an unfinished manuscript at his desk."

He nodded, as if knowing about sorrow. "I did not know there was a daughter..."

"Two — my younger sister, Violet, and me."

Without knowing how it happened she and Huda ended up at Khalil's table. The band launched into another number.

"Abdulwahab," Khalil said.

"What did you say?" Camellia asked.

Khalil cocked his head to listen. "Egypt's greatest composer. They almost do him justice."

The band struck up another one, but this time provoking murmurs of disapproval. The mood of the crowd grew ugly. One man waved a fist, then he stood and shouted down the musicians.

A strained silence ensued while the ruffled Greeks shuffled through their sheet music.

"What were they playing?" Camellia asked.

"'Hava Nagila'." Khalil sounded amused. "A Semitic tune — but for the wrong Semites."

"This is a *hafle*," snapped Huda, "not a Jewish wedding."

"But what a rousing tune," Camellia said. Orange lips weighed in: "Yes, and so is 'Fiddler on the Roof'."

Camellia felt sorry for her, forced to endure Huda's all but venomous stare.

Finally the band tackled a sprightly Turkish melody and the crowd moved to the buffet. Khalil helped Camellia sample the delicacies. Stuffed grape leaves dripped with lemon oil. Ripe tomato chunks topped mountains of parsley and chopped vegetables. Chicken, pine nuts and spices transformed rice into hearty pilaf. Baklava — thin pastry layered with filling and nuts — oozed syrup and honey. It was all delicious.

Huda was arguing and picking at her food. "We must defend our art, our poetry," she said. "How can we enjoy Jewish culture when the Jews have our land?"

Before Camellia could decide whether the question was rhetorical, a drumbeat throbbed and someone said, "the dance." A mass of quivering flesh, flying hair, angled arms, crashing finger cymbals, swirling veil and thrusting hips — the dancer whirled on-stage. "An American," someone whispered. "You can see her bones." Angled rather than ample, she couldn't duplicate the fleshy, wide-hipped look of Egypt. Lacking anything authentic, she tried with enthusiasm and — "yella!" — she could dance.

Camellia sat fascinated. What power in the rolling hips! What promise of fertility in the undulating belly! The veiled breasts shimmied above an orchestra of jangling coins; the pouty lips and narrowed eyes hinted of the consequences of female sexuality denied. Sexism or sexuality? Exploitation or raw woman power? Her mid-'70s consciousness newly raised by the '60s tumult, Camellia couldn't decide.

"My word! Is this *really* how poor virgins once danced for a dowry in the street?"

Khalil laughed. "Now it is the poor man who must offer gifts for the bride."

"It's about time," said Huda, slamming down her fork.

"Why must you take it seriously?" Khalil answered her. "This crowd is no more Semitic than — than Camellia. Covered-dish dinners and belly dancing — that's all they know of being Arab."

The music faded slowly, the clarinet almost making sensuous foreplay with the drum. The dancer swayed like a cobra adrift on the languid music. Lips curved in pleasure, she arched until her hair fell behind her to touch the floor. Coins rattled on her rippling belly. Her heavy breathing carried to the corners of the hall.

Now, mimicking the repetition of cycles and seasons, the music tempo became brisk. The dancer responded, leaping and whirling and flinging aside her veil.

Camellia jumped, bit hard into a grape leaf, sending strange-tasting lemon oil trickling down her chin. The gracious Khalil dabbed at it with a snowy napkin. "A good start." He smiled. "But when you acquire the taste you will never be satisfied. You will never have enough."

****

Soon Khalil dropped the woman with orange lips to pursue Camellia and she wondered how he could prefer wide-eyed Midwest charm to the smoldering earthiness of someone like Huda, but she knew better than to ask him. He would never have answered a direct question anyway; he would simply choose not to hear. Camellia could never decide whether this was a personality quirk or indication of deep character.

But it was undeniably easy to respond to him purely on a physical level, to be drawn by his beauty, his arrogance, his sensuality — all of which made him seem like Mr. Rochester, Max de Winter and Dr. Zhivago rolled into one. He carried himself with dignity; something about him proclaimed "stand back." The aura of forbidden sexuality made him irresistible. He was alluring to some women as a celibate priest.

She loved him so much she danced for him, a dance that had become an obsession for her. She sewed translucent harem pants, a bodice and a veil. She listened to "The Joy of Belly Dancing" over and over. To "Unhappy Wanderer" and "Lawrence of Arabia," she choreographed hip twitches, rib cage rolls and seductive flutterings of the veil. She imagined the dance as they made love; imagined its frenzy, joy and undulation — and all this while working by day as a newspaper reporter.

When finally she felt ready to dance for him he watched with an amusement he might have reserved for a child in a school play, but "you could make a fortune in Cairo," he muttered. Then he made love to her with the dedication of a marathon runner, committed but essentially alone. She wondered if ever she would get to know him.

But she had mastered the dance, for someone not born to it. There was a joy about the accomplishment, stirring emotions she had not felt since her father died. Of course no one could measure up to Marshall. Camellia more or less accepted her mother's dictum: "You two can't go wrong with husbands just like your father," although it seemed she said it less often since his death.

Career-oriented Camellia wasn't looking for a husband. She liked reporting and writing news and was more than half-satisfied with her job at the News. Her best friend at the paper was tough-talking Myra Wendt, the city editor and her boss. Long ago Myra had worked as a feature writer for the late New York Herald Tribune — a job, she was fond of saying, that was about all any woman was going to get from the men running New York's city rooms.

"I never knock it," Myra told her; "New York then was really Baghdad on the Hudson — to me — and I worked with some of the legends." When the Trib was put to death in 1967 Myra fled New York and surfaced in Ann Arbor where within three years she became that paper's first woman news executive.

Young reporters idolized her for what she had been and for her fairness and ability to teach them nuances of reporting and editing they would not otherwise have found on a paper such as the News.

When Camellia told her she probably would leave with Khalil she snorted. "Sleeping with him here was exotic, Camellia," she said. "In Beirut he won't stand out in the crowd or likely the bedroom either."

Camellia refused to be baited by her boss or her caustic younger sister, Violet. "Khalil's better than some you've brought around," Violet opined, "but to me he seems to have evolved from a separate species." Her tone indicated that the species had no great appeal to her.

For that matter Camellia had doubts of her own. He was handsome, self-assured and smart as hell. She was always nagged by the indefinable sense that something was missing in his makeup but she always ended these introspections with a mental shrug. What relationship was perfect?

Already she felt her love had taken her past the point of no return and tonight they would tell Angela, her mother, at dinner.

****

The dinner table was a bizarre medley of gravy bowls, salad bowls and silver clanging against flower pots and terraria. "You cannot fill a home with plants and expect it to resemble anything but a damned greenhouse!" her father once bellowed after tripping over a Japanese laurel and cutting his head on the table's edge.

On such points Angela was unflappable and adamant. "Marshall, dear, that's just the point," she said, dabbing at his forehead with a napkin. Long ago she had made a near total commitment to what one of her naturalist authors called "the web of life." To her, plants were living history. The living room's rubber tree was reminiscent of the '50s, growing among a burst of Victorian-style palms, ferns and aspidistras. In the kitchen there were always bouquets of cut flowers, harking back to the Flapper era.

Her mother, Camellia thought, would have made a hell of a street marcher had she not been a faculty wife and a botany professor in her own right. Plants were her living art and architecture.

Camellia had removed the sansevieria centerpiece from the table to make room for the plates but her mother had put it right back. Violet was pouting about something, sitting there like a frog on a lily pad ready to jump.

"Violet, pass Khalil the chicken," Angela said. She was cheerful, just in from digging in the garden and smelling of outdoors. "If you're going to be a regular around here, Khalil," she said, "we'll have to come up with a nickname. I still get caught on the 'Kh' sound."

"A difficult sound," he agreed, "unique to Semitic peoples. The Nazis are supposed to have given sly screening tests, forcing people to recite lists of words, some of which contained Hebrew words using the 'kh.' The Aryan, of course, could never pronounce them."

"Extraordinary," Angela said.

"It was told to me by a Jewish professor of history."

Violet's laughter was cut short by Camellia's glare.

"When Muzz learned you were an Arab, do you know what she said?" Violet asked.

"Not now!" Camellia hissed.

"She said, 'Violet, don't you take up with an ethnic. That's all we need, Camellia with an Arab and you with a Jew — an Arab-Israeli war in Ann Arbor!'"

Angela reacted quickly. "Khalil," she said, "tell me about your grandparents. Camellia says the Turks nearly starved them during World War I."

Khalil paled; Violet seemed to have upset him. "They survived," he said slowly, "by eating grass and roots. They were lucky. At least 100,000 Maronites starved to death."

"Who are Maronites?" Violet asked.

"They're Christians," Camellia spoke out. "Lebanon's Christians. Even the Pope recognizes them."

"Well, I don't," Violet said. "What's so surprising, anyway? Arabs kill each other all the time on television."

"Mother, we were talking about the Turks. Sometimes I think the electronic years have given Violet a two-digit IQ."

Khalil was impassive. His standing as a romantic figure rendered him no less a child of the tribe — polite and honorable despite outrageous provocation from the unwashed. "Five years in America have exposed me to so many stereotypes."

Violet giggled. "You mean you watch Abdul the wrestler too?"

Abdul was a paunchy, hair-stubbled American who masqueraded as a brutish sheik. He specialized in vicious, below-the-belt punches. His fans believed this was the natural way for Arabs to fight.

"Khalil — when are you returning to Lebanon?" Angela asked.

She was blunt. Camellia worried that Khalil might take offense. But he only laughed. "My father never stops asking me that. Not since I arrived in America five years ago."

"Are you part of a dynasty?" Angela prodded. "Will you inherit a fortune?" echoed Violet.

"My father is a government official. He works in the Ministry of Finance."

"Ooohh." At last, Violet was impressed. "A pasha."

"That's Turkey," Camellia said.

"Surely you don't expect me to make distinctions. Not between competing barbarians. Not just because you've decided to marry one. Don't look at me like that, Camellia. You know what I mean."

"Do I?"

Angela ignored them both. "Will you follow in your father's footsteps?" she asked Khalil.

"No." Khalil smiled. "I intend to avoid government service as ambitious men do. Power in Lebanon is wielded informally. It is tribal chiefs and religious leaders who are influential."

Camellia squinted and thrust out her jaw. "I'm going to Lebanon," she told her mother in a low but firm voice. "With Khalil."

Her mother's jaw dropped. She looked first at her daughter, then at Khalil. "But, but, but..." was all she managed to get out.

"Camels! Harems! Sheiks!" Violet giggled. "What a honeymoon. Can I go, too?"

Khalil gave them his most inscrutable gaze. "Will my people never outlive Hollywood? I am Lebanese, descended from Phoenicians. My ancestors *invented* civilization. I am not a Bedouin, not a sheik."

He put a cold eye on Violet. "You, my little sister, are in the desert with Rudolph Valentino. Lebanon is now — 1975, maybe even 10 years ahead of the rest of the world."

Khalil plunged on. "High fashion begins in Beirut before New York. Beirut has more banks than Bern, more restaurants than Paris. Our gambling casino is bigger than Monte Carlo's. Beirut is..."

"So very far away," said a tearful Angela.

"Beirut is the Paris of the Middle East, Angela," he replied, ignoring her sad face. "We combine Europe's flair with what you Americans call Yankee ingenuity. And we know what we are about. Our family is strong, ongoing. We have values."

"Look out!" said Violet, munching green beans; "the AY-rabs are coming."

Khalil ignored her. "Kuwaitis make million-dollar deals. Saudis indulge in pleasures for which they'd be flogged at home. Jet setters flit from casino to casino like so many bees, dropping money at the tables, catching the European pop stars and ogling the showgirls. The Swiss come to speculate, the Israelis to spy. Americans do a bit of all of that."

Camellia ate without tasting the tender, fragrant Captain's chicken falling from the bones. Surely her mother wasn't about to cause a scene, was she?

She had been a strong tiger of a mother for her daughters. They had been given discipline and nearly every privilege including the greatest of all, love. Angela the botanist had named her daughters after flowers. She regarded them as rare specimens best left to flourish in their natural state whenever possible. Marshall, the old soldier, saw untrained troops with hearts and minds in need of hardening to face life's battles. "You've turned them into marigolds," he'd chide her, then hustle them off to museum or hardware store. They were welcome apprentices in his workshop. At the rifle range, he saw to it they learned to shoot straight. And always, he expected — demanded — that they learn about all of the life around them. He would not tolerate fragility in them that was a big part of Angela's charm, or appeared to be.

By the time the two flowers were ready for college they could fix a faucet, pick a lock, drive a stickshift or do long division in their heads. Marshall had assigned chores, supervised homework, screened friends, but he died before he could help them choose husbands.

Distracted, Angela reached for a table plant and began pinching back its stems. "What if you're not happy?" she exhaled audibly.

"Mother!"

"Life is difficult, among foreigners...."

Khalil reached for the mother's hand and began to speak. He made her see mountains rising from the coast, rivers springing from headwaters, neat terraces holding fast the soil. The *masyef*, his family's summer home, was included: fertile farmlands thick with peach trees, grape vines, the hardy olive grove and lucious figs.

"I know figs as dry wrinkled things in wrappers," Angela said.

Mother is being a good sport, Camellia thought.

"What I would have given these last five years for the delicate sweetness of a green *khadari*," Khalil said, almost in a whisper.

Damn, Camellia marveled, what a show he is giving for her. She was reminded of a profile in the Detroit Free Press about a Lebanese-American, a famous criminal lawyer of whom it was said he had never lost a case. "Mentally I make love to every woman on the jury," he confessed to the reporter.

Khalil wasn't finished. "Camellia will know the flesh of pomegranates, baby lamb ... coffee from brass samovars ... bread cooked on open fires...."

By now Angela was fluttering her hands.

Violet wasn't finished, either. "All right, eat the pomegranates," she said, "but if you *must* marry an Arab, why not a sheik?"

Camellia glared and Khalil chuckled, then said with exaggerated politeness, "As we say in Lebanon, 'the tar of my country is better than the honey of yours.'"

2

Baraka

"Tell me more about Lebanon."

Camellia repeated this phrase often. It was "open sesame" to Khalil's world and to his heart.

Khalil unfailingly responded. When he spoke it was as if Camellia had never before experienced the world.

She and Khalil tossed peanuts to the gorillas at the Detroit Zoo. The gorillas made faces and threw things back. Back in Ann Arbor, she and Khalil would stop for ice cream at Gelato's. Camellia always ordered *coppa mista*. Friday nights found them at the jazz joints on West Liberty.

Sometimes they simply lay entwined in bed and listened to the howling wind.

Throughout it all she listened, absorbing the rhythms and cadences of his speech. His narration, like a subterranean river, was filled with undercurrents.

"My family ... my *family*...." His voice would trail off, his eyes mist in memory. Sometimes the linking of his historic past and personal history seemed to overwhelm him. He spoke stirringly of his Phoenician ancestors — the glorious seafarers of antiquity — until they became as real to Camellia as his living relatives. (Or at least no less strange and indefinable.) Most of them, she gathered, had intermarried. Generations of intermarriage had given many Lebanese surnames meanings that could be put into words. Associated with the predominant attributes of family members, a family name could be synonymous with, for example, business acumen, physical strength or overarching foolishness. Khalil's family — bearing the surname Majdi — was especially noted for bravery, ambition and pride. By intermarrying, they claimed to have preserved the bloodline.

In addition, a special vocabulary defined relatives. Informal titles at once identified the sex, relationship and tribal importance of the person in question. Familial titles were used in direct address. For example, everyone always called Khalil's mother Om Mousa; his father was Abu Mousa. Each bore the name of Mousa, their first-born. Mousa, their son, who had died in infancy. "Om" meant mother of. "Abu," father of.

"But doesn't that needlessly remind them of tragedy — the death of a son?"

"They would not think of it that way." He continued with his involved explanation. He would never merely say "aunt," for example. He would instead say (changing the antecedents as the situation warranted), "wife of my uncle." Or "son of my brother-in-law," which was much more specific than "nephew." Though cumbersome in English, the Arabic phrases were short and lyric.

Camellia giggled. "You have as many friends-and-relations as Pooh's Rabbit." Her relatives of various Northern European extractions were scattered around America. Many she had never met. "Do they meddle?"

He smiled a little sadly. "What child could fail to thrive with so *many* mothers, so many men who are like fathers?"

She never mentioned it again. The clan was part of him, and she would never fully understand the strange mix of loyalties that motivated him. Western mannerisms could not erase tribal values any more than the teachers who had drilled him in French and English were successful in usurping Arabic. No matter how well she grew to know him, some part of him would always exist beyond her reach. Certain segments of his consciousness she would never be able to control or even influence. She only hoped one day it would be as easy to understand him as it was to love him.

The East-West mix made him alluringly unpredictable and endearing. Despite his Beirut sophistication, he carried a debt of gratitude impressed on him since birth: that he should *owe* something to the parents who had brought him life, the community that nurtured him.

Summers, he was simply a boy.

"We would leave Beirut for the *masyef* ... the summer home."

It was morning. They walked together on the icy sidewalk — she to work, he to State Street to do last-minute errands. "I remember my mother making preparations, wrapping blankets around our clothes. She never even took them off the hangers..." He tilted his head, remembering. "I will take you there ... to what we call simply 'the mountain.'"

Everything he described seemed unreal. Terraced hillsides. Nectar-drizzled figs.

Around her, on this fine March Michigan morning, sun glittered on the pristine snow.

She walked faster to keep up with Khalil. His stride was swift and gliding on the frosty sidewalk.

"Lebanon." Her breath crystallized the air. "Tell me ..."

"Have I not told you everything?"

He was beautiful — an onyx set in white sand. She imagined him bounded by miles of shimmering desert, astride a stallion, his hair covered by a *kaffiyeh*, his smoky-hued eyes fixed on some horizon. He was so fragile, so other-worldly — yet so resilient, here among the Bad Axe farm boys and Detroit dandies who dug the sidewalk with their earth-caked boots.

She shivered, numb with the cold. "In the desert ... does it snow?"

"Desert?" He smiled indulgently. "In Lebanon, there is sand only near the sea."

"But I thought...."

"The desert is for Moslems. God gave us Lebanon."

"Aren't there Moslems in Lebanon too?" Eager to demonstrate all that she had recently learned, she added: "Don't the *fellaheen* of both faiths lay claim to 'the mountain'?"

But Khalil was thinking of the land. Of how *she* would view the land. "The sun shines 300 days of the year. In spring, the valley — Beirut is a valley — will be alight with sun while snow shimmers on the surrounding mountain peaks. It has become a cliche in Lebanon — to say that one can water-ski and snow-ski on the same day."

"My kingdom for a bikini," Camellia said longingly. She blew into her mohair scarf for warmth. "I'll bet it's 16 below if you count wind chill. Nineteen seventy-five may not be the coldest year on record, but it seems that way."

"Come close." He put his arm around her. Camellia looked up in surprise. He was never demonstrative in public.

"Ummm ..." She snuggled against him, matching his stride as he slowed for her. "Tell me more ... "

"Have you heard about the Lebanese boy? His teacher asked him the sum of two plus two. The boy deliberated, then asked, 'Am I buying or selling?'"

She laughed. "I bet that kid made a fortune in used camels."

"Camels!" Khalil jerked away. "You still don't understand my people. We're not 'desert niggers' ... not Bedouins or Moslem fanatics ... our women don't wear veils."

He stopped, scooping up a snowball in his camel-gloved hands and flinging it at the white-crested oaks. "We have not a drop of oil. And yet we prosper."

"Because of the ingenuity of your Phoenician ancestors?"

"Don't laugh. The Phoenicians...."

"I know. I know. Invented the alphabet. Sold Solomon the cedars for his temple. But what about *today*? You and Huda never talk about the same things. *She* talks about *The Arab Awakening*. And nationalism. Forgive me, but you seem caught in the past."

He waved an imperious hand. "Nationalism is a joke. The Egyptians are a joke. Forty million of them, clutching at the tatters of Pharaonic greatness. The Saudis? They were Islam's bodyguards — until the world discovered oil. Now the royal family profits by studying at Harvard."

"And the others? The 20 Arab countries? You dismiss them, too?"

Again, he gave a peremptory wave of the gloved hand. "Libya and Syria can't decide whether to make love or make war — and thus are impotent at both. Jordan is impoverished, the Palestinians displaced. All the rest wallow in their oil. Brotherhood? With such as these?"

He turned at the corner.

She drew her fingers lightly over his chin. "You're lovely when you're angry."

He blinked impatiently. "Go to work and learn."

Impulsively, she kissed him, catching a whiff of sandalwood. Momentarily, she stood watching his eyes glitter, the kiss glisten on his cheek. Ah, Khalil, she thought admiringly. Not even the friction of that fur-lined coat could make you sweat.

****

That Khalil loved his country endeared him to Camellia. That he loved hers made her admire him all the more.

Subtle differences reminded her he was Arab, not American. He didn't wear special jogging shoes but he took brisk walks in well-worn loafers. He didn't drive to a lookout point to see dazzling sunsets. He stopped wherever he was to watch them unfold.

She wanted to show him everything about her world. There was so little time before departure. A month. Then two weeks. Now 10 days that seemed like 10 centuries. Their time together was lyrical, unbroken, like snow at daybreak. Mundane things would tear them apart — her news reporting or errands or temporary need for solitude. Camellia would as a result suffer; disproportionately, she knew. After all, the deprivation was brief. Then an eager conjoining. Time would flow as if it had never been disrupted. To Camellia, everything but being with Khalil seemed so irrelevant.

Also, she wanted to show Khalil her proficiencies. She could ski, so she proposed a trip to Pine Knob. There, the world outside would be fresh and glittery — and cruel, like the white-capped mountains of Khalil's description. Love was a safe haven.

The day of the trip Khalil sat in the beanbag beneath the living room window. Rabbit tracks dented the snow-covered lawn. Khalil had come too late to see the rabbits. He looked funny in the beanbag chair. His spine was too stiff. He couldn't slouch, and beanbag chairs require slouching.

Violet looked up from a solo game of checkers. "Oh! Can't I go, too? I'll call Bret." Bret was her boyfriend.

"Maybe next time." For Camellia, smug, dreamy, the magic number was two. She was stunned when Khalil overruled her.

"Of course you may go," he said firmly. He gave Camellia a look of reproach. Briefly, she wondered if she *wanted* to understand that Eastern mind. "And Angela, too — if she wishes."

"Why stop there?" Camellia asked. "I could call Stockbridge and invite my cousins." Gone were images of a lovers' afternoon — of kissing in the snow, of dodging the wind.

"Don't be silly," Angela said. "In Stockbridge, they prefer snowmobiles."

An hour later they were in the ski lodge, suiting up. Bret — Violet's steady since November — had come, too. He and Violet had met at a doctor's office. Violet was having a wart removed. Bret had a hernia. "Shoveling snow," she explained to Khalil.

On the slopes, Khalil was graceful.

Camellia fell twice on her way to the tow ropes.

"It is simply a matter of balance." He helped her up. Icy wind drove color into his face. Life's-blood coursing through marble.

A light snow fell like feathers.

The wind abraded her cheeks. Her hat fell to the mud-slush. It lay there, absorbing water.

"It's no fair. Physiologically, you're all wrong. You're — what we call lanky. With a high center of gravity. *I* should be the one upright and *you* should be down there trying to untangle your legs!"

"Never mind. You will learn. Say, when the *donkey* climbs to the top of the minaret." He winked and dashed away. She brandished her ski pole. "I love you, too."

Later, in the lounge, they sat beside the picture window, admiring the Grandma Moses landscape. Skiers grabbed the motorized rope. When Camellia had grasped it, her mittens shredded. It bore the experienced skiers to the upper reaches of the slope.

It looked effortless. Higher they rose, lifted toward the sparkling summit, to paths, higher reaches, steeper slopes. The snow had become a drizzle. Camellia had made one perilous downward slide. Each step she took to slow herself resulted only in increased acceleration. She had slid the last 20 yards on her rear and crashed against the brick wall of the lodge.

"You took quite a tumble." Bret, of course, wasn't skiing because of the hernia. He, like everyone else in the lounge, had witnessed Camellia's fall.

Khalil had ordered pizza.

Violet, throwing off her sweater, was still stamping her feet from cold. Smugly — "Camellia got the brains. But I got the coordination and grace."

"The mouth, you mean."

Violet snuggled against Bret, who kissed her, happily and noisily.

Camellia took another sip of Coke. "I knew there was good reason to leave the country."

When Violet came up for air, she stuck out her tongue.

"You've got your Arabian knight. But Bret is a king."

Softly, so only Camellia could hear, Khalil whispered, "Every man is a king who is loved." The comment was so startlingly disingenuous, so revealing, so unexpectedly vulnerable from someone so poised, that she kissed him as noisily as Violet was kissing Bret. Momentarily, at least, he seemed no longer remote.

****

So much to do! To prepare, Camellia read all the important stuff. *The New York Times. Mademoiselle.*

Mademoiselle told her how to be contemporary. A woman of 1975. This would require squarer-shaped nails. A natural-look eyebrow. A well-defined, no-shine mouth. The parfum of the moment: Yves St. Laurent Rive Gauche. Jeans were indigo blue, with yellow seams.

The New York Times, or, rather, Evans and Novak, told her about Kuneitra...for centuries the commercial and marketing center of lush farming lands on the Syrian Golan Heights.

"Destruction of the shuttered city by dynamite and bulldozer started two weeks before it was handed back to Syria."

Kuneitra. Israel had captured Kuneitra during the 1967 war. It stood, deserted, for seven years. There were three mosques. Christian churches. A single hospital — "shuttered against cold Golan winds blowing off Mount Hermon." Occupied but empty — "its population of 53,000 scattered, a new drop in the brimming bucket of Arab refugees."

Pressured by the United States, Israel gave Kuneitra back to Syria.

But not before destroying it.

"The city looks as though a vast iron boot had stomped it down with crushing force, leveling 40 percent of it pancake flat. The hospital, which the commanding Israeli general promised would be spared, was gutted, its staircases now deep in rubble and its ceilings pitted with rifle fire.

"It wasn't the Israeli army that wanted this," Syrian Brig. Gen. Adnan Tayara told us. "We think it was a political decision."

Political analysis. What the "meticulous, house-by-house destruction" of Kuneitra meant to nearby Israeli settlers. To Syrian officials in Damascus.

"Kuneitra is dead and so is the reason for its existence. To skeptical Syrians, that does not lead to 'relaxation of tension' but to rage and a thirst for revenge — dangerous emotions, as Israelis themselves should know from Munich, Maalot, Beisan and Kiryat Shmona."

What was this geopolitical cauldron called the Middle East? How could Camellia go there, knowing so little, trusting so much?

****

Angela seemed increasingly reconciled. If not happy, then curiously excited. Her knowledge of the Bible was better than Camellia's, a fact she insisted on demonstrating.

"Listen to the *Song of Songs.*" Angela began to read aloud. Camellia admired Angela's ability to immerse herself in a world of her own making, a world without contingencies or danger. "His lips are as lilies," Angela read. "His aspect is like Lebanon, excellent as the cedars."

"How biblical," Violet said. She gave a little sigh.

"That's the point," Camellia said. She couldn't resist responding to every idiotic thing her younger sister said.

Angela, although seeming resigned to her daughter's going, stopped watching the news.

Camellia didn't. It came out that Arab governments were boycotting Rothschild and any other bank "extending military or economic assistance to Israel." The U.S. Department of State confirmed the docking of a Soviet freighter bearing six MiG-23s to Egypt. George Habash of the Popular Front for the Liberation of Palestine called for war in the Middle East as the only way to establish peace. Any new conflict would, he said, "be a grave threat to Israel's existence and U.S. imperialist interests."

None of this seemed directly related to Lebanon. Or to Camellia. But Camellia couldn't be sure. She listened to anyone who could offer insight or objectivity.

"What do you know about Kuneitra?" she asked Huda.

But Huda was busy with her own priorities.

"Why don't you ask me about Dr. Hanna Nasir, president of Birzeit College? That's on the Israeli-occupied West Bank. Have you heard of it?" Huda could be overbearing. "Nasir was deported — taken to the border and told never to return. Whenever leaders emerge on the West Bank, Israel expels them — and then Israeli officials say there are no Palestinians to negotiate with."

"Nasir?" Camellia asked.

"Why don't you ask me about Luffiya Hawary? Just released after six years in Ramle prison on the West Bank. She is a 30-year-old woman. Victim of torture."

"Hawary?"

"Why don't you read Felicia Langer's *With My Own Eyes*? She is a lawyer in Israel. She defends the Palestinians. And she is Jewish."

"Langer?"

Huda's intensity could be off-putting.

Camellia was delighted when Khalil asked her to go with him to Dr. Elias' home on Saturday night. Perhaps she could learn from him. And from Khalil's contemporaries.

All Arab students had a standing invitation to Dr. Elias' home on Saturday night. Khalil usually avoided going. It wasn't that he was a loner so much as that he was Lebanese. Many of the students were Saudis or Egyptians, Jordanians or Palestinians. Their world view differed from his. But he would go, if only to say good-by.

The house was filled with students. The scent of incense. Ice clinked busily in the glasses of the Saudis. Glasses filled with Scotch, which Moslems are forbidden to drink.

The sight of Khalil inspired the others to bring up the subject of Lebanon.

Dr. Elias was not kind.

"You, the Lebanese, have never forgiven God for putting Lebanon in Asia."

Dr. Elias was a burly Palestinian. His articulate mass-class lectures were a must for American students wishing to know about the Arab Middle East. Among Middle Eastern students, Dr. Elias was known for his Saturday-night *sahras* — literally translated, by Dr. Elias, as "evenings of pleasure."

"Lebanon deserves a continent of its own!" Dr. Elias was deliberately provocative. It was his trademark. "Or at least a spot in Europe. Unspoiled by primitives."

Khalil sat cross-legged, aloof.

Camellia, sitting beside him on the blue-and-russet Persian carpet, wondered why he didn't speak up.

"Aren't you being unfair?" she asked Dr. Elias.

"Unfair?" he echoed.

Attentive students sat around him, forming a circle. Like Mohammed's *halqa* of listeners, Camellia thought, remembering her research. Frequently of a Saturday night, Dr. Elias puffed on his meerschaum pipe and let the food grow cold, the eight-track tape play Abdel Wahab over and over. Camellia, who had made previous visits with Huda, knew his passion for politics. It was quintessentially Arab.

"Lebanon's newspapers promote half a dozen economic theories. Nationalism. Socialism. Ba'athism. A dozen languages. A hundred political parties. A thousand points of view. In Lebanon one finds a curious commingling. The refined. The glamorous. The bankrupt. Your poets are the most artful. Your holy men the most hallowed. Your dancers beyond peer, even judged against Egypt's. But you, the Lebanese — you lack integrity."

Camellia had no idea what he meant.

Khalil flicked a nervous hand across his forehead. Moments earlier, Khalil had praised Egyptian President Anwar Sadat. Sadat had declared Egypt "will never start war unless Israel attacks us." Khalil remarked — rather innocuously, Camellia thought — that Sadat commanded the respect of the American media. Most commentators, when they thought of Arab leaders at all, thought of them with contempt. Sadat was a refreshing change.

Dr. Elias had responded immediately. "Sadat? He licks Israeli boots. You will see. He will allow Israel access to the Suez Canal in return for Israeli pullback from Mitla and Gidi passes and the Abu Rudeis oilfields. And the world will be that much closer to war."

All but Khalil and two young Egyptians — who suddenly seemed to wish they were somewhere else — concurred.

"You are jealous." Khalil's tone was soft and cutting. "You call us, 'You, the Lebanese.' You single us out. You despise us because you envy us."

Dr. Elias bowed slightly. A polite, self-deprecating gesture. This was America. He was Arab host first, political enemy and intellectual adversary second. Surrounding him were glittering mementos. A mother-of-pearl Dome of the Rock. A porcelain-and-copper landscape of Mount Ararat. A panoramic sepia print of turn-of-the-century Jerusalem. All suggested a dozen countries but laid claim to not a single one.

"My people are desperate," he said. "Outnumbered. Disenfranchised. Poor. But we're not like you, the Lebanese, who kill because you have always killed, for God knows how many generations."

"Beirut — " Khalil began.

"Beirut." Dr. Elias' laugh was a snort of derision. "Beirut is a center for spies. Headquarters of a dozen smuggling rings. A hundred armed camps, a thousand mercenaries."

Animated, he sat forward. Jutting chin and upturned palms complemented his crisp diction. "Your government is inept. Permissive. Corrupt. Your people say of their own officials: 'Any one of them would set his country on fire to light his cigarette.'"

Music wailed from the stereo. A woman sang, husky voiced. Om Kalthoum. Camellia knew about her. She had thrilled the Arab world for 50 years. Millions of mourners thronged to her funeral. Even so, her singing sounded to Camellia like a credible response to extreme pain.

Dr. Elias relit his pipe. "Imagine Bella Abzug marching a private army down Pennsylvania Avenue. Or William Colby, CIA director, firing on anti-war demonstrators. Instead of two political parties, imagine 42. And 17 conflicting religions. Such is Lebanon."

"It's a wonder there's a government at all!" Camellia said.

"For several months in 1969, there wasn't. No one noticed. Even the newspapers were slow to catch on."

The students tittered. Only Khalil sat silent, jaw clenched, beads of perspiration massing on his forehead.

Camellia said, "I can't quite grasp ... *private* militias? Do they really threaten the army?"

"Several could *defeat* the army. The army, you see, is demoralized and badly split along religious lines. Many top officers have deserted — to join militias or even to establish autonomous commands."

Dr. Elias paused. There was no denial. Was there a case for the other side? If so, why didn't Khalil make it? The professor bit the stem of his meerschaum pipe and went on.

"Anyone who blames the Moslems for inciting trouble in Lebanon hasn't seen the stockpiles of the Christian Maronites. Latest acquisition: black-market M-16s. No doubt to be aimed at anyone who prays facing east. Pierre Gemayel, they say, admired Hitler."

Khalil's nostrils flared. "*Ten thousand* Palestinians in Lebanon carry guns. And do they give a damn about my country? In search of their own land, they would destroy mine."

"Lebanon." Dr. Elias looked amused. He chided Khalil as effortlessly as an old man kneading worry beads. "What is Lebanon but a collection of hermits and persecuted minorities? A last frontier for religious fanatics? Druzes, Maronites, Alawites and Shi'ites — each claiming supremacy." He jabbed at the air with his pipe. "You, the Lebanese, won't even admit you're Arab. You claim Phoenician blood — and, as we all know, Phoenicians didn't give a damn about *anything* but the price of silk!"

Khalil seemed not to have heard. "Palestinians have ruined Lebanon. Look at the south. You cannot deny it," he said stubbornly.

"The Palestinians ... or Israel? *Whose* air raids carry out a policy of 'scorched earth'? *Whose* 'rain of terror' sends refugees streaming north, by the thousands, where they cluster in camps, in a 'belt of misery' girdling Beirut?"

The front door slammed.

"*Marhaba! Marhaba!*" The voice, penetratingly familiar — followed by a blur of gold and magenta. Huda had arrived.

She plunked her bowl of *tabbouleh* on the table. "*Keef hallek!*" she said cheerily.

"*Ahlan wa sahlan*," Dr. Elias responded, equally hearty.

Inexplicably, Khalil looked relieved.

"How are you, girl?" Huda stood just long enough for Camellia to squeeze her hand and inhale her perfume. Then she quickly tottered away awkwardly on her fashionable high heels. Glossy lips and hair festooned with ribbons gave her the air of a Moroccan carpet. Serpentine necklaces and stacked bracelets completed the Beirut-Paris look.

"So — everyone must be talking about Watergate. Or the collapse in Saigon. Can the Vietnam war really be ending?" "Dr. Elias thinks *we* are on the brink of war." Khalil, sardonic, had regained his equilibrium. "We — the Lebanese. In *Lebanon*," he finished triumphantly.

"*Haram!*"

Dr. Elias blew a ring of smoke. "Disenchanted Christians. Disenfranchised Moslems. Impoverished refugees. Uprooted Palestinians. War? It is only a matter of time."

Again, angrily, Khalil began, "The Palestinians...."

But Huda turned on him. "Thirty years of war, *ya* my brother, and you still can't see the enemy." She sounded wistful. When crossed, Camellia knew, Huda could be a formidable adversary.

Khalil didn't heed the gentle warning. Undeterred, he said, "I understand the Palestinian wish for self-determination. You want land. But not at any cost...."

Dr. Elias looked at Camellia as if for the first time.

"Do you know what you're getting into?" he asked. He glanced from her to Khalil.

For an answer, she lifted her hand to show its twinkling diamond. Set in white gold, Khalil's ring looked beautiful. It sat new and strange. It signaled a formality she would rather have postponed. But Khalil had said they could not travel, in his part of the world, without it.

The professor exhaled smoke. "Being an American, of course, you have no concept of danger. Or, one might argue, of reality."

"*Haram*." Huda cut in quickly. "We cannot solve the problems of the world in one night." She motioned toward the table. "Let's eat."

Camellia sniffed appreciatively. The aromas were tantalizing. She was even beginning to appreciate the taste. Flavors and textures of Mediterranean food were no longer strange and overbearing. Khalil had been correct at the *hafle*. Her mouth now watered when she so much as thought of grape leaves.

Hummos, or pulverized chick peas, smelled lingeringly of garlic-laced lemon. Dr. Elias' *kibbeh* — cracked-wheat- stuffed meat carved into the pattern of diamonds — looked equally delicious. So did Huda's *tabbouleh*, its fresh parsley, cucumber and tomato chopped by hand, by people who believed good food came from the heart.

Camellia picked up a plate. "Give me some of everything."

Khalil, glowering, left the room.

"*Haram*," Huda whispered comfortingly. "He'll get over it."

Camellia stood uncertainly, ready to put down her plate and follow him. But when Dr. Elias urged her eat, she was too inexperienced to resist the ritual of his repeated invitations. He spoke in Arabic, as if to break her in. She didn't fully understand. But she heaped her plate so full there was no room even for the Arabic bread. She carried it, a flat golden triangle, in her hands.

She sat on the sofa. Dr. Elias ate bread but was too busy to fill a plate. He brought her a small glass of clear liquid.

"Have you tasted *arak*? Try it straight ... before I add water."

Camellia swirled the liquid. She noticed it created legs on the glass, like brandy or fine wine. She sipped, then shuddered. "Smells like licorice. Stings like whiskey."

"Eighty proof. Watch." He poured water from a crystal pitcher. Hair grew from his knuckles, black as the hair on his head and of his eyebrows, which were now raised, implying mischief. He bent seriously to the task. He blended the water with the *arak*, and the mixture became white. What had been clear was now milky and opaque.

She squinted. "Magic?"

"For shame! Alchemy. Or, more accurately, *al-kimiya*." His teeth gleamed beneath the black slash of his mustache. "While Europe burned witches, Arab chemists discovered everything from nitric acid to talc. Avicenna learned to extract the essence of a flower's perfume while trying to isolate a rose's *soul*."

"You were clever in the Dark Ages." Camellia took another sip of the now white *arak*. "Water weakens it," she added.

He nodded approvingly. "I, too, prefer it straight. Things Arab should never be diluted. Arab nationalism today is all bluster and faded glory — a shame. Do you like the music?"

"I'm trying." Listening, she tilted her head. "She sounds near death."

He chuckled heartily. "Such richness! Listen. The audience cries for more. She repeats, repeats, repeats until the music drives them mad."

He blinked dreamily, savoring the wavering phrases. Then he noticed Camellia's expression and sighed. "Om Kalthoum. Her funeral made the cover of *Life*. But today everyone demands a Western beat. They prefer Fayrouz."

He fiddled with the stereo and a clear, sweet voice flooded the room. Steady four-four time carried the Oriental melody.

Beating rhythm with one foot, Dr. Elias translated softly:

> *We shall return*
> *The nightingale told me*
> *When we met on a hill*
> *That nightingales still*
> *Live there in our dreams*
> *And that among the yearning hills*
> *And people there is a place for us*
> *O heart then*
> *How long has the wind scattered us?*

"Fayrouz." The name was almost a sigh. He added dreamily, "I suppose you consider the lyrics excessively romantic."

"You can always tell an Arab by his syntax," Camellia teased.

"Arabs!" The professor chuckled. "We are the poets of the earth." He motioned to the shelves over the piano. "You see, here, I keep my mother-of-pearl creche. An uncompromising symbol of Christianity. Beside it hangs a Moslem prayer rug inscribed with the *shahada:* 'There is no god but God: Mohammed is the messenger of God.'" He ran one knuckle along the silk. "Together, they give my home *baraka.*"

"*Baraka?*"

"A quality of mysticism ... Oh, how shall I explain it? You Americans are pragmatic; you don't live anywhere or own anything for long. *Baraka* is a blessing, an indwelling force. Saints have it. So do charismatic leaders ... and, sometimes, things. My sculpture and my prayer rug ... they are from my grandfathers."

"But — then — what does that make *you*? Are you Christian or Moslem?"

"Does it matter?"

Khalil cut in: "Of course it matters." He stood beside Dr. Elias. He glanced nervously at Camellia. "If you've finished eating, we'll go."

"Not before I tell you the latest joke about Sadat."

Khalil looked like that was the last thing he wanted to hear. Dr. Elias ignored his expression and, full of mischief, pressed on.

"Sadat's chief of staff had arranged for an aerial inspection of Egypt. Shortly after takeoff, a junior officer threw a five- pound note out the window. Sadat asked: 'Why did you do that?' 'To make five Egyptian families happy,' the junior officer replied. Then a senior officer threw a ten-pound note out the window. Again, Sadat asked, 'Why did you do that?' 'To make ten families happy,' the senior officer replied, getting one up on the junior officer. Suddenly the pilot took a nosedive and began hurtling toward Earth. Sadat screamed, 'Why are you doing that?' The pilot's answer: 'To make *all of Egypt* happy!'"

Khalil opened his mouth but said nothing.

Jovial, Dr. Elias began the ritual of goodbye, protesting their leave-taking, shaking their hands — "What *baraka* to have met you," he said to Camellia, and she wondered if she imagined the curious look of regret his expression seemed to convey.

As they walked down the gravel driveway, she could hear the sounds of a party in full swing. Someone had turned off the stereo. She could hear drums, compelling and primitive, quicker than her heartbeat. *This* music was live. The rhythms were irresistible, inexorable as the moon orchestrating tides. She imagined Huda dancing, her bejeweled fingers curving gracefully, palms held high above her head.

In the car, Camellia pulled her jacket tightly around her. "Why were you defensive?"

Khalil bit his lip. His teeth indented soft flesh.

She sighed in exasperation. "This is America, you know," she said. "Ideas are free-ranging. Speech is expressive. Dr. Elias..."

"Dr. Elias." He snorted, slashing in and out of traffic. "Those damned Palestinians," he muttered. "They are ruining my country."

****

The sidewalks were thick with mud-slush. Everything was a blustery gray. But to Camellia the world was spring, spring, spring. Age 26 and in love — love gave it all a bitter sparkle — like winter's first freeze or the last drops of champagne.

Khalil walked fast. Exerting herself, she matched his stride. She hardly noticed the ricochet of ice making blotches on her boots — black suede. Violet had talked her into buying them. Why had she worn them in the snow? To impress Khalil. It was still rubber-boot season. Yet she had thrust her ugly rubber boots to the back of the closet. She would be as sharp as any Beirut beauty in Magali silk and strappy heels. At least for the moment.

She hooked her arm through Khalil's, bunching up her mohair scarf as if it were a muffler.

"Must you be so mysterious? Where are we going? Couldn't you let me sleep in on my day off?"

She smiled up at him. She wasn't an ingenue, or she would've winked. But Khalil wasn't looking and would have missed the subtlety anyway.

"You need to work more than you need to sleep."

"How dreary! Are you going to be dreary in Lebanon?"

"I do not have one set of manners for Lebanon, another for America. If that is what you mean."

"At least in America, there are checks on how domineering a man can be. Women are liberated. If you act like this in Lebanon, I may have to form into colonies and rebel!"

"Save your Yankee ingenuity for a time when it is needed."

"Ha!" He glanced at her. At last.

"Your boots are a mess," he said. "Wet through."

"You don't miss much. Where *are* we going?"

"We are almost there."

"You're maddeningly short with me. If I didn't love you, I'd be devastated."

He stopped suddenly. Camellia lurched into him.

"Do you mean it?" He grabbed her by the shoulders. Harsh reflected snow-light made his eyes look almost black.

"Well, I'd probably overeat for a day or two. Join a support group — "

"Do you love me?" His cheeks were flushed, magenta. She could feel his fingers through her coat. "Have you said it before? To others?"

"Oh! You are my one! My oasis! My Lawrence..."

He spoke in Arabic, short and cutting. Then English: "I will be damned if I believe a word."

He was walking again. Faster.

"Wait!" She hurried to catch up.

Catching hold of his sleeve: "Let's forget about errands and studies. Let's go to Detroit — to the Science Center. We can speak love poems into the parabola. You can whisper on one side of the room and hear it on the other. Lawrence! Lawrence! Then to Greektown for *mousakka*...."

"You amaze me. Your parents are scholars. Yet you are utterly unserious of nature."

"Not compared to Violet. Compared to Violet, I'm sober as a judge. Or as an *imam*, I guess I should say."

"And *Americans* condemn *Arabs* for intermarriage!"

"You, by contrast, are the product of several hundred years of flawless breeding, I assume?"

"At least."

"And I suppose your parents are second cousins?"

"First cousins. My little hedonist." He grinned crookedly. "The women of my family have always been exemplary. Full of energy and common sense. For that reason, turning away would-be suitors has always been a troublesome task for the men. This despite the girls being jealously guarded and often promised to a male cousin almost from birth! The marriage offers start coming in when the girl reaches puberty and ends only when she is safely married off. Preferably to a cousin."

"I can't believe you're not exaggerating."

"To a degree. The old ways are changing — for which I am grateful."

"Even so, I shudder to think of the damage I'll do to the bloodline."

"As a man, I have greater freedom of choice. That is simply a fact. Have you forgotten what day is today?

"Gosh, yes. I mean — no! Today's Huda's speech."

A ten-speed bike sliced by, splashing slush on her boots. The black suede was becoming even more blotched.

"Oh, Lord." Camellia sighed. Her warm breath turned to vapor. "Huda could incite the peace-loving to World War III over coffee! Can you imagine her haranguing the State Street crowd before lunch? The average uninformed businessman headed off to a three-martini meal, inclined to a moderate hostility toward Palestinians and disinclined to anything that might interfere with his digestion?"

"Ummm."

"And Huda is the quintessential Arab — Palestinian and proud of it."

When Camellia was nervous, she had the urge to chatter. When Khalil was silent, the urge intensified.

"My father was always discreet in conversation," she continued. "I think it was because he'd lived around the world so much. After a distressing argument, he would say, 'Ask anything of the average American, but don't ask him to examine his beliefs!'"

Khalil looked worried. "If the average American were all we had to contend with, I would not worry. I have seen posters on campus — posters announcing Huda's speech."

"But these speeches aren't *announced*! That's the whole point of the exercise — to get up and let fly and hope you can hold the crowd."

"So many Jewish student organizations.... If each sends even only one representative — "

"I see what you mean."

Khalil kicked at a stone. "I am afraid that is what her professor had in mind."

"Bentwick Schapp? Impossible. He never behaves callously — at least not toward students. He's one of the few profs who sets office hours — and actually keeps them."

"Did she tell you the title of her speech?"

"Something about the guerrilla movement?"

"'The PLO Terrorist: Madman or Freedom Fighter?'"

"Mine was 'Coffeehouses and the Pre-Rafaelites.'" Camellia added wistfully: "I'd have killed for a heckler."

"Huda is not experienced enough to turn a heckler to good advantage."

"Relax. I'm telling you, this audience lacks imagination. They won't formulate a question, much less a protest. Remember — these are anti-establishment times. To the three-piece-suiters, we're all subversives. Huda's just a subversive with olive skin."

"You are incredibly naive," Khalil said.

"I know what I'm talking about. These business types — they somehow think the whole experience is a sort of student spontaneous combustion. That knowledge acquired so rapidly and urgently somehow demands release. Little do they know how long we've crammed, searching for words, deliberating over phrases to appeal to their lizard brains, to engage them, to make them *think* — all to satisfy the minimum requirements and get the hell out of Speech 401!"

Khalil exhaled slowly. "Look at that crowd!"

Then, in the next breath: "How I envy the Jewish students their organization!"

Camellia had misjudged. In some ways, the onlookers represented a microcosm of Ann Arbor. A blue-jeaned couple with long hair looked as if they'd made a wrong turn on the way to a peace march. Women in coatdresses carried little purses and looked ready to leave at any moment. Two businessmen watched sorority sisters make angel wings in the snow. A student government contingent, politically aware, fashionably indifferent, had turned out. There was a scattering of Palestinians. A professor or two.

The Jewish students outnumbered them all. They stood apart, looking belligerent and uncomfortable — aware their presence gave legitimacy to speech as a vehicle for change but nonetheless unwilling to miss the delivery. Their movements were purposeful. Some wore skullcaps.

Khalil murmured, "I have always believed chutzpah to be overrated. Names, addresses, phone numbers — an organized response — these are the keys to success."

"Hush! Huda's speaking."

Huda stood on a wall. Her breath came in crystalline puffs. The crowd was alert, waiting.

She began, tremulous of voice.

"We all have seen the terrorist on the 6 o'clock news." Her hands trembled slightly. "When you hear him identified as a member of the PLO, what do you think? What images come to your mind?"

A discontented swelling arose. The sound was that of an orchestra tuning up. Words were bitten off, voices strangled. The sound died.

Huda lifted her chin. Her voice was crisp now, as if she'd just had a shot of Southern Comfort. A shot that had warmed her but not yet reached her brain. "What do you see?" she insisted.

"Murderers!" A young man raised his fist. His hair was bushy and black. "A killer of children and humanity!"

Huda considered briefly. Then, eyes fixed on some distant point, "You probably see a man dressed in military fatigues. He wears a tablecloth on his head. He carries a machine-gun. He is a terrorist — yes. But have you ever considered him a person? Wondered why he fights? Wondered at the justness of his cause?"

A man in a corduroy jacket took a step forward. Camellia recognized him. He was slight of build, and his skin was like parchment. He was an archaeology professor, well known on campus. A survivor of the Holocaust.

"He has no cause!" The professor thrust his fist into the air. "The Arabs — " he muttered, but his voice weakened. He lowered his arm and stepped back into place.

"No cause?" A gust of wind had dislodged Huda's fur-lined cap. She grabbed it and tucked it under her arm. Dressed in black, white and red, she looked simultaneously stalwart and slight.

"I am a Palestinian."

Camellia glanced at Khalil. He was staring ahead, fascinated.

"I am a college student, studying in your country. I would like to share some of the things I have learned. I would like to explain — briefly — *why* I am here. My university, Bir Zeit University — the Israelis have closed it many times. The last time they closed it for good. The closing — it is only one example of the injustices ... if I could just speak of ... of the people...."

"There is no Palestinian people!" The individual voices became a chorus. "Terrorist! Go back to your country! Go back to the desert!"

Camellia looked around frantically. Where was Professor Schapp? He must have stationed himself somewhere nearby, to evaluate and grade. Why wasn't he putting a stop to this? Would Arab and Jew have a showdown in Ann Arbor — with

Huda the casualty?

Eyes downcast, Huda stood holding her hat, listening to the crowd's collective voice.

"Do something, Khalil!" Camellia elbowed him. "This isn't rhetoric — this is life!"

But he, like the crowd, stood mesmerized.

There was a lull. Huda held her hat aloft like a scimitar.

"You have been misinformed!" she cried. "You have been trained to see Palestinians as guerrillas or refugees — or worse! You do not sympathize with him. You cannot feel for him even the twinge of guilt you sometimes feel about the conquered people of *your* homeland — the American Indian!"

Camellia had seen enough of Huda's prepared speech to know she was departing radically from it.

"More than likely," Huda continued, "you do not know the Palestinians have the highest literacy rate in the Arab world! That we have produced more university graduates than any other Arab country! You are unaware that many of us are Christian. That all but the most recent generation once lived in the land called Palestine...."

Her voice grew more forceful. She was back on track.

Damn, Camellia thought. Incapable of stoicism, she admired the stoic. Momentarily she wondered why Americans so often interpreted passivity of expression, the great patience of tribal peoples, as indifference.

Brisk, furtive, Huda wiped away a tear. The blue vein at her temple throbbed. Camellia recognized anger. Huda didn't cry from sorrow, ever. Only from outrage and despair.

"The PLO is a political fact brought about by historical tragedy. It thrives on a vision of a national homeland. The PLO was not born in the desert where a new generation of martyrs now trains. It was founded 10 years ago, by *students*, at the University of Stuttgart. Who does it represent? The Palestinians — all three and a half million of us."

The crowd had quieted. Curiously, it stayed quiet. The young women making angel wings sat in their forms; the 9-to-5 crowd had stopped looking at their watches.

"We were forced from our land, stripped of our national and human rights. But we are no less powerful in exile!"

There was more: Huda spoke of the PLO's hospitals and schools, its archives, its parliament in exile. She described the Red Crescent with its network of hospitals in Syria, Lebanon and Egypt. She held her hands clenched at her sides, speaking as if nothing but exhaustion could stop the flow of words.

She spoke until a snowball hit her in the face.

"Yes — Zionist!" someone shouted. The snowball disintegrated against Huda's skin.

The word "Zionist" — that was the trigger.

"We were betrayed by the Europeans," Huda had said. "Uprooted by the Zionists—"

Like a backgammon player who plays skillfully, offensively and well, the crowd was ready to retaliate. The merely curious began to edge away. Those who remained were the core of the committed.

Huda wiped snow from her eyes. She continued, describing the resistance movement, composed of lawyers, doctors, journalists, poets. Many had abandoned their careers as they had been forced to abandon the land. But none would abandon the cause. During fighting in Lebanon, PLO soldiers had guarded fleeing Americans. The soldiers in escort had "roses in the barrels of their guns to show their commitment to peace."

Fearful Camellia moved closer to Khalil. The time to intervene, to influence the outcome, was gone. The incident had taken on a life of its own. Curious, that Khalil had not somehow rescued Huda. Had he, too, come only to listen?

"The facts are clear. Arabs and Jews must live in peace. We must share the dream — as we must somehow share the land." She touched her chin in a gesture Camellia recognized as a plea for indulgence; then she opened her arms in a gesture of expansiveness everyone recognized. "I am not asking you to join the boycott against retailers of goods to the Israelis. I am not asking you to write to your congressmen. I am not asking you to *do* anything. All I ask is for understanding. I ask only this: When you hear the word PLO or see the Palestinian on television, don't say, 'Goddamned terrorist.' Ask, 'Oh, God — why?'"

The second snowball seemed to come from nowhere.

The Palestinian students needed no further excuse. Huda had been hit.

Without anyone having given a signal, the fight turned physical. It was Khalil, in fact, who tackled the young man who had thrown the second snowball. He was the young man who had spoken earlier. The scuffle was fast becoming a full-fledged fight. Even the archaeology professor was flailing indiscriminately.

Camellia stood on the sidelines, paralyzed, ineffectual. "My God! Khalil...."

He was being pummeled. But he quickly disentangled. Blood was oozing from the corner of his lip. He spat in the direction of the combatants who had already forgotten him.

"It is pointless. Let us go to her...."

Huda stood dazed. She hadn't even bent to pick up her cap. They linked their arms through hers.

They heard someone mutter: "She should not have been allowed to speak."

As they put distance between themselves and the crowd, they could hear the sirens of the campus police.

Farther away still, a second sound overlaid itself. Weirdly incongruous, it floated from the center of campus. A harpsichord. A recorder melody. Other oddly familiar melodies and remote notes blended in harmony.

"The Academy of Early Music!" Camellia said. "What a day for an open-air concert!"

"Oh!" Huda's giggle pushed hysteria. "I guess at one time or another everyone must practice in the 'real world'!"

The music grew louder. The sounds of the melee di-minished. Or perhaps it is our hearing that is diminishing, Camellia thought.

She looked back. There was Bentwick Schapp, Huda's professor, staring after her, looking slightly awed and embarrassed, as if he had fathered an illegitimate child.

****

In a week she would be in Beirut.

So many details! Her passport came — at last! — in the mail. A sympathetic Myra Wendt agreed to waive the usual two-week notice at the Ann Arbor News. Camellia was sure it was easier for the publisher and general manager to be so considerate, especially since she had waived any compensation for accrued vacation time.

She thanked Myra for offering her the chance to freelance articles when she reached Lebanon but Camellia felt she needed a clean break from all that and probably from journalism itself. "Nah, Camellia, you're too good at what you do. I can tell you that now." Myra grinned. "Somewhere, and soon, you'll be doing this again. That whole damned Arab shtick isn't you and you'll find that out soon enough."

Farewells in the newsroom were brief and perfunctory. Aside from Myra, Camellia had made no real friendships there and was, in fact, relieved to be leaving a group of average newspeople she considered to be too smug and parochial for her.

One afternoon, she pounded on the door of Khalil's apartment. When he let her in, she pranced around the living room, hugging to her chest a stack of magazines she had borrowed from Huda.

"Ah, the Middle East! I'll be a gazelle among the dromedaries!"

"In those clothes? You look like a refugee."

"You mean there aren't any flower children in Beirut?" She skidded to a stop against a bulging suitcase. Dubious, she patted the soft denim of her favorite jeans. "And they're such a perfect fit!"

Khalil looked up from The Wall Street Journal. "That long straight hair is strictly '60s. And those eyebrows — somewhere there must be an arch. See if you can find it. For Beirut you will need — " He considered. "Stockings. Jewelry. Designer jeans, if you insist on jeans..."

"Just what I need. A pasha who thinks he's Pygmalion."

"*Turks* are pashas. If you must insult me, at least get the continent right." He put down the newspaper. His eyes were alight with affection. "You are lovely. But raw charm will take you only so far."

"Oh?"

"Many things add to a woman's allure. The slope of her shoulders. The arch of her foot." Ironically, "The lilt of her voice — "

"Beast!"

"My beauty. With a little help from me."

"You're sure of yourself."

"Tweezers alone would make an incredible difference."

"Ha! Twiggy should have my eyebrows." Doubtful, she surveyed her running shoes: scuffed Nikes. "Whatever will your mother think?"

"She is familiar with Americans. She will understand your — how do you say it in English? Flakiness?"

She stuck out her tongue.

But she let him take her shopping. Setting feminist principles aside, she let him pick and choose. She let him pay. Cultural accommodation and all that, she thought. Got to meet him halfway. Relinquish the notion of American cultural superiority. And loving every minute of it, as he lavished her with clothes and gifts — although accepting them contradicted everything she believed about the role of liberated women.

Khalil's taste was exquisite. He favored fitted suits. Clingy dresses with tiny chain belts. Purses of soft leather with matching shoes. He didn't just choose an outfit. He pulled together an ensemble.

Stocking up on necessities, she had picked up a bottle of Sweet Earth cologne. She liked the pleasantly fruity smell. But the scent was all wrong for the clothes. She now realized she should have bought the kind of perfume that sells by the quarter ounce.

Khalil didn't shop at stores; he patronized boutiques. Camellia was intimidated by the elegance of the coifed salesladies. They gushed over Khalil.

"I'll bet the words 'permanent press' never cross *her* lips," Camellia muttered as one of them trotted off to search for her size. Khalil followed, and in consultation they settled on a crisp, navy three-piece suit.

"Impressive." Camellia twirled in front of the boutique mirror. The outfit didn't twirl with her. Its lines were severe above and below the wasp waist. "But — don't I look like someone in search of something to command?"

"*Now* you have style," the saleslady asserted.

Khalil nodded admiringly.

Camellia inhaled, straightening her spine. Her hair, now blunt cut with bangs, skimmed padded shoulders. In the dressing cubicle, a two-piece champagne-and-russet creation lay, discarded, on the bench. It had been her choice. She couldn't help thinking how well its muted colors complemented her. Iridescent green eyes. Rose cheeks.

"Garish," Khalil had said.

Then, back at his apartment, in the soft half-light of dusk, he unwrapped a purchase she hadn't yet seen. From white tissue paper he withdrew a soft, sheer nightgown with a stretch-lace bodice and tiny straps. She unfolded it eagerly and draped it across her body.

"It's lovely," she murmured. "So sensual and soft."

Then, impulsively, she pulled off her clothes.

"What are you doing? It is freezing outside."

"But so warm here. I can't wait to try it." She stepped into the gown and stood before the full-length mirror. "Ooh. It's indecent." Her flesh was visible, from breasts to shadowy thigh-junction. The rise of her belly and curve of her hips softly silhouetted.

"Make me warmer?"

But already he was kissing her nape, stroking her skin, pulling the thin straps and knitted lace from the white swell of her breasts, kissing her nipples and savoring every moment of the kissing, until finally he made love to her with the gown spread around her like a casing. They lay until dusk grew heavy. Drowsy, Khalil watched her dress. But when Camellia left for home the glow turned to a feeling of vague irritation. Was she regretting — what? Loss of innocence? *Now?*

There was nothing left in his apartment that was not boxed and ready for removal.

Next day, Violet helped her organize and pack. Pastel-colored luggage and strewn apparel created a look of soft disarray as Camellia's bedroom became the scene of an intimate soiree.

Camellia was pawing through nightgowns and underwear when Angela poked her head in to exclaim, "How bride-like you look — such high color!"

Camellia balled up her flannel pajamas and stuffed them back into the drawer. "Just get me to the jet on time." She slammed the drawer shut.

"Cold feet?" Violet asked. "Grab some extra socks."

"Hardly."

"You're the center of attention. Romance ... travel ... You should make like Snow White. Not like Grumpy!"

"I just don't want anyone rushing me into marriage. Not Khalil — and not you." She bunched up a pullover and tossed it into an open suitcase. "A woman can have adventure without being married," she finished in a tone of superiority.

Angela walked over to the bed, pretending not to be shocked. "I always wondered why Snow White bothered with all those funny little men," she said absently. She finished putting an antique lace scarf into Camellia's peach-colored garment bag. Pieces of lace stuck out in tufts where Angela had forced folds in the fabric. She patted it dreamily. "Nina's stole," she said. "I've never been attached to *things*. But this scarf is practically our only family heirloom. All I have to remember your grandmother by."

"No fair!" Violet stopped pairing socks. "Muzz, you should save that for *me*. I'm the one left behind. I'm the comfort of your old age. Camellia won't need it. Not in Lebanon."

"Aargh! Mother, if anyone sends you to an early grave, it'll be Violet."

Violet sighed. "I've always regretted sibling rivalry existed. I was deprived of the pleasure of inventing it." Laconically, she twisted a pair of Camellia's kneesocks into a knot. "Well — where *would* you wear that stole of antique lace? To the camel races?"

The suitcases were filling rapidly. Camellia, lost in thought, was still trying to decide between the mohair sweater and the suede jacket with fringe. "Too bad you have to miss it," she murmured.

"Miss what? Camels on the straight-away?"

"The wedding, idiot. *If* I decide to get married."

Angela seemed distracted. "Don't the Lebanese believe in June weddings?"

"I have no idea. Why?"

"In June, Violet and I could make a Grand Tour...."

"No way! You're not dragging *me* to camel-land," Violet exclaimed.

"Hold that thought." Momentarily, Camellia forgot her packing. "The Lebanese have survived earthquakes, conquerors and plagues. I'm not sure Lebanon — or my relationship with Khalil — could survive the two of *you*."

Angela's fluttery kisses, Huda's damp hug, Violet's wan wisecracks — and a gift of a dozen red roses from the three of them.... The good-bys were brief, but the ambivalence was piercing. Sensations of loss and longing, nostalgia and eager anticipation — there was little time to think. The jetway retracted, groaning. Aloft, the wheels retracted with a thump. Camellia and Khalil sat together, unspeaking during takeoff, fingers entwined, and soon were thousands of feet in the air, streaking across the Atlantic, riding the wings of adventure....

They drank champagne from plastic glasses and Camellia grew numb. But as the trip wore on, her limbs regained sensation. With every vibrating hour she knew more completely the dry-lipped, bone-weary fatigue of travel.

"The travel agents call this flying *straight*?" she asked, incredulous. For 18 hours, they had done nothing but fly, land, deplane, refuel, take off. Fly some more, then land, only to trudge to an airport lounge or waiting room to slump onto one of the vinyl-covered benches. On such stops they rested briefly, inhaling the acrid smoke of smoldering cigarettes. Then change planes and begin the cycle again.

On the final leg of the journey, she retreated to the lavatory. There she removed her pantyhose and threw them away. She rinsed out her mouth and dusted herself with baby powder. What a first impression she would make! She returned to her seat and gave Khalil's hand a squeeze, thinking: this trip would make Juliet snappish and Romeo hold out for a prenuptial agreement.

Nozzles above her seat let loose a blast of cold air, and everyone seemed to come alert at once, lifting window shades and groping for belongings, restless energy relayed in shuffles and bumps. In Athens, a dozen or so Greek passengers had boarded, young men with shirts unbuttoned to reveal tufts of hair and chain-encircled necks; they reached for a final cigarette.

Camellia's watch showed midnight. But it was morning. The plane — emerging from the swirling fuchsias and mauves of sunrise — moved toward a new horizon, into the hard glare of sun on uncut rock, on steel and glass, and white roofs dotting dusky mountainsides.

"Beirut." Khalil was exuberant. He gestured at the window as if frustrated that she could not see as *he* saw. "Look!"

It was a panorama of shaggy mountain ranges crowding a conquered terrain, villas like pearls clustered on slopes where the mountainous encroachment stopped short, allowing a valley. There lay Beirut. Like a stalwart occupier, it stood jammed with buildings that covered flat land, dotting it with beige walls and red-tile roofs; the gray of roads supplanting the cool colors of the hills. White skyscrapers rose abutting the sea, surrounded by land and clusters of transplanted pines. The highrise windows were like sightless eyes overlooking the Mediterranean. "Magnificent," Camellia said softly.

He seemed not to hear. "We are hours from Moscow ... minutes from Jerusalem, with Europe and North Africa just beyond. Camellia! I have brought you to ... to the center of the world."

She reached for his hand. He seemed oblivious.

"Think of it, my love! We are circling ... the origin of civilization! Greeks and Romans ruled here. Assyrians, Persians, Egyptians — all called this valley home. Phoenicians launched ships here. The Crusaders ... God help us, the Turks — once it was theirs.

"Now" — his eyes became fixed on some distant point — "it is for the Lebanese. Lebanon for the Lebanese," he repeated firmly.

Camellia craned her neck for a last view of the mountains, but she saw only the rushing-up ground; the engines roared final resistance and the wheels touched, jolting on the runway.

Her hand lay limp in his.

For the first time, she imagined herself in Beirut, wandering alone in the *souk*, the labyrinth of ancient streets that Khalil could navigate by heart, but that she would know only as an endless, pitted maze.

Once, in Ann Arbor, with Lebanese friends, he had told a joke, the premise of which she could not remember. He had laid out the situation in English, but, at the punch line, switched to Arabic. She sat witnessing his laughter, unable to understand, to share. He refused to translate. It could not be translated, he said. The meaning, the spirit, the subtlety would be lost.

She wondered if Khalil, unknowingly, held something from her now....

"I've missed my night's sleep." She stared uncomprehendingly at her watch. Then she dug her fingers into the taut muscles of her neck. "My circadian rhythms will never be the same."

Khalil's face was blank with pleasure, with unself-conscious savoring. Did he now think in Arabic? In the language of the heart, of dreams?

He gave her hand an answering squeeze. "Come, my love!" He smiled forgivingly. "What is one night ... in the land of a thousand and one nights?"

3

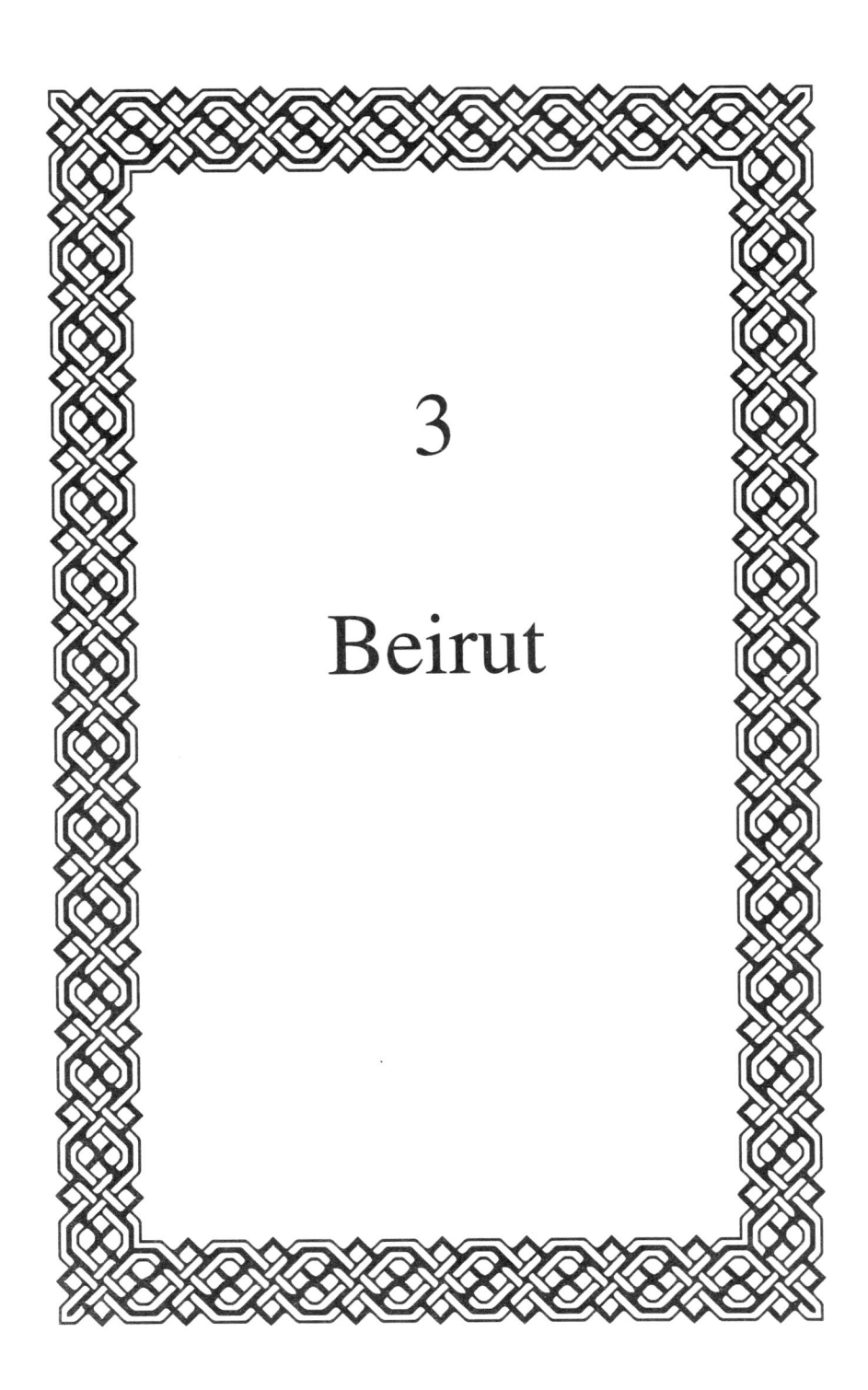

Beirut

"*Ahlan! Ahlan! Ahlan!*"

The words were like the opening notes of a symphony, welcoming Camellia to Khalil's world.

"*Ahlan! Ahlan! Ahlan!*"

Strong repeated triple-beats, expressive as bells.

There was touch, too — lavish touch; successive kisses, handshakes and hugs. Throughout it all came the soft echo: "*Ahlan! Ahlan! Ahlan!*"

Abu Mousa — Khalil's father. Om Mousa — Khalil's mother. Their titles carried the name of their first-born — Mousa, long dead.

Samir! So handsome. Young. Vulnerable looking. Strong bones, like Khalil's. But wider eyes. Less rigidity around the mouth.

Abu Mousa never stopped stroking his mustache, even as he maneuvered through the Beirut traffic.

"*Y'allah. Ya habibi. Hamdullah as-salaamah!*" he exclaimed whenever the thought occurred to him, which was roughly every hundred meters.

"Oh! Translate for me," Camellia begged.

At first Khalil refused. But then, reluctantly: "Welcome, my darling. Thank God for your safe return."

Camellia shivered, both at the words and the way Khalil's voice caught, repeating them. There was something grand about phrases repeated in prescribed order, in rhythms developed over time through centuries of language-building. Of course, Camellia couldn't distinguish the words. But sound alone gave them poetry.

Suddenly an even stranger sound — .

An eerie chant arose from somewhere high and distant.

"The *muezzin's* call to prayer," Khalil said. He seemed more comfortable explaining things that were objective and dispassionate. "The Moslems blast that call to prayer five times each day throughout the city, at intervals set by sun and moon. Get used to it."

The rise and fall of the wavering voice left her mystified. She had never heard the call to prayer. But the strains seemed familiar, like a dream that suddenly makes sense.

At the airport perimeter, she had been dimly aware that the volume of dusty ground about equaled the amount of paved area. Concrete was clearly the foreign material, set in intervals, spliced into the roll and rise of hard earth. But the dust couldn't conceal the smell of spring.

Sun glinted on jets. Families — extended families — stood clustered. They gathered to wait, standing not on the paved area but on the hard dust of the earth. Women wore shapeless dresses in terra cotta colors. Scarves tied around their heads.

A wild-haired child looked her full in the face — but quickly averted his gaze. What sensitive thought had occurred to him?

Om Mousa crushed her in brief possession. Camellia felt salt tears and bosomy maternal weight.

So many others: cousins and uncles, friends and aunts. Loving gestures and moist eyes — the emotional tumult of welcome. Cars — at least four carloads of relatives and friends. Abu Mousa drove a red Mercedes Benz.

Samir was olive-skinned and young, just her height, disarmingly awkward and shy. She had kissed him, and he had grinned.

As the caravan began its zigzag journey through the chaotic Beirut traffic — and *home*, Khalil's home — she had no time to ponder. Taxi horns blared in frequent blasts. They ran together, making a cacophony of street noise, brakes-on-pavement and horns, some of which were programmed to make melodies. Background noise rendered unintelligible the many conversations going on at once — not that she could have understood a word in any case.

Would they never stop exclaiming over her? The phrases fell like rain. She could hardly tell one person from the next. Faces and names blended, then blurred. Few identities registered. And all while still at the airport! This must be what it's like to be in shock, she thought, as she sat quietly beside Khalil for the rest of the drive, unable to formulate question or response.

Entering another country was like being a traveler in time. It gave the word "disoriented" new meaning. Camellia was unaware of being tired, though her mind was sluggish and numb.

She squeezed as close to Khalil as she could get. She held tight to his wrist. Quick impressions registered as scenery changed from street to street. Dingy fabric-topped, misaligned buildings fronted with ragged, fluttering wash signaled poverty. Then the squalid area cleared and gave way to gleaming glass and skyscrapers.

Abu Mousa veered east to the Christian suburbs.

Khalil's family lived in Ain Rumaneh. It was every bit as neat and bright as

Khalil had described. Pastel-colored apartment buildings abutted glass-fronted stores and shops with steel shutters. Villas had balconies whose angles hinted of inner courtyards. Here, the wash fluttering on balconies wasn't ripped. Boys kicked soccer balls. But even here the alleys were full of trash. It was shocking, like seeing a beggar-lady at Saks.

Marble stairs made a path to the third-floor flat.

A formal living room. Camellia was sitting on a scratchy divan. She understood nothing of the hurried conversations and softly shouted exchanges. Excluded from the dialogue, she couldn't build new words or ideas in her consciousness. Only the ritual of welcome still rang in her head — "*Ahlan! Ahlan! Ahlan!*"

All at once, cookies and tea were brought. Cigarettes offered. Drinks replenished.

Then a strange thing happened. As if alerted by some sixth sense, everyone looked at her. Parents, brother, aunts and uncles, friends — all who filled this room apparently became simultaneously aware. They had neglected her. Caught up in affectionate greeting, they had been attentive exclusively to Khalil.

Mortified that they had forgotten her, even for a moment, they baptized her anew with questions of concern.

Was she hot, cold ... hungry? Would she like a pillow to soften the divan against her back? What could they bring her? Did she speak *any* Arabic? No? French, perhaps? No?

Ma'alesh. Never mind.

She was amused, profoundly touched — and slightly overwhelmed. What could she do but smile in thanks? If only Khalil had prepared her! He had once said, rather clinically, "You will find the art of welcome highly developed among ... among my people. Westerners say of us, we are an easy people to love." He had made the assertion with such unself-consciousness that it had seemed fact, not boast. There seemed nothing more to say.

"Please tell them — " she whispered to Khalil — "tell them I am comfortable and very, very happy."

What she told *herself*, silently and firmly, was: Love like this can surmount any barrier. Even language barriers.

Concern faded with the half-drunk drinks and the half-smoked cigarettes. Thinking they had forgotten her again, Camellia nudged Khalil.

"I can't believe it!" she said. "Your family — it's like watching Masterpiece Theater in reverse!"

"The British show?" he asked absently. He was too immersed to either recall American television or appreciate the comparison.

She stifled a giggle. "Rigid British family manners — how strange and cold they seem! Your family is openly affectionate. Like aborigines."

"Naked in the rain forest? Hardly. Do not forget; this is a society of conventions.

You cannot hope to understand my people so soon. But you will understand them. I will help you."

She squeezed his hand. "And I'll love you for it."

"Starting now." He withdrew his hand. "Public displays of affection between men and women ... would not be accepted or understood."

She sighed. The way he said *my people*, giving the words powerful resonance ... he had spun a cocoon of warmth around her with those words. Even if he refused to hold her hand in public.

So vast was the depth of Khalil's bond with his family, so unreserved their embrace of her, and so childlike, fanciful and secure did she become as a result — it was some time before she realized that Khalil's family had not been told. Not been told about *her*.

No one had known she was coming.

****

The living room was starkly elegant. Wine-colored Persian carpets carried motifs of stylized birds. A gold-threaded Damascene cloth covered a nearby table. Themes and rich hues were repeated throughout the room. The furniture was all gleaming wood and polished marble — it could have been Italian. A few pieces were intricately carved, recognizably Ottoman: corner chests and drawers, wood inlaid with glittering mother of pearl, fabric lavishly embroidered. Walls were unbroken except for religious adornments. All were hung too high — a jeweled crucifix, an ivory Madonna. Even the peacock-blue tapestry of the Last Supper was positioned just below the ceiling.

Two vital functions of this room were immediately apparent: Providing seating for, easily, two dozen people. And shielding the less formal quarters of the flat from view.

People sat everywhere. The chairs were strung in rows along the walls. Ironically, they created a circle. Did the decor mimic the nomadic circles of the past? Camellia wondered.

When Khalil had first entered *Camellia's* home, in Ann Arbor, he had asked: "But where is the furniture?" Now she understood his astonishment. Angela's beanbag and love-seat arrangement created space that must have seemed vast.

Composition, balance, style — here, all gave way to practical necessity. People came — and people sat. The decor existed only to serve their sociability.

"*Biddek ahweh?*"

Om Mousa stood in front of her, holding a silver tray. On it were white cookies and painted china cups that were handleless. They looked like tiny tulips. Fragrant coffee filled them to their gold-lipped rims.

Camellia shifted uncomfortably. The fabric of the red-and-ivory divan scratched her legs. Where was Khalil? He had left the room 10 minutes ago, following Samir lugging suitcases. She hadn't let him take her shoulder bag. She had clutched it as if it were a talisman.

"*Biddek ahweh?*" Om Mousa's voice was surprisingly birdlike and mellifluous. It rose slightly in repetition.

Patrician features, an abundance of upswept hair ... low light from the lamps cast crescent shadows on her cheeks. How lovely she must have been — before bitterness had hardened.

Dazed, Camellia looked from Om Mousa to the tray and back again, understanding that "ahweh" must be "coffee," and that she was being offered some. For the second time.

She couldn't speak. She couldn't think. Inhibited, embarrassed, she could only wonder why she was utterly incapable of formulating a reply.

Om Mousa stood patiently. How strange, Camellia thought, that this woman would always bear the name of Mousa, the son who died at birth. Yes, Khalil had explained that Arab mothers and fathers always assumed the titles Om and Abu, "mother of" and "father of" their first-born sons. But surely no one could have blamed Om Mousa for breaking the rules. For choosing to become not "Om Mousa" but "Om Khalil." For taking the name of the son who lived....

By now Om Mousa had lowered the tray to the level of Camellia's chin. An unfamiliar scent, aromatic and exotic, wafted from the coffee.

"No ... no thank you," Camellia stuttered.

Om Mousa looked puzzled. She spoke again, this time in French.

"Ahweh!" "Cafe!" "Coffee!"

Suddenly the coffee was being offered in three languages. Half a dozen people interceded, crowding close, each trying to end the social impasse, some translating, others gesturing or quizzing. A balding, middle-aged man a with reddish-brown mustache — one of Khalil's uncles — attempted broken English.

The meaning was clear. What could be wrong? Who would refuse coffee after such a long journey, after setting foot across a strange threshold?

Khalil emerged from the bedroom area looking irritated. "What is going on?"

Camellia shrugged her shoulders. Ruefully, "Three years of high-school French, and I don't understand a word."

"It is *coffee*."

"But I want to sleep."

"You must drink it. Once, at least. It is the ritual...." He gestured helplessly, impatient with her lack of understanding. "I cannot explain. Just ... There!"

He nodded approvingly, watching her balance the hot tiny vessel between her fingertips. "Smell the cardamom," he invited.

She did, then sipped. The coffee was sweet and bitter. "Gee. Am I supposed to drink it — or eat it with a fork?"

"Drink it in good health." His tone of gentleness became emphatic. "True, it is strong. But then the cups are small." And, more expansively: "There is nothing like the rich, bitter smell of coffee beans roasting over a fire. Or the rhythm of Tayta, my grandmother, pounding them."

Abruptly, Khalil turned back to the family, to the audience of flushed, expectant faces. The interlude had ended. Camellia knew nothing about Lebanese social conventions. But she began to sense the strength of social custom and expectation. Khalil's attention seemed focused by external forces that excluded her. More curiously, as he re-embraced the family, ending a five-year absence with an outpouring of news and an exchange of anecdotes and gossip, she could see how much he loved it. Khalil the urbane, the independent, was also Khalil of the tribe.

She wondered how long it would be before she would stop feeling like a stranger. And, more immediately, how soon she could find a bed and sleep.

Everyone laughed raucously. Khalil had been telling a joke. He looked pale but astonishingly unrumpled.

More coffee ... more laughter ... more talk.

"Khalil — "

Cool as a snowy egret on a hillock, he came naturally to his Beirut elegance, unaware of physical discomfort, seemingly unaffected by private want. He sat with his legs crossed. His trousers were crisp. Occasionally, he leaned to light someone's cigarette. His cheeks shone porcelain-doll pink; a vein at his temple throbbed. He seemed more alluring, more unattainable than ever. What did he draw from the mutual exchange of information, anecdote, loving recount of shared memory? What attentiveness, what respect flows in what unalterable pattern when people sit in circles — the beginningless and endless circles of society — that give resonance even to banter?

Could any single lover compete with the potent chemistry of family, of clan? Would Khalil ever crave time — alone with her?

As the voices mingled and chattered, laughed and demanded, Camellia became more mystified by language. In compensation, she became attuned to tones, vibrations, inflections. With growing sensitivity, she began to read meaning even in pauses. Om Mousa put a question to Khalil. In his insouciant reply, she recognized tossed-off evasion.

Everyone laughed.

Everyone except Om Mousa. She seemed distant, genuinely puzzled.

Oh, Camellia thought. Now she's looking at *me*.

Camellia nudged Khalil with her elbow.

"What was your mother's question?"

"Nothing important."

"What have you told her — about me?"

"Camellia...." Khalil's voice was pleasantly modulated. His palms were upraised in innocence —

"Your mother knows about me. *Doesn't* she?"

Still no definitive statement from Khalil —

"Can it be true? Did you bring me to the end of the earth without telling anyone? Not even your mother?"

"Why declare more than is necessary? They say in Morocco, 'Among walnuts, only the empty one speaks.'"

"How can you be so cavalier, so — " She stopped short. "You're not even Moroccan," she finished in a burst of foolishness.

He ate a white cookie and brushed away crumbs. Then he downed a cupful of the bitter coffee in one gulp.

"My mother is not worried. She is bringing up an ... an agreement between Yasmina's family and mine. Unwritten, of course, but understood by certain family members since her birth. That we would marry." This time it was Khalil who finished in a rush.

"Marry? You would marry? You and *who*?"

"Yasmina, of course." He continued in a tone of ennui. "A Maronite bride ... it would have pleased the traditionalists." He yawned, then scooped up a handful of cashews and began to munch thoughtfully. "My parents knew I wanted to marry. They did not know I had already chosen the bride."

"Oh! A minor technicality."

"Camellia — "

"Are you trying to tell me your marriage has already been *arranged*?"

"Of course not. I have told you before. This is Beirut, not the desert. No one is forced to marry against his or her will."

Unable to resist: "Is she beautiful?"

"Heartbreakingly so."

"And the arrangement — . You'll break it off, just like that?"

Yawning again, he extended three fingers to cover his lips. "Yasmina is my cousin. Second. Or perhaps third. It is no longer fashionable to marry cousins. And Yasmina is rarely unfashionable."

"What if she's got her heart set on you?"

"Then her brothers will kill me."

"You will deserve it."

"I would rather die, if I could not marry you."

Camellia looked at him, not knowing whether he was teasing, too much in love to care.

"If you are promised to Yasmina, and *they* don't kill you," she muttered, "I will."

****

At last, as if responding to some abrupt signal, the welcoming party left. Their departure cleared the room of at least thirty people. These were only a fraction of the Beirutis bearing Khalil's family name, Majdi. The Majdis who had come to the airport were only the Majdis with whom Khalil's family had an ongoing, daily social relationship.

Abu Mousa knew how to fall asleep speedily when opportunity permitted. He slung his legs over the arm of the couch. He closed his eyes. Almost immediately, he began to snore.

There was a maid. Bahija — they referred to her simply as "the Moroccan." She washed and dried dishes, thumped and bumped glasses and pans with a clattering echo, making no attempt to stifle the noise. She sang to herself.

Working swiftly and silently, Om Mousa briskly repositioned cushions and emptied ashtrays in the living room. Samir and Khalil talked quietly.

Camellia was now sitting upright on the stiff divan, mostly vertical but half-asleep. Travel, new experience, the spectacular realization that she couldn't communicate with anyone — all combined to create a sensation of utter enervation. Background noise lulled her almost into a stupor.

A delighted exclamation from Khalil brought her quickly awake.

"Tayta!"

Startled, Camellia blinked. Khalil's grandmother had moved, whisper-quiet, unnoticed, to the center of the room.

She moved on noiseless slippered feet to where she stood, alone. A shapeless black dress shrouded her. A band of fabric wound like a wimple across her forehead. When tears glistened on her cheeks, she made no move of her gnarled hands to wipe them away. Half-coherent cries caught in her throat as she swept Khalil into her arms.

Then she turned to Camellia, regarding her momentarily with faint surprise, then crushing her in an embrace no less fervent.

Camellia hugged back. The old woman smelled of talcum and fragrance, as if she had bathed in rosewater. Camellia could also smell the mustiness of old cloth.

That black garment — what did its opaque fullness conceal? Withered breasts, milk-white skin that had never seen the sun?

Tayta briefly pressed Camellia's plump cheek to her own dry one and, after soft, repeated kisses, cupped Camellia's face in her bony hands.

Now *this* is scrutiny, Camellia thought.

Tayta's eyes, faded but intelligent and deeply set, missed nothing. Camellia knew intuitively that, with Tayta, the language barrier would be irrelevant. As Tayta analyzed, judged and sought confirmations of the first impression Camellia had made — whatever it might have been — language would be only one of many sensory means of assessment.

To Tayta's repeated *"Ahlans!"* Camellia stumblingly replied, *"Marhaba!"*

After several exchanges, Camellia took one step backward, then another.

Am I beyond the point where Tayta's vision blurs? she wondered. Suddenly embarrassed, she shoved her hands into the pockets of her suit. The metallic polish on her fingernails now seemed garish. Why had it ever appealed to her? She could imagine how the plum eyeliner and taupe eyeshadow looked in this light, especially to Tayta, who wore her years unadorned, like a mantle of dignity. Camellia's own grandfather, in America, would have called it "paint," Camellia a "shameless hussy." No matter that the year was 1975 and Camellia more than old enough to vote.

But Tayta smiled as she lowered herself to a cross-legged position on the wool carpet, awash in the innocent pleasure of the aged when presented with the young. She issued a soft order and Samir brought pillows and a glass of hot tea. Tayta's voice, slurred but precise, overrode the rasp of her breath. The voice was accustomed to being heard.

"Come closer, so she can see," Khalil translated.

Camellia squatted on the carpet. Leaning on a chair leg, she tried to mimic Tayta's easy comfort on the floor. She caught her breath at the sight of Tayta's gnarled hand, outstretched and reaching, steady and sure.

Her fingers trailed over Camellia's cheek.

Camellia exhaled. She was almost afraid to speak. While still in high school, she had once been introduced to her best friend's aunt. As the aunt stood by, Camellia's friend set about describing her. "Camellia's not too ugly," she said teasingly; "though she's on the short side. Most striking feature ... ummm, would have to be the green eyes. Pale green eyes. The rest is standard issue."

Camellia had blurted: "Cut it out, you idiot! Let your aunt make up her own mind."

Camellia had never been so mortified as the moment she learned the aunt was blind. Camellia's friend, out of mischief, or simple forgetfulness, had neglected to prepare her in advance.

Camellia had then and there resolved never to commit a similar gaucherie. Unsure of the status of Tayta's eyesight or health, she decided not to ask any questions. Or to blurt out anything.

There was life in the old woman's expression, and cleverness in her eyes. Her smile was earthy and forgiving.

The soft voice continued its litany. Then another order, to Khalil.

Khalil blinked sardonically. "You are precious, she says. Your mother must weep, letting you travel so many miles from home. We must cherish you."

Camellia clasped and unclasped her hands. What to say in response that would not sound sentimental? Or simply dumb? She felt the prick of tears. The sight of

Khalil's irreverent expression inhibited them.

"Smirk and I'll kill you," she said.

"Just do not take her literally. You are conceited enough as it is."

"Me?" For no good reason, tears were streaming down her face.

He touched Tayta lightly on the shoulder, then took Camellia's hand.

She followed him out of the room.

****

Clean sheets! They had never seemed so glorious!

She tucked herself into Khalil's boyhood bed, alone, luxuriant in scented sheets. But sleep was a forgotten dream.

She lay alert. Her nerves were tight as the spring buds on Om Mousa's zinnias on the windowsill.

Somnolent breezes of afternoon should bring on drowsiness. Or was it no longer afternoon? Had day dissolved abruptly into night? The gray-blue window-light could signal either crepuscule or dawn.

Someone cracked the door. Khalil. Camellia sat upright, startled.

"The door seems grown onto its hinges," she said, pulling the sheet up under her chin. "That sound was sudden as a gunshot."

"I was trying to be quiet. I thought you were asleep." He entered the room. He was walking almost as softly as Tayta. He carried something. She couldn't see it in the dimness.

"I can't. I'm so tired, but ... What's all that?"

"Delicacies. To tempt you." Gray light bathed his face. He set a woven basket on the night-stand. It held bananas and pears, plums and cans of 7-Up, Jordan almonds and expensively wrapped chocolates. "From my mother."

"What a spread! Your family is unbelievably considerate."

"My mother has been cooking for three days. They are insisting that you come to eat dinner. But I told them you are tired. That all you want to do is sleep."

"Suddenly I'm wide awake. But thanks for making my excuses."

"And when you refused to eat even a cookie ... my mother concluded, naturally, that you are shy — or too well bred to admit to hunger in a stranger's house."

"Stop laughing. How do you know it's not true?"

"Have I ever said anything that was, later, not proven absolutely correct?"

"Don't you *dare* say anything to affect their opinion of me."

"If their opinion of you is good, it is because of everything I have told them."

She held out her arms. When he sat down on the bed, she kissed him on the nose. "It's infuriating — the way I never know when you are kidding and when you are serious."

He kissed her, lingeringly, and she lay curled against him, letting him pin her down. How good to touch! Muscles, emotions, taut nerves — all became soothed in tactile response.

"Where are you sleeping?" she murmured.

"In Samir's room. He on a mattress, me in the bed."

His hands began to play, lovingly, on her skin, first on her throat, then on the rise of her breasts, then moving to graze her erect nipples.

Curiously, an indefinable sensation of unpleasantness coursed through her body. She sighed and made a wedge of her fists.

"Out! Before you ruin my reputation."

His hands tensed. He withdrew them.

To her surprise, he left. Abruptly. His shoes rat-a-tat tatted on the marble floor.

Distant voices, cries, the chatter of evening drifted from the street, carried on the wind, muffled by the fluttering curtain.

She lay with mind awhirl, body damp with frustrated desire, and wondered if she should have let him into her bed.

****

She woke to the disembodied dawn wail of the *muezzin*.

It was holy summonings: the *adhan* — the call to prayer.

Loudspeakers blared from the minarets of countless mosques.

"Wake up, my love." Khalil opened the door gently. It didn't so much as creak.

"I'm awake." She sat up, brushing her lanky hair from her eyes. Ruefully, she waved at the half-open window. "How could I sleep?"

He laughed. "True enough. Not even a late-sleeper in the Christian suburbs can escape the Moslem wailings."

It was incontrovertible, the *adhan*, set to the rise and rhythm of the sun, inexorable as the universe in all its patterns. It carved the day into worshipful intervals, echoing throughout the city. "God, the Great, the Merciful, the Compassionate." The first cry came at dawn, the last at dusk.

"Actually, I enjoy the chant," she said perversely. "The name of Allah is all but drowned in those mournful and unearthly syllables. I find it evocative and mystical. Somehow you Arabs manage to make even spirituality sensual."

"It gets old." Yesterday, indoors, even when barriers and city noise obscured the distant wail, Khalil had been irritated by it, as by a fly in a closed room.

"You should count yourself lucky not to have been born Moslem. Then you'd not only have to listen, but you'd also be forced to stop and kneel."

Puffs of morning air ferried in the noise. Camellia could almost hear industriousness: Christian entrepreneurs getting the jump on Moslem counterparts still on their knees. Metal shop shutters crunched open, brooms swished on dusty sidewalks. Somewhere, a caged canary squawked.

She rubbed her temples, where yesterday's jet lag seemed to have migrated and settled into a dull throb. It played a countermelody to the tenor of the morning background noises, sharp and lively even filtered through the third-floor window. Trilingual greetings ... hurried steps on pavement ... the thuds and shouts of boys in the courtyard.... And traffic. By now it had intensified into a steady screech of tires and blaring horns.

"Did you think Beirut would be a sissy place — like Ann Arbor?"

"I don't remember what I thought."

"*Ma'alesh.*" Khalil's tone was solicitous. "There is Turkish coffee. And food."

"Just what I need: my fiance transformed into a Jewish mother."

He smiled and looked somewhat annoyed at the same time. "Get dressed." Forehead furrowed, he scanned the room disheveled by her suitcases and accouterments of travel carelessly flung.

"You have not yet unpacked?" Distracted, not waiting for an answer, as if she were but one of many problems competing for his attention: "There will be visitors."

"Visitors? When and how many?"

"How could I know?"

"I experienced enough visitors for a month — yesterday."

"It will be like that — for a while."

"What am I supposed to do? What am I? Hostess or guest?"

"You can be and do whatever you like." His distracted air returned as he looked around the room. "Where are your clothes? I am sure you will want to look — how do you say it? Sharp."

She pushed away covers. "Will you settle for inner glow?"

****

The *muezzin's* cry burst forth repeatedly, then faded, like something that lives and dies in a day.

Everything else conspired to make time run together. The grandfather clock in the hallway could have been an hourglass fed by endless desert sand.

"*Sabah el-kher?*" Camellia's "good morning" became a question as she tried to master the difficult Arabic word.

Khalil's family smiled indulgently.

"Good morrrning," replied Abu Mousa, rolling his r's and straightening his spine. The unfamiliar language made him remember himself, and attend to his posture.

"Good morrrning." Now Tayta repeated the English salutation in her soft voice. She looked quizzical and pleased, as if she were tasting a new fruit.

Breakfast was omelet, *hummos*, *khobis*, marmalade, olives and fried potatoes.

"Everyone thinks you look skinny and starved."

Khalil helped himself to the potatoes. He watched, amused, as his parents and his grandmother admonished her to eat. Her plate had become community property. Each family member deposited choice morsels there. Even Samir tried to tempt her with a wedge of ripe tomato.

"They wonder how you have any strength at all."

"Are you kidding? I still haven't lost the five pounds I gained at Christmas."

It was an unfair contest. She knew little of complex Arab social manners but sensed she shouldn't refuse food. Unfamiliar with custom, she was helpless to resist. Obligingly, she ate more than she wanted under their watchful eyes and pleasant badgering.

When Abu Mousa loaded her plate a third time, she was beginning to feel green.

Tayta was sensitive. She said something sharp, which Khalil laughingly translated as: "Leave the girl alone."

Khalil ate hungrily, with enjoyment and appetite. Oblivious of her discomfort, delighted at the way his family pampered her, he said, "You will soon learn to deal with everyone insisting that you eat. In fact, you should refuse at least once or twice, even if you are hungry."

"And I thought learning the *language* was going to be hard!"

But he was lost in memory. Laughing, he recounted his own naivete in America: "I went to a dinner party — in Ann Arbor, in fact. It was my first. A friend took me aside and said, 'Look, things are different here. Do not turn down what is offered. The Americans will believe you mean it, and you will starve!'"

It was the last private exchange before the visitors came. Khalil was right.

They swarmed, drawn by the nectar of Khalil's homecoming. Om Mousa met them like a queen bee. Pushing the sleeves of her gray sweater to her elbows, she worked constantly, issuing staccato directions to Bahija, the Moroccan maid.

That first day Camellia learned two things: Arab social customs were so intricate and the political situation in Lebanon was far more volatile than even Dr. Elias' pessimistic assessment had led her to conclude.

The highlight of the afternoon was Yasmina's visit.

From the morning onward, coffee or tea was either being made or being served. There were two kinds of coffee. One was the standard sweet Turkish coffee sipped from handleless cups. The other was stronger, drunk from the same sort of cup, but larger. Samir served the second type. He stood before the guests, holding the coffee pot in one hand and a stack of maybe three cups in the other. He would pour the cup maybe a quarter full, then wait while the person served drained it. Meanwhile he would fill another cup in the same manner. The ritual would continue until everyone had drunk. The coffee was fragrant with cardamom.

From the kitchen Bahija toted a seemingly inexhaustible supply of 7-Up, cigarettes and fruit. Food preparation became a morning-to-evening affair. Lavish trays of eggs, meats, fruits and spicy sauces emerged from the kitchen at conventional times, complementing the steady service of breadsticks, date-filled cookies and mixed nuts between.

When the time of day or the amount of food justified calling a meal, the guests of the moment were invited if not exhorted to join the family as they ate. Everyone encircled the food. They squatted around low tables to eat goat cheese and olives from a platter. Or they stood at a laden table. The *khobis*, or triangles of Arabic bread were wielded like a primitive spoon, becoming an extension of the hand, wrapped in yeasty shreds around chunks of omelet, sugary *halva* or sauteed lamb. The arrangement heightened the communal aspects of feast.

Talk ceased as serious eating began. Camellia remembered Huda's observation: "If you cook for them, don't expect compliments. The Arabs will never say they like this dish or that dish. They do not praise the food. If they like it, they will eat."

Tea or coffee and *khobis*, the Arabic bread, were omnipresent. Visitors never left before the ritual of coffee.

Just as the visitors came, abruptly and unannounced, so they left. Their departures seemed triggered by some bell outside Camellia's range of hearing. The oldest male in the party would rise; the others would quickly stand and begin shaking hands. Everyone shook hands, even the women. Always, Khalil's family urged the departing guests to tarry. Always, they resisted. The good-bys were said, at which time every guest — some quite forcefully — issued a dinner invitation. Khalil turned them all down.

"But why can't we go?" Camellia stood on the balcony watching the departure of a couple who spoke good English. They were Khalil's contemporaries. The man was also an engineer, like Khalil. His wife was an architect. They lived nearby. "We might have a lot in common. And he is your cousin. Why turn *them* down?"

Khalil frowned. "It is complicated. If I accept his dinner invitation, I must accept the others. My parents would be obligated to return the hospitality ... our social calendar would be horrendous. We would have no time for anything else. Maybe after things settle down...."

"Why is everything so rigidly controlled? I'm beginning to feel like a bee in a hive. Each assigned its own task. Except that there's no work for me."

He laughed, pinching her cheek. Then the bell rang again and Khalil went to answer the summons of a new round of visitors.

He found a moment to whisper: "*Ma'alesh*. The heaviest visiting will be over soon ... in a day or two. Then we may slip away quietly and do as we like."

A neighbor brought round loaves of delicately wrinkled home-baked bread. Om Mousa accepted them with hurried, murmured thanks. Then she quickly passed round a box of elegant Damascus chocolates.

Khalil's contemporaries sat comparing doctorates. Relatives introduced themselves to Camellia in terms of their relationship to Khalil. Some were aunts to

Khalil's father's side. Sons of his mother's sisters. Third cousins. Wives of uncles. A unique Arabic title defined each: *mart 'ami*, wife of my uncle; *ibn silfi*, son of my brother-in-law.

They shook her hand, kissed her cheek, admired her diamond ring and called her *habibti*, my darling, as if it were her name.

"Who are all these people?" she whispered to Khalil at one point. She was sitting beside him. To cross the room was to dodge gesticulating hands and protruding knees.

Khalil was too busy to answer. He spoke French with ladies and talked politics with men, translating for her only now and then. The news monopolized the conversation. Someone had brought three of Beirut's more than half a dozen daily newspapers. They were all in Arabic.

It was hardly necessary that Camellia read them. People talked of little but the news. Henry Kissinger's peace mission had ended bitterly in Israel. President Assad of Syria had snubbed Egypt's President Sadat at the funeral of King Faisal, slain by a crazed nephew in Riyadh. The Geneva Conference seemed doomed to failure.

Little wonder — the eyes of the world are on Vietnam. North Vietnamese forces advance to Saigon; South Vietnamese forces retreat in confusion ... the refugee airlift ... scenes of desperation as soldiers mob rescue aircraft ... President Lon Nol fleeing the country — all this in the last 10 days.

Despite the somber events, political trivia was appreciated. From America, a leak: The CIA had asked a Mafia family to assassinate Castro in Cuba. The operation had occurred in the early '60s. The disclosure was treated as if it were fresh news. In most Third World nations, rumors about the CIA are rampant, and proof of its activities is always welcome, partly because what the CIA has done to one country can be experienced vicariously by another. Any evidence serves to vindicate the many who theorize about the agency's involvement in domestic affairs of state.

When Yasmina came, she was accompanied by her brothers. Khalil broke free of a heated political discussion, interrupting himself. He stood to kiss Yasmina on both cheeks. He also kissed Yasmina's brothers — Faize, Farouq and Foud — who shook hands vigorously with Camellia. Om Mousa's eyes brimmed with affection.

Camellia retreated to the kitchen, ostensibly to make the Turkish coffee.

Yasmina followed her.

"You see — it is like this." Her English was crisp, her instructions pointed. "You must let it boil three times."

Yasmina was fair-haired and hazel-eyed. Apparently she was one of the many Mediterranean Arabs who were living evidence of the Crusades. Beirut was full of them, Khalil said: the blond offspring of black-haired parents, dappling an otherwise uniform brood. They emerged, fair or redheaded, with irises of varying pigments. Yasmina's smoky eyes were kohl-lined with Pharaonic precision, her nails carefully sculpted. Gold jewelry, crafted in the image of fallen leaves, added to the image of lissome fragility. Her brothers, hardy as thorn-covered bushes, were darker and more rooted.

Yasmina grasped the painted wood handle of the copper pot, edging Camellia aside. Dewy morning had crisped into the white of afternoon. From the herb garden beneath the window rose the fragrance of parsley, cilantro and sun-warmed earth.

"Three times, you see," Yasmina repeated. Her French-accented English was stilted and precise. Her sleek skin exuded a musky perfume.

The aroma of coffee soon was overpowering.

Three times, the black liquid boiled. Each time Yasmina snatched it promptly from the flame, at the precise moment it would otherwise bubble over. Then she coaxed it to a further boil.

"There." At last she was satisfied. She smacked her lips. "It is ready."

Yasmina's sharp nails skimmed Camellia's fingers as she relinquished the wooden handle. Camellia extinguished the flame and poured the coffee into handleless cups.

"Is there a strainer?" Camellia glanced at the peelers and scrapers hanging from the wall. Sediment from the pulverized beans was running into the cups.

"*La. La.* Of course not." Yasmina's laugh was lilting and mocking. "You Americans do everything the easy way."

"Do we?"

Yasmina had pulled a clear bottle of water from the refrigerator and tilted the carafe above her head. Camellia watched, fascinated, as nothing but the dribbling water touched Yasmina's lips. The process was both delicate and crude. Yasmina swallowed rapidly as she stood in front of the refrigerator, door ajar.

Only a small number of newcomers remained to drink the coffee Camellia carried in on a tray. A cousin had hurried back to work. An uncle had been drawn away by the exigencies of family.

Yasmina dropped down beside Tayta. Tayta sat cross-legged, seeming to drowse. Her eyes were deliberately unfocused. Absently, she kneaded worry beads. Little in the room could be heard but the gentle clicking of the mother-of-pearl orbs.

"Why does everyone wear expensive watches when nobody keeps track of the time?" Camellia asked.

She expected Yasmina to chortle in derision. But Yasmina only gave an elaborate, Levantine shrug. Some questions were, apparently, unanswerable.

Other things had been puzzling Camellia.

"Why do men kiss so enthusiastically — and so often? It doesn't seem fair. Khalil and I can't even hold hands." It was true. If she came too close, he grew edgy. Once he had almost slapped her hand away.

Yasmina shook with suppressed mirth.

Tayta answered. Somehow she had understood. Or, at least, she had caught the drift. She spoke in the insistent, hypnotic rhythm no one dared interrupt.

"Never mind." Yasmina translated. Her tone was nonchalant. "There will be time for that later, behind closed doors."

"But why," Camellia pressed ahead futilely, "does everyone say, *'Ma'alesh'*? Even when the air seems heavy with the importance of things, no one can push to the heart of a matter. Anyone who tries will be told, 'Never mind'!"

"*Ya habibti...*"

Yasmina blinked rapidly. She repeated the term of endearment. She tossed back her blond hair, but she didn't explain.

No doubt she thinks such questions are best met with polite silence, Camellia concluded. She has no way of knowing how maddening it is to be faced with silence. Of Yasmina, "She is very much in love with her Phalangist militiaman," Khalil had said. Camellia, admiring both Yasmina's honey-lipped Oriental beauty and also her sense of timing, of knowing when to talk and when to be silent, fervently hoped this was true.

They drank tea and ate sliced peaches, then washed white cookies down with coffee, all the while making conversation in soft delighted voices.

Only Camellia, increasingly restless, seemed aware of the passage of time.

A new swell of visitors arrived before sunset. The business day in Lebanon ended well before 5 p.m. Workers were free for the remainder of the day. Retailers rested, then reopened for the evening trade. Many government workers held second jobs, evening jobs.

So Om Mousa's parlor was full when the machine-gun fire began. No one seemed unduly alarmed. Bursts of it punctuated the stillness of afternoon. The sounds came intermittently, like fireworks, and stopped an hour later.

"A local election," a cousin said carelessly.

"No!" protested another. "The Palestinians are restless in their camps."

"Don't be foolish!" said a third. "It's test-firing by the army. They wish to prove — to those who argue they are emasculated — that at least they are armed."

The explanations began in English — for Camellia's benefit. But the talk soon switched to Arabic. Voices grew bitter as ideas, thinly suppressed, oozed like blood through a bandage.

The conversation became a thing alive. Camellia was sitting on the floor beside Yasmina, who murmured translations into her ear.

"As long as the Palestinians are here, Lebanon is doomed." The speaker was young, younger than Khalil. His tone was absolute. He leaned forward, holding a glass, aggressively swirling the scotch and ice filling it. His voice was like an engine forced to ignite on a cold day. "We must finish the job, if Israel cannot...."

Listening to Yasmina's translations was like reading a newspaper account of a horrifying event. You pick it up intending to read only the headline. But then you read to the very end.

The voices of Khalil's uncles grew vehement as they brought him up to date. The details had not escaped him in America. But he listened eagerly to their recounting.

Last summer had been a time of chaos. Explosions. Robberies. Abductions. Assassinations. The trouble had spread north to Tripoli and south to Sidon and Tyre. But mostly the conflict centered in Beirut.

To think, the problem might have been solved two years ago. The Lebanese army had launched air raids against the Palestinians. The attacks were carried out virtually at rooftop level. Target of the bombs: refugee camps ringing Beirut.

According to Khalil's friends and relatives, the attacks had not gone far enough. Instead, the conflict had been left to fester, and now, two years later, there was no telling who might do what to whom. One Felliniesque development followed another. One example was the current massing of training camps in Baalbek by the Imam Musa al-Sadr. He was preparing thousands of Shi'ite Moslems to fight Israel. Who could have predicted such folly?

Had she ever read such stories in The Detroit News? Had Associated Press covered them? Reuters? Had Camellia read the news accounts and failed to absorb their significance?

The consensus in Om Mousa's parlor was this: the Imam Musa al-Sadr was foolishly suicidal. Like the Palestinians, he would invite the wrath of Israel. Even now, the Palestinians were setting up permanent bases, storing armaments in the hundreds of caves on land bordering Israel. In the Arkoub — the barren, rocky land at the foot of Mount Hermon bordering Israel and Syria — Palestinians had turned Lebanese villages into supply centers.

And of course those villages were now dreadfully at risk.

It was also agreed: Israel would have its way in Lebanon. Following an attack by the Popular Front for the Liberation of Palestine on an El Al airliner in Athens (an Israeli engineer was killed), a helicopter-borne task force was launched from Tel Aviv. It landed at the Beirut Airport. Thirteen aircraft and a gas storage tank were blown up. Israeli commandos ordered a Lebanese gendarme out from under his desk — and extracted from him some 25-piastre pieces so they could get soft drinks from the machine!

The act of remembering greatly upset Khalil's uncle Abu Ferhan. He stood at the balcony, raking his gray beard with his stubby fingers. From this balcony two years ago he had seen smoke curling from the bombs of the Lebanese army as they attacked the Palestinian refugee camps.

"Every good Lebanese should kill at least one Palestinian!" He raised a gnarled finger skyward. "The army should have killed them all!"

Camellia thought of her friends Huda and Dr. Elias and was horrified. She drew her sweater more closely around her shoulders. To Yasmina: "Does he mean — ?"

"*Ma'alesh*," Yasmina murmured.

"Yasmina, please!"

She shrugged dismissively. "Politics is life and death to them — even when it is not."

"Well, that certainly makes a lot of sense. Life and death to whom?" Camellia persisted. "To all the Lebanese? Just to the Christians? Just to the men?"

"Who can say?" Yasmina asked.

"Dr. Elias — my professor in Ann Arbor — compared the Phalangists to Hitler."

Khalil had overheard. "Dr. Elias is a fool." He made the motion of spitting.

Camellia suddenly needed something to do. She jumped up to help Bahija and Samir clear away the scotch glasses and empty the overflowing ashtrays. The tasks were mindless, and for that she was grateful. She passed her hand across her forehead and felt its oiliness. But she didn't stop to wash her face.

She poured coffee, carried trays of fruit and candy, replenished glasses of whiskey and beer. Dinner was cooked, served and eaten. More coffee was drunk.

When it was dark and the visitors had gone, she dropped onto the couch. Memories of gentleness juxtaposed with memories of fear.

Om Mousa's pungent stew was still warm on her tongue. During dinner, Abu Mousa, with great tenderness, had planted a morsel in her mouth.

She blinked back tears at the intimacy. Abu Mousa looked at her, and she knew that her effort during the afternoon had not gone unnoticed. She asked for *arak*, a request she knew would please him.

He grinned. He had to unlock a cabinet to get to the *arak*.

The drink was delightfully numbing. At once she became warm and secure within the circle of Khalil's family. How foolish were her fears. How distant they all were from any ugliness!

She suddenly realized she had spent the whole day waiting for people to leave — so she and Khalil could be alone. Ironically, she had never been so comforted as she was now, surrounded by family. Was she becoming culturally transformed, believing, like the Arabs, that she could bear anything but aloneness?

Their language flowed around her, pleasurable and rhythmic.

"Khalil." He passed within reach. Ignoring the social taboo, she pulled him down to the scratchy divan beside her and hung on. "Are we — " The world seemed pleasantly fuzzy. "Are we in any danger?"

"Of course not, my love."

She had laced her fingers around his sinewy upper arm. He patted her hand.

"Tomorrow I will take you to Beirut."

****

But in the morning, more visitors came.

Camellia had dressed in pants, a turtleneck, boots and the suede jacket with fringe. She had eaten breakfast (at Om Mousa's insistence). Then, giggling, hand-in-hand with Khalil, she had skipped to the landing — only to meet a contingent of visitors ascending the stairs.

"*Bismallah!*" The Arabic exclamation came almost instinctively to her lips. "Have they seen us yet? Godammit, Khalil — can we go down the fire escape? Don't *look* at me like that..."

But there was nothing to do but file back into the flat, shake hands all around and become acquainted with Aunt Basma and her teen-age daughters. Aunt Basma, apparently inspired by the sight of Camellia, began to pontificate. She spoke good English but insisted that her daughters speak only French. She had no desire to visit America, she said. People who walked in public places risked being mugged. And in America everyone ate from cans. Arabs who traveled there returned transformed in unwholesome ways.

Nothing Camellia said could dissuade her from a picture of America as a most unhealthful place.

"How do you find Lebanon?" The question was standard, phrased always that way. Camellia bit her lower lip, trying to think of an original response. Something more definitive than "very nice."

"I'm not quite sure yet," she said in a rush of truth. "It's all so strange. I'm dying to see the city, of course, and — " Breaking off at Khalil's look of reproof: "I love it already. I look forward to a greater understanding," she finished.

Aunt Basma was pleased. At last the sorority departed. It was all Camellia could do to count to 10 before following on their heels.

She did not feel fully free even when she had taken her place in the red Mercedes and Khalil had started the engine. Abu Mousa had given them the car for the day. Soon they left the placid Christian suburbs awash in the dust of wheel-spun gravel. Ahead lay downtown in all its gritty splendor.

"Beirut! Beirut!" she caroled.

Khalil drove cautiously at first, then more quickly as he regained familiarity and confidence. The onrush of wind was glorious. It ruffled her hair.

"How could you leave it?" she demanded as they sat at a traffic light near angled alleyways and buildings with Byzantine architectural flourishes. "How could you come to Ann Arbor when you have all this?"

The question was unanswerable. But Khalil's expression, always so guarded, softened and his gaze held warmth.

The city sparkled with nascent spring. Water gushed from spouts in the balconies of concrete-and-glass edifices as maids whooshed the floors within. Children in gingham uniforms strolled on the streets to school. Old men maneuvered donkey-drawn carts among the gleaming tour buses. Strange sounds echoed, from the clop of hooves to the impatient *"It la! It la!"* of a soldier bullying traffic. The honking never ceased, not even for the *muezzin's* long-drawn *"Allaaaahu Akbar."*

Khalil's driving escalated from proficient to reckless.

"It didn't take you long to get the stampede spirit," Camellia remarked.

Within minutes, he had negotiated several dangerous points of entry to the city. He traversed streets that narrowed suddenly, then angled into nowhere. Rammed his way through intersections that were nothing more than circuitous free-for-alls. Nipped ahead of a Datsun pickup. Cut off a zigzagging trolley. Careened through traffic that ran three deep in lanes designed for two.

He held his own among the ubiquitous taxi drivers in battered black Mercedeses who drove with one hand on the gearshift, the other on the horn.

"You, the Lebanese —" Camellia began.

Khalil laughed. "Who taught you to start a sentence that way?"

"I suppose I picked it up from Dr. Elias."

"You are truly becoming an Arab. It is the Arabs who say, 'You, the Lebanese,' as if the Lebanese were of a different species. Everyone envies us."

"I was just going to say you need three hands to drive. Both of yours are otherwise engaged. There's nothing left for the steering wheel. Oh, my God!"

Khalil refused space to a driver intent on nosing in. The driver, honking as if the right of way were his, was trying to turn left from the extreme right lane.

"Ibn el-kelb!"

The driver turned straight into Khalil's path, and there was nothing to do but slam brakes and horn simultaneously.

It took Camellia several moments to recover. Her hands lay crossed against her throat. "Are there *no* rules?"

Khalil considered. "Maybe: 'Who gets there first, proceeds.'"

"Since when do you know Latin?"

He glanced at her and smiled. His hands were relaxed now, draped across the wheel. "Latin? That is not Latin. That is a Lebanese kid's high school English. Since when is wisdom confined to one dead language?"

Beirut was thriving and urgent, vast and crowded, busy; lively as the Semites, half-breeds and foreigners who peopled it: an exotic hybrid of a city, with European skin but Asia's insistent, throbbing pulse. Everything here negated the warm, lingering social life within the walled garden of the home. At home with friends, looking at one's watch could be a breach of etiquette. By contrast, the city was frenetically intense. Could it be collective memory of faded glory had not paled? Did willful residents thrive in a civilization living on borrowed time?

Khalil sped past the thousand sprawling shacks of a refugee camp. Between them children walked hand-in-hand, seemingly oblivious of misery. The old strode slowly on the dusty streets. Their faces reflected poverty. Their posture spoke of defeat. In scarf-wrapped heads their shrouded eyes stared here ahead or at the sky, anywhere but at the dilapidated walls, torn roofs and shabby vegetable stands that had been built to last weeks but had become permanent in one of history's grim encores. Months... years....

On the outskirts, small beds of flowers flourished under sightless eyes — the eyes of boys. They had been photographed on black-and-white film, their images blown up on black-and-white poster paper. They were the martyrs. All that was left of them now was image.

On the outskirts of the camp, where everyone could see, the posters hung, beneath them the cemetery.

Khalil drove determinedly past, but not before Camellia saw those filmy eyes, dewy and dark, desperate.

"The faces ... so young."

Khalil shrugged contemptuously. "Not too young to hate."

He directed her attention to banks and ministries, pizzerias, public gardens; to Barbir Hospital and the new Soviet Embassy under construction on the Corniche Mazraa.

"Look at the storefronts." Hamra Street was opulent. It drew Khalil like a beacon. "Fashions fresh from Paris and Rome. Sidewalk cafes with cut flowers, flown in fresh each night. And the women — "

"Something's missing in the equation." The change of subject was intentional. Khalil as man-of-the-world sometimes overwhelmed her. "This is *West* Beirut — the Moslem part. You've always attributed Beirut's prosperity to the Christians."

He didn't answer; the city was his. West Beirut — Moslem Beirut — all of it was his.

"You can eat a hamburger," he said. "Buy a yacht. Change dollars to yen. See a belly dancer. At any hour or the day or night. Beirut never sleeps. There is money to be made. We have no industry, few resources and nothing to sell. Yet we thrive."

"Who's getting rich?" Images that had troubled her since passing the refugee camp surfaced again. "Certainly not the Palestinians."

Khalil shrugged. "Bankers. Lawyers. Brokers. Middlemen. Anyone shrewd enough to spot a need and quick enough to fill it."

"And to think Violet wanted me to marry a sheik. An *oil* sheik."

Khalil laughed reassuringly. "Lebanon has no oil. Yet it handles billions of dollars of oil money — related to transporting, storing, refining, loading. And, of course, profit. Foreign profits always need investing. Why not here?"

He swung north to the waterfront. Beirut, glimpsed from the air, had seemed harsh and spare. White skyscrapers and red tile roofs, barren avenues and craggy cliffs — the details had added up to a city of angles and hard surfaces. By contrast, the Avenue de Paris was startlingly lush. Street lights arched over a shore-hugging avenue. Sculpted medians split the boulevard gracefully in two. The Mediterranean rippled to shore from a vast horizon.

The American University of Beirut was a sanctuary of gentle hills and Islamic arches. It overlooked the water. The American Embassy, the Hotel St. Georges, countless large buildings and small cafes — all shared a view of the sea.

"Slow *down*."

"Later. I want you to see everything."

They parked at Martyr's Square, where (Khalil explained, savoring his history) the Ottomans had hanged sixteen Lebanese nationalists. But Camellia could think only of life as she and Khalil walked hand in hand through the square. It was alive with the bustle of morning and the smell of spring. The air was fragrant with aromas and blends. Incense. Cardamom-flavored coffee. Perfume from the street-level clock whose face was composed of flowers.

"I told you Lebanon is beautiful in spring," Khalil said. "April — "

"Is the cruelest month," Camellia interrupted.

"Latin?"

"Poetry. Whose, I can't remember." She furrowed her brow. The words had sprung to mind in order. At some point, she had memorized them. Now, she could place neither author nor literary allusion.

She was, however, far too exuberant to remain lost in thought.

People were everywhere. Some walked decisively, others milled without purpose. Several continents were represented in this city square: sarongs and saris, three-piece suits and veils — the national costumes of a dozen lands. Half a dozen regions within Lebanon itself were represented as well. With Khalil's help, Camellia soon became an accomplished amateur, placing the wearer by his costume. Khalil could establish identities immediately. He recognized them at a glance: self-conscious village *fellaheen* dispatching town affairs. Mustachioed businessmen fingering worry beads, hurrying, looking longingly at the cafes. Raven-haired girls in designer jeans sauntering. Veiled women forming hulks. A turbaned Druze standing at a newsstand, flipping through the pages of *An-Nahar*.

Khalil pointed out a mufti, a "keeper of the faith," recognizable from his mustache, trimmed beard and well-tailored coat hanging to his knees. Christian priests were equally conspicuous. They wore full beards and long black cassocks.

A strangely familiar melody floated from a music shop. The music sounded like Mozart — but in a minor key. And there was singing, too. A woman's strong, sweet voice followed the melody — or did it swell, following her?

"Where have I heard that voice before?"

"Hush," Khalil said, " — the languages — "

It formed a babel: the intermingling of half a dozen conversations. Rhythmic Arabic played a counter-melody to bland English and mellifluous French. She could distinguish few words.

"Why so much French?"

"France owned us, remember. And, under Ottoman rule, speaking French was one good way to insult the Turks. But Arabic will survive."

"But no two people speak alike!"

"Regional variations. Jordanians and Saudis speak classically. We Lebanese drop certain consonants. And the Egyptians — no one outside Egypt can understand them!"

"Will I ever learn?"

"Not easily. Once you have mastered spoken Arabic, you must learn a completely different version: the *written* language."

"Oh, joy!"

Three white-robed Saudis pressed past. The loose fabric of their skirts swished with the motion. Camellia had an impression of dark eyes quickly hooded. The Saudis established eye contact that hardly registered — then swiftly averted their gaze.

Laughing, "Can't they even look at me?"

"They're good Moslems, avoiding sin."

She looked at Khalil; smiling, amused, proud, superior. And *hers*. They stood in the fresh morning air, inhaling it, reveling in the potency of breezes. They swirled down from where mountain currents met the coastal winds.

A man roasting meat on a open-air spit ... he wore white, but he wasn't a Saudi. He was a chef and wore a white chef's hat, matching his coat.

The meat — the *shawarma* — sizzled. The shank hung like merchandise, clearly visible from the street.

The chef wielded a broad knife, deftly slicing away the thin outer strips of meat, exposing the pink middle to the flame. The grilling and slicing took place in the public eye; customers who stepped up to order watched the assembly as meat married spice, sauce and tomato in a pocket of bread.

It was early, still morning, so Khalil ordered just one.

He gave it to Camellia.

"I hope you don't expect me to share. This tourist business has me famished."

"You are crude, but enchanting." Khalil dabbed with a napkin at a spot on her chin. "But at least after Saturday, you cannot claim to be a tourist."

"How so? I intend to sightsee for no less than a year."

"I am going to marry you."

"Saturday?" Camellia choked on the meat.

He ignored the interruption. "You cannot be my wife and still consider yourself a tourist. Are you not pleased?"

"Of course not. I mean, of course — "

"And I thought you were the impatient one. The one who ... who wants life at her fingertips."

She opened her mouth. Then closed it.

"It is awkward, to have you living in my father's house." He grew serious.

She chewed, appreciating the truth of what he said. "I guess I've still got one foot in America. I didn't realize Lebanon would have no place for the 'unmarried woman.'"

"If she is single, working, on her own — no problem. But if — "

Saturday?

Sure, setting a date had been a vague goal all along. But "the wedding," when Camellia thought about it at all, seemed a distant milestone. Ceremony was superfluous. Wasn't that the message of the '60s, from which Camellia had only recently emerged? All in all, matrimony seemed unrelated to the current adventure. Marriage meant settling down. It meant the end of the honeymoon. It occasioned thoughts of plans and children and career and future. The end of youth.

Khalil bought *An-Nahar* from an open-air newsstand and settled into reading the day's news. They were, by now, sitting in a coffee shop where the aroma of coffee and the flavorful scent of tobacco were strong.

Camellia sank into a state of dreamy tranquillity. Her legs ached; she hadn't realized how out of shape she was. She sat alert but unobservant. Her gaze was fixed but her eyes were unfocused. She wasn't quite asleep. Or totally withdrawn. More like stunned. In reaction to an overwhelming wealth of stimuli.

When Khalil finished reading, he translated the headlines. Would she ever stop being startled by such details?

Lebanon's Christians feared becoming a "defenseless and persecuted minority" as Moslems pressed for political reforms.

Palestinians had fired rockets at Lebanese army barracks in Tyre.

In Sidon, an army corporal had been killed in a fishing dispute. This messy affair involved former president Camille Chamoun and resulted in extending the territorial war off shore into the sea.

Had such things been reported in America? Could Camellia really have been so inattentive?

There was more:

Rashaya Fuqhar, once a prosperous Lebanese village famous for its pottery, had become a ghost town. Unluckily situated near Israel's border, its demise no less certain for being slow and measured, Rashaya Fuqhar was gone. Bombs devastated it.

The 6,000-mile migration of birds of prey down the great Syrian-African rift had been disrupted by young men of the armed militias shooting into the air.

"My God! Why didn't you warn me in Ann Arbor?"

He laughed at her sudden panic. "Such things happen ... always."

"Not on State Street!"

Still, he was amused. "Did you think I would expose you to danger — or bring you anywhere that is not safe?"

Apologetic, feeling slightly foolish, she squeezed his hand. Then a cheering thought occurred.

"Oh, I simply must send a telegram to Angela. About the wedding, of course!"

She thought about what she would say. Then she began to scrawl line after line on Khalil's copy of *An-Nahar*.

The wedding is Saturday STOP This is what an Arab wedding is like STOP First Mass, then the priest chants, blesses the rings and spreads incense STOP We actually wear crowns STOP There will be music, dancing, hundreds of guests, tons of food STOP Don't worry in Lebanon the groom pays for everything STOP We are in downtown Beirut STOP Off to Martyr's Square, the Umari Mosque, Pigeon Rock STOP Wish you were here STOP Love and kisses STOP Camellia.

Completing the message, she felt continental and polished.

Infuriatingly, Khalil broke into uproarious laughter. "Have you ever sent a telegram before?" he asked.

"None of your business!" She had never even received a telegram, much less sent one. She wasn't about to admit that to Khalil.

"A simple period at the end of each sentence would do."

"I read somewhere that telegraph equipment is incapable of punctuation."

"Maybe when first invented. Or maybe you're confusing Western Union and Morse code."

But he paid for the telegram, and she forgave him the mocking laughter. Who could resist a man who so loved his neighborhood? Khalil was at home everywhere in Beirut, whether having his leather shoes polished — hardly noticing the grubby boy who knelt to do the polishing and, grinning, pocketed the tip — or choosing hand-worked 22-karat gold earrings for her from the Street of Gold.

She, in turn, loved the *souq*, its maze of streets and disreputable air. Sweat, incense, meat, leather and dung — the wind smelled earthy. In Ann Arbor, all such smells would have been Lysoled and Saran-wrapped out of existence. Here they lent pungency to the air.

An extraordinary sense of history and disorganization attended the *souq*. Pitted streets tunneled past open-air stalls where merchants for centuries had parted foreigners from their money. Spices as well as jewelry sold by the gram.

Westerners in blue jeans strolled arm-in-arm. Syrian women — eyes veiled, but vision sharp — were the most aggressive hagglers. Each sales transaction was an act of theater. At its conclusion, the woman would thrust her paper-wrapped parcel under her arm and march off. Looking after her: the defeated proprietor, who clucked his tongue while pocketing coins.

There was a Street of Fabrics. Camellia exclaimed over French brocades. Pakistani cottons. German knits. Syrian silk. There were sequins and satins, the machine-worked and the homespun. White for the Saudi men. Gray for the Egyptian men. Black for the Syrian women. Jacquards and sheers and gold thread for the wives of rich Lebanese men. Camellia ran her fingers across bolts of stiff shiny taffeta, soft chamois, rough damask. The proprietor began eagerly unrolling them for her inspection. His expression betrayed sudden brief disappointment, then indifference, when she admitted she couldn't sew.

"But won't I need a wedding dress?"

"My mother saved hers ... an heirloom of satin and pearls. It will look lovely on you."

"But Om Mousa is taller than I am. And stout."

"She married at age 14."

"Oops."

Around the corner, another street. This one overflowing with copper pots and inexpensive household wares. That one like a farmer's market, full of tables laden with fish and fresh vegetables. Plastic souvenirs. Persian carpets. Was there nothing one could not find somewhere in the *souq*?

On the Street of Spices, aromas wafted from open barrels. Camellia stepped closer and Khalil translated the Arabic labels: cinnamon, cardamom, ginger, coriander, cumin and *sumac*. Khalil composed a *baharat*, a custom blend, for Om Mousa. He chose and weighed the assorted spices like a connoisseur. He laced the mixture heavily with pepper.

While he was occupied, a boy sidled up to Camellia. He carried a basket; he lifted a cloth to reveal shampoos and powders. She reached for her purse. But before she could make a selection and pay, Khalil wheeled on the boy and, cursing, ran him off.

"But he's just a kid!"

Khalil ignored the protest. He stood, vigilant, watching until the boy had disappeared into the crowd. "Street urchins," he muttered.

Camellia wondered if they were Palestinians.

Later, when they passed a crone sitting cross-legged on the sidewalk, peddling pistachios, Khalil tossed her a coin. She grinned, revealing blackened teeth. The blessings she shouted after them seemed to linger in the air.

Khalil, she could see, was tiring of the chaos. But Camellia couldn't get enough of the freedom and the flux. The crowd moved, trudging shoulder to shoulder on the stone floors of the cavernous streets — and its movement provided a wonderful anonymity. Why not make it last? Once she and Khalil returned to the flat, she would be captive to whoever rang the bell.

A young man, rounding a corner, barreled into Camellia. He knocked her flat — but the bread-tray balanced on his head somehow stayed steady. He swerved, called an apology, repositioned the tray and rushed on. Not a single loaf fell.

Khalil helped her up. "Now you know what they mean by 'East meets West.'"

Camellia laughed, dusting herself off. She had been afraid Khalil might kill the guy.

On another street, in still another store, where the bolts of fabric were interspersed with samples of dresses already sewn, Camellia lingered. One of them had caught her eye. It was a high-collared Palestinian dress. She recognized its origin because of an article she had read on Palestinian women and their activities. The fabric was a rich black. Tiny red x's were embroidered in swarms on collar, hem and cuffs.

"Huda tells me the women put in every stitch by hand." Camellia grazed the fabric with her fingers. "They consider it a sort of passive resistance ... preserving the Palestinian folk arts."

"What is there in this Bedouin gaudiness worth preserving?"

"Red on black — it's striking. Every culture has a right to survive, doesn't it?"

"Not at my expense."

If she wanted a dress, he insisted, they would return to Hamra Street. There, over her protest, from the racks of high-fashion, he selected a frothy green import triple the price of the hand-sewn black.

"It won't survive three washings." It had frills and flounces and a tiny hem.

"Ah, but look at the color. See how it illuminates your eyes."

She thought of the Palestinian dress and gave a little sigh. But she took the bag with the Italian green dress and carefully placed it under the seat of the car.

Khalil became ebullient. "You were right about Lebanese weddings," he said, behind the wheel again. "But your telegram only hinted at the magic."

He himself had witnessed many weddings — on moonlit nights in courtyards awash in floodlight; in elegant hotels; in the mountains; beside lakes and pools choked with exotic flowers. He recounted details: costumed couples and cascades of flowers; zither music and crashing cymbals; motorcades and gunplay and theatrical processions with men and flaming swords drawing up the rear. Marriage was sacrosanct and even the poorest family celebrated it with opulence.

He talked and time passed quickly, reminiscent of Ann Arbor. For Camellia the description was less important than the recapturing of the days of their courtship, the mood of her plea: "Tell me more about Lebanon."

"Aren't people killed with so much gunfire?"

"In Beirut entire neighborhoods must sometimes duck for cover of a wedding night — all the militiamen are shooting into the air."

He was still lost in description when they pulled into a parking lot near Pigeon Rock, the best place in Beirut to watch the sunset. They decided to avoid the crowded cafes. Instead, they strolled on the rock-rich embankments near wavelets lapping at the shore.

The sun glared against the city's white-brown hues. A spring wind blew down from the tree-thick mountains. It met the off-shore breeze of the Mediterranean, restive and chill. Afternoon drifted into evening.

Pigeon Rock rose like a behemoth from the sea, its textured granite like a thumbprint whorl, encrusted here and there with moss.

The scent of jasmine clung to the air.

Weary, happily affectionate and oddly nostalgic, Camellia rested her head on Khalil's shoulder.

"You know what I liked best about today? The old man on the street corner selling *sous* from a silver tankard. Who would think you could make licorice into a drink? He rattled brass plates together to draw a crowd — and everyone drank from the same cup. I know, he washed it between customers, but still —" "You were thirsty," Khalil said.

"Beirut." She said it lovingly. "It's an enchanted forest. And yet I feel at home." She smiled up at him. "My proud Semite. My ..."

"Camellia." He drew out the syllables, giving himself time before continuing. "Do not romanticize me."

Quickly: "Are you having second thoughts? Everyone says American women can't cut it here, they're..."

"Likely to leave their husbands at the first sign of disenchantment? Can you deny it?"

She gave a little sigh. She remembered Yasmina and *her* cause. "Why didn't you marry someone like you? I understand about Yasmina. She wouldn't tolerate an arranged marriage. But why didn't you marry Huda? Huda loved you."

Speculatively, he looked out to sea. The horizon shimmered. A lone ship was a white blip on aquamarine.

"I take what I can from the world as it is. Huda is caught up in a world that will never be."

"Why do you fight what you *are*?" She tightened her fingers on his arm. "You pull me away from the refugee camps. You turn away from ugliness as if it did not exist. How can I understand if you don't let me see?"

She blinked rapidly against a swelling, suffocating feeling that produced dryness, not tears.

He kissed her lightly on the forehead.

"I wish we could stay here forever," she whispered, "just as we are now."

She was gratified to hear him answer: "I wish so, too."

****

To prepare for the evening, Camellia opened her makeup kit. She was alone in Khalil's bedroom. (He hadn't slept here in five years, but she still thought of it as his.) After twenty minutes of work, she closed the containers of powder and shadow. Freckles showed through the extra matte finish makeup — freckles dusted across the bridge of a decidedly upturned nose that wasn't Greek or Roman or anything remotely resembling Lebanese. Green eyes looked absurd lined with kohl. Or in this case eye liner, applied with a heavy hand, creating smudges and shadows. She looked like a hung over cat.

Dr. Elias had once said, following some fixed assertion she had made: "There's such charm in a 26-year-old who thinks she knows everything." What had made her think Ann Arbor girl-next-door cute could compete with Semitic beauty?

The *muezzin* called into the deepening night sky.

Khalil and his family were in the parlor with guests. Would there always be guests? Camellia didn't know them. The voices raised in greeting were unfamiliar. At least, that was her impression as she virtually fled to the back of the flat. Khalil had promised that today was hers, and she intended to dress for the duration.

I'm as useless as a spray of jasmine, she thought, pulling on the frothy dress that had been Khalil's choice. She doused herself with something floral, then rubbed it off and reapplied perfume that smelled of musk. She completed dressing, then draped gold chains around her neck.

She wasn't dark and exotic, she knew.

But if she lacked some quintessential Eastern element — like a baby without a 24k crucifix pinned to its tee-shirt, or a soup without parsley — the comparison seemed to escape Khalil.

If anything, Khalil was more alert, more vibrant, more intent on showing her his city. Mercury vapor arc lamps illuminated the streets. Shoppers thronged to the city's centers. On the outskirts, darkness cloaked the refugee camps, obscuring them as black rings might encircle a vile planet.

Khalil was restless. They settled into one cafe only to move to another. On from there to a restaurant, then an ice-cream shop for Italian ice, then for a drive through a district called Zeitouni with its street of Egyptian whores — quite legal. Then on to another nightclub where there would be Western music and, later, belly dancers.

The nightclub was smoky, and diamonds glittered on the watchers' hands. White-robed Saudis sat together like daffodils in the dimness. Shouted anecdotes and grating coughs and clinking glasses made background music.

Midnight came and went. By this time Camellia was drinking *arak*, straight. Khalil smoked Rothmans and sipped Scotch. He grew increasingly detached.

The smart European band finished a salsa. Arab performers took the stage. They played instruments that looked primitive — strings and simple woodwinds and a drum played with the flat of the hand. The *oud*, the *nye* and the *derbecki*, Khalil said.

They came on like a fervent secret saved for last; the music was elaborate, expressed in grieving subtlety, in quartertones.

By contrast the belly dancer had a fleshy, savage, simple look. Voluptuous and wanton, she undulated savagely. There was a jewel in her navel — a carry-over from Egypt, where belly dancers had invented them to circumvent public nudity laws passed by Moslem elders.

Camellia could think only of the half-naked wild women who were love interests on an episode of Star Trek. They spat and clawed and growled, protecting coveted terrain. They were said to be irresistible to men. One member of the crew had succumbed.

Khalil, who surely had watched it with her, said he didn't remember.

Scotty? Kirk? Surely not Spock. Not the Vulcan.

She had forgotten the question by the time they returned to the flat. It was nearly dawn.

Khalil seemed withdrawn. All night she had been unable to recapture the intimacy of afternoon, when they had stood hand in hand near Pigeon Rock. Amused and frustrated by his stiffness, she pulled him into her room and kissed him playfully, rubbing his chest and nipping at his ear. The strap of her dress slid down, baring her shoulder.

He broke free of her clasped hands. "Women here are stoned for less."

"Why should you care, my proud Phoenician?"

He pinched the white skin of her upper arm. "*Bint el-sharmoutah!* No one forgives a whore."

She lifted her chin rebelliously. Then she grinned. "May the fleas of a thousand camels...." she began.

He raised his hand as if to slap her, then lowered it — reluctantly, it seemed to her.

"Just remember where you are," he said.

She fell back on her pillow, laughing.

****

Day four. Beirut had been a respite. But it was over. Camellia was more impatient with the visitors, not less. The flood had become a persistent trickle.

Khalil went out in the morning. When afternoon came, he was back. But a covey of French-speaking aunts, arriving at the same time, kept him occupied. By the time they left, sun through the windows carried afternoon heat. Camellia, tired of sitting on the hard embroidery of the divan, in a fit of rebellion dug out her Nikes from the bottom of the suitcase, put them on and laced them up.

Khalil sat drinking tea with Tayta.

"Later!" Camellia called out the good-by swiftly and cheerily so she wouldn't be stopped. Then she left for the street before their surprise could turn to disapproval.

Rubber soles on marble stairs ... jogging shoes on pavement ... release. Camellia brushed her hair from her eyes as she ran. I won't live my life following their complicated logic and inhibition, she thought. Even so, she began to experience the strange unease that comes with violating social convention. Streets in Lebanon were for comings and goings. They were for work and traffic. Women walked in pairs or groups. The housewife on an errand carried a basket or packages; she struck a brisk stride; no one could mistake the businesslike quality of her outing. No one strolled or ambled or jogged — certainly no woman alone.

This Camellia knew because Khalil had told her: Women didn't walk solo unless necessary — not because of any particular danger. To the contrary, streets in the Arab world were incredibly safe because Arab men romanticized women. Dozens of protectors would spring to any woman's defense if needed. But the respect accorded an Arab woman would not necessarily be extended to her, she knew. Western women, assumed to be loose, drew leering looks and loud appreciation from passing males. Khalil for all his worldliness warned her off the streets.

Who cares? I'm an American. Fearless. Unassailable. Camellia ran faster, recognizing the unreasonableness of her own logic but believing it anyway.

She shivered at first. Down from Mount Lebanon the air was scintillating — bracing and brisk. She ran past boisterous boys. Wilted shoppers. Shopkeepers rolling down their metal shutters to close for prayer. They wouldn't reopen until the evening, when people were off work and when arc lamps gave a carnival look to the street.

After a few blocks she began to sweat. The sun was strong. She stripped off her jacket. What eyes watched from behind balconies and through mullioned windows? She didn't care.

The rain came. A sudden, exhilarating wind announced it. The streets emptied of all but housewives snatching clothing off lines.

Water ran in rivulets into her eyes. She turned back toward the flat. The drizzle was a downpour by the time she reached it.

Damp and perspiring, she thudded up the stairs.

Khalil stood alone on the landing. He wore his jacket, and he stood there bundled, his hands clenched and thrust into his pockets.

"You look like the Lord High Executioner," she said.

"What were you trying to prove?"

"Am I on trial?"

"Tayta is worried."

He opened the door. Inside, Om Mousa and Tayta sat waiting — incredulous and alert. At the sight of her their voices melded to a high pitch. Did she want to catch her death of cold? Could she, so thin, withstand a fever? Did she not know the consequences of foolish behavior?

Khalil translated verbatim, after which there was nothing more to say.

"They cannot believe you went out in the rain," he finished. "And they cannot believe I let you."

Camellia spoke anyway. "You know darn well that *viruses* cause colds." Combative, she shifted her weight from foot to foot. Lord, she wanted their good opinion. She hadn't realized how much so until this very moment. Still, she wouldn't succumb to old wives' tales. Not in the face of hard science. "Tell them," she urged. "Explain to them that the weather has nothing to do with whether a person gets sick."

There was a hard look in Khalil's eyes. But he turned to his mother and grandmother and said something in Arabic. His tone was dismissive rather than explanatory, and Camellia suspected her message didn't get through. But whatever he said silenced them. He turned away and lit a cigarette.

In the bedroom, Camellia flung her shoes at the wall.

Lebanese brides were expected to blend with the family of the groom. This she knew. Hell, they were expected to *live* together. Mothers prized their sons because the daughters, one day, must go. She must go to the house of the husband.

But why should Camellia, an American, be bound by archaic rules?

The closet door was ajar, as Camellia had left it. She stared at her clothes. There was the navy suit Khalil had chosen in Ann Arbor. And the frothy green creation he'd fancied in Beirut. A silky blouse ... a piece of jewelry. Little remained of her student look. The jeans ... the suede jacket ... the shoes....

Huda knew a student, a girl named Julia, who had married an Iranian. In Iran, of course, they wore the *chador*. Julia's mother-in-law had sold off all of Julia's clothes. She had replaced them with "suitable" garments.

The marriage lasted ten days.

In Lebanon, thankfully, no woman wore a *chador*. Beirut was modern and cosmopolitan.

But one thing was sure: People would *always* be there, watching her ... loving her. Could she bear it?

****

The dawn *adhan* came filtered through her stopped-up ears.

She sat up slowly, her breath coming in labored snorts. Her sinuses ached. Five serial sneezes confirmed the presence of a virus.

"Stay back." She held out an arm when Khalil came to see why she still slept. "Don't let me breathe on you."

He arched one eyebrow.

"Go away." Sniffling, she burrowed back under the sheets. "I'm bloated and itchy."

"Hmm. The sun is shining. So it must be a virus."

"Go to hell."

"As they say in America: Never underestimate the power of a woman."

She peered over top of the covers as he left.

"Are we still getting married Saturday?"

"We will see. They will make you chicken soup."

But if there was an Arabic equivalent of "I told you so," she didn't hear it from Om Mousa — who went to the market for fresh chickens — or from Tayta — who brewed chamomile tea and sat at bedside clicking her worry beads and praying to the saints.

Listless, sweating, Camellia drifted in and out of sleep, waking at intervals to the tedious lament of the *muezzin*.

Khalil left without telling her where he was going.

****

She ate soup and slept. When she woke it was afternoon. Tayta, chin sunk to her chest, sat dozing in the bedside chair, lulled by the afternoon breeze.

Camellia stretched carefully. Then she got up and carried the teapot to the kitchen. She wasn't entirely ready to credit the old wives' tales. But she certainly felt better. Fresh air, chicken soup, chamomile tea — their combined medicine seemed to be holding the germs at bay. The snorting and swelling had diminished to a slight sniffle.

Om Mousa was working in the kitchen. A mustache of sweat clung to her upper lip as she mixed dough with a wooden spoon.

"*Ghraybeh.*" It was cookie dough. Cookies for the wedding. Om Mousa gestured invitingly toward the mix.

Camellia pinched some off to taste. She had always liked dough, raw before baking. Om Mousa's dough was grainy, buttery and fragrant with orange blossom water. Om Mousa's square hands were brisk at their task: forming the dough into delicate crescents, circles and tiny squiggles.

Camellia gave a little sigh. Cookies for the wedding. A crowd to feed.

"I suppose it's time I learned the husband-pleasing arts," she murmured. It was fun to speak English around non-English speakers. You could say ridiculous things. You could say anything you pleased. She pushed up her sleeves.

They were up to their elbows in flour when the bell rang. Om Mousa looked up like a deer sniffing the wind. The bell was a domestic imperative. One must answer it. Custom allowed no variance. And one must display no hint of inconvenience or impatience. People came first. Always.

"Go on. I'll finish. Cookies I can handle." Camellia made shooing motions with her hands.

Nodding understanding, Om Mousa rinsed her hands, snatched up the coffee pot and left.

Alone, Camellia imitated Om Mousa's deft shaping of the *ghraybeh*. But Camellia's crescents came out lopsided. Her squiggles looked like lumpy snakes. She pressed almonds into the centers of Om Mousa's perfect rounds and slid the tray into the oven. Then she cut some honeydew onto the good china.

"Good morning." Yasmina sat perched on the red-and-ivory divan.

"*Sabah el-kher.*"

"*Sabah el-noor.*" Yasmina's response was emphatic. She stood up as Camellia set down the tray. It landed with a clank on the marble-top table.

Yasmina's handshake bony and brief.

"So you have learned Arabic." Yasmina tilted her head in apology. "You must think us strange: so many salutations. So many responses. Such a complicated way of saying 'good morning'..." Yasmina's English was charmingly stiff. "America is not like this."

"But you are enchanting! Little phrases — names and customs for everything. It's the social grease of human..." Lost in metaphor, Camellia trailed to a stop.

"When you go back to America, you will *still* stand up when someone enters a room. You will do so instinctively." Yasmina's kohl-lined eyes crinkled pleasantly.

"I'm not going back."

"*Wallah*? You intend to stay?"

"Well, for now. Khalil must find a job...." The words, again, were rushed and defensive.

"But Khalil chose you. He chose *America*. Life is complicated here. Especially for Americans. It is even difficult for us, the Lebanese. The Christians — "

"The Christians?"

Yasmina nodded vigorously. "Life is impossible for us."

"You don't seem different from anyone else."

"Danger is invisible, like luck." Yasmina waggled a jeweled finger. "The Moslems are unpredictable. They hate us. They have hated us for centuries. They need only opportunity."

Camellia bit her lip. "People still talk about two years ago — when the army bombed the refugee camps. What did the Christians have to do with it?"

"Two years ago! I am talking about today. The commandos clashed with the army in January. The fighting in the south never ends."

Camellia blew her nose reflectively. "And this will hurt the Christians?"

"Of course."

Yasmina's tone was authoritative. It discouraged give and take. Camellia handed her a plate of melon.

"You know," Camellia began, "Khalil is protective of me here."

"Is that strange?"

"I would like to see a refugee camp. We pass them all the time. But Khalil won't let me near."

"Do you have business with refugees?"

Camellia shook her head. "That's not the point." She was unable to organize an explanation. "Anyway, Khalil's *changed*. He's possessive. He's protective. And he's political. He wasn't political in Ann Arbor."

Sharp sounds intruded. They were harsh, like the blow of a mufti's cane against shutters still open at prayer-time. Thuds, shouts and scattered curses emanated from the courtyard. They violated the mellow afternoon with their shrillness.

Yasmina ran to the balcony. Camellia ran after her.

Tayta had been startled awake. She stood leaning over the rail. She looked frail as she stood mewing reprimands. The sounds of the scuffle swallowed them.

"*Ya hiawanat!*"

Yasmina's staccato insult was breathy as a war whoop. Sun glinted on her dusky hair and red, contorted lips. Her breasts strained against her sweater. She inhaled energetically and whooped again.

Her target: a dozen boys. They lay tangled in the courtyard like larvae, arms and legs flailing.

Faces appeared at windows and balconies. Audiences of watchers clustered like lights in a chandelier.

Yasmina kept up a piercing narrative. Men came running from shops. To the disorder of the children, they added adult turmoil. They pulled the boys up one by one until they formed a line, upright and sullen. Camellia recognized one or two from impromptu soccer games held beneath her window.

The boy at the bottom emerged.

He stared straight ahead, face swollen, one eye beginning to purple.

Yasmina's voice made his head jerk.

"*Ya walad.*" She poised her lips to spit but seemed to think better of it. "Return to Tel Zataar. Never come back!"

He didn't look up again. He limped into an alley and was gone.

Yasmina, muttering, sat on the red-and-ivory divan and, lips glistening, ate the melon.

4

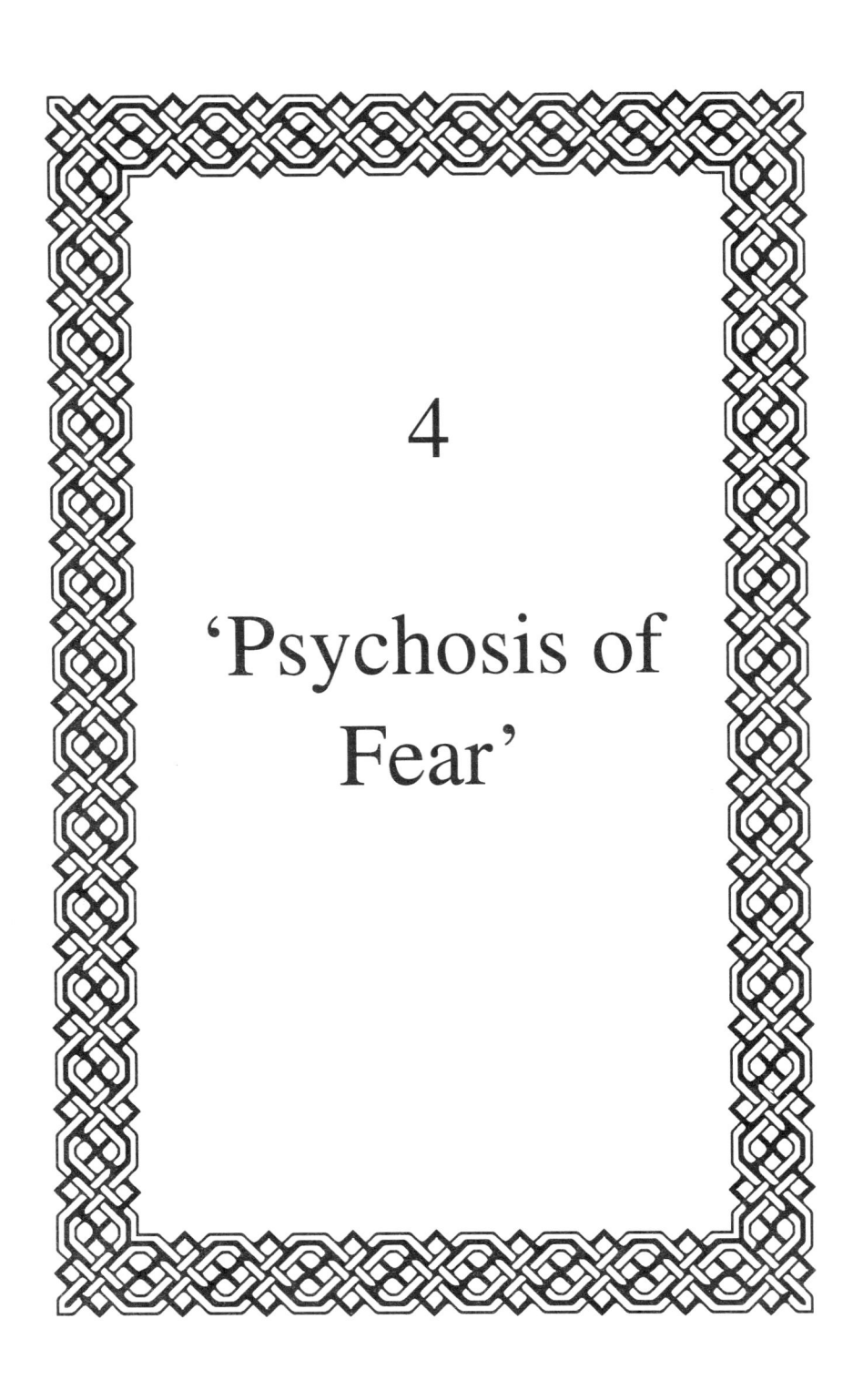

'Psychosis of Fear'

The Mediterranean was breathtaking at noon. Large picture windows framed a scene of white-on-aqua as skiers' wake bisected the expanse. From the restaurant, Camellia could see the flowers on a woman's bikini before she fell. She bobbed and quickly surfaced, like a creature of sea.

West Beirut.

The water shimmered, placid and benevolent. The sheen of sun on flat surface reflected in the dining room, brightening its interior. The effect was of a sidewalk cafe encased in glass.

Camellia did not feel benevolent. She sat twisting her napkin. Khalil sat ignoring her, shutting out the view. Resplendent in his Pierre Cardin suit, frowning in concentration, he perused the headlines of An-Nahar. At length he finished with the paper, folded it, and folded his arms across his ribs. His expression was thoughtful and subdued. He looked off into space, beyond Camellia and slightly to the right, as if he were contemplating something private and difficult. His body language said: You have no place here.

That's what I get for inviting myself, she thought. She had refused to be left home without him. She wouldn't stay cooped up in the flat, not for one more hour, alone with the family. Khalil's free range across the city left her home drinking tea with visitors, deprived of experience.

But considering the checkpoint, maybe he had been right....

"What a harrowing experience!"

"Sons of bitches." Anger overtook Khalil's expression. He drew a breath, remembering.

The roadblock was no more than a pile of tires and several sandbags, manned by two teen-age boys. They forced Khalil to stop; they did so by positioning themselves in the center of the street and holding up their hands, as if they were herding goats. They were armed, rifles of some sort slung across their shoulders. Even so,

Khalil waited until the last second to brake, so that the Mercedes bounced as it came to a rest, bumpers inches from knees.

Shouts began immediately — orders, queries, and general cursing, in Arabic — but, astonishingly, as soon as the boys spotted Camellia, they switched to English, which infuriated Khalil.

A "chickenpoint," one of the boys informed Camellia. You must stop at the "chickenpoint." What on earth did he mean? But then he explained, "Everyone must stop and show proof of ID."

They looked at Khalil's identity card. Camellia tensed as one of the boys thrust his hand into his pocket. But when the hand reappeared, it held only a piece of candy. He handed her the sweet. It was white, covered with pistachios. She sat looking from it to the boy. Grinning, nonchalant, he waved Khalil through.

He had not asked for her ID.

They drove 100 meters before she realized what had happened. They had emerged, safe and alive, from one of Beirut's infamous checkpoints, set up at streets that bounded political or religious zones, enclaves, neighborhoods, or camps. Her knees shook.

The seaside restaurant was ersatz Italian, designed for intimacy. Cut roses atop the red-checked tablecloths might have been flown in from Rome. The waiters were dark and thin and discreet. Piped-in Arabic music and scattered conversation as background noise made the atmosphere even more private.

A place for lovers. Or old friends. And Khalil hadn't planned for her to come.

"Talk to me." Her voice was wistful, urgent. "You have dark circles under your eyes. And you've been on the phone all morning."

"What do you want me to say? Look — have you noticed the skiers?"

They made trails of froth on the blue-green sea, zigzagging near the Hotel St. Georges. The St. Georges, a landmark, roosted on a sandy spit of land where sunbathers clustered.

"Look how they change position, to escape the shade."

"They follow the sun like remoras clinging to a shark."

But Khalil wasn't listening. "Now that is a grand luncheon spot." He was talking about the St. Georges.

"It looks just as Dr. Elias said it would."

According to Dr. Elias, you could walk through the Hotel St. Georges and spot, on any given day, "a deposed monarch drinking Turkish coffee and smoking his *nargeila*. Political exiles, journalists, spies — at the same lunch table. The discredited and the disloyal, the powerful and the impeached — all find it useful to do business at the St. Georges."

With a flash of intuition, Camellia imagined Khalil there. Cool and elegant, watchful, he would have fit with the crowd. She banished the image as disloyal.

"What were you trying to accomplish on the phone? You sounded ... as if you were sweating. Not like a cool job seeker."

Presumably, Khalil was pulling strings to land a suitable job. That's how things were done in Beirut. Through connections. Khalil's graduate degree in his field was almost beside the point. Family identity, religion, political leanings and loyalties— these were the crucial factors.

On the phone, his voice carried an intense, wheedling quality, as if he were asking for things he had no right to expect. What quid pro quo did he offer? On which tribal loyalties did he seek to trade? And for what? He had slammed the receiver down, cursing Beirut's notoriously poor phone system. But Camellia suspected something more profound had caused anger.

He didn't answer. Maybe he had nothing to deny. Maybe the calls were related to his search for a job. Somehow she doubted it.

She gave a little sigh. "Don't worry. Beirut is dynamic. A good engineer can work anywhere in the world. Isn't that what you told me?"

Khalil folded the newspaper as if it were a losing hand of cards.

"Damn!" Camellia released the balled-up napkin; it fluttered to the table in a wrinkled heap. "You're so protective of me! I love you for it, dammit. But I can't fathom your world — or my place in it — if you won't talk to me."

"I do not think you want to listen. I think you want to talk."

"Damn right I do," she continued, ignoring the contradiction. "This morning I experienced my first real moment of freedom in Beirut. I bought something from a street hawker. Do you want to hear about it?"

"Ummm."

Alone in Khalil's bedroom, she had heard the shrill cry of the vendor. She heard it every morning. He was a laconic neighborhood regular who pushed a cart loaded with pots and pans, sundries, and plastics. Today it was a siren song.

She leaned out the window. Trained and quick like an auctioneer, he spotted her. From the balcony, she haggled with him — speaking mangled Arabic, which he instinctively understood. She made her order; then, grabbing up a handful of piasters, she ran barefoot to the street. She was masterful. She concluded the transaction and bore her dozen gewgaws back upstairs like booty. A sense of independence flooded over her.

But at the recounting, Khalil looked only baffled. "Have I ever prevented you from buying anything?"

"That's hardly the point."

"Oh?" Khalil raised an eyebrow.

"First you don't want me to go anywhere. Now you won't tell me anything...."

His response was rushed, passionate. "You have been to Pigeon Rock ... to every dress shop on Hamra Street ... to the Casino du Liban. I have taken you to places no woman of my family has ever seen...."

She had challenged his image of himself as an upstart: open-minded, unfettered by tradition. Still, she accused.

"You think I'm a harem doll!"

Out of the corner of her eye, she saw a man in white. He was too large and overbearing to be a waiter — could someone possibly have sent the chef? She declined to acknowledge him; she refused to be distracted from argument. "You go places and do things, and *I'm* shut up like ... like Rapunzel...."

Khalil, elbow on the table, supported the weight of his head with one long, graceful finger at the temple.

"Of what am I depriving you? Dust? Donkey dung?"

"I love the stench." Now Camellia was passionate. She lifted her arms in an all-encompassing gesture of rebellion. "I love Beirut. I love everything about it you find gritty and objectionable."

She ran out of declarations just as the man in white began to get seriously close. Why did he intrude?

"Doctor Marwan!"

Khalil's eyes flashed in recognition, interest and, indisputably, relief. He stood up. He pumped the man's hand. He spoke to him effusively. Phrases of greeting and welcome were
unmistakable. The two men — Marwan, was it? — kissed each other in the Lebanese way: short, repeated pecks to the cheeks.

At last remembering her Lebanese manners, Camellia stood up, too.

"So sorry to be late." Dr. Marwan's slight bow in her direction was decidedly Old World. He was stocky, muscled, plump — but hardly out of breath. His unhurried words belied the apology.

"Dr. Marwan Attiyeh. *Ahlan. Ahlan. Ahlan.*" Khalil was still repeating phrases, heartily, as Dr. Marwan and Camellia shook hands. "*Yallah! Hamdullah as-salaamah!*"

"*Ahlan fik*. Please call me Marwan." The hand was rough, the smile a show of teeth, the voice like sharp cheese melting in the mouth. In Arabic, he sounded guttural, but he spoke English with a slight British accent. "Welcome to Lebanon. How do you find our country? Quite unlike America ... we're not nearly so sprawling."

He stood rim-lit in the noon sun, a half-smile playing on his lips. His face seemed at odds with itself. Too skewed for beauty, his features were rough, raw terrain; thatched eyebrows guarding the eyes, jutting chin challenging the nose, laugh lines girding the cheeks and the well-formed mouth. The eyes shone, iridescent and red-gold; incredibly, they matched his beard. It was a face content with middle age.

Before Camellia could formulate a response, Khalil snapped his fingers. The waiters pulled back the doctor's chair, produced a decanter of chablis and briskly laid out plates, napkins and food.

Still smarting from Marwan's having caught her in argument with Khalil, and annoyed at her own transparency of appearance, Camellia asked, "How do you know I'm American? How do you know I'm not a daughter of Isis?"

"Daughter of Isis?" Settling into his chair, Marwan looked startled, then amused. "I couldn't help but overhear what sounded very much like a declaration of independence." A deep chuckle rumbled in his chest. "Besides, Mrs. Majdi, surely if you were an Arab you wouldn't attribute an Egyptian god to the land of Lebanon." He sighed theatrically. "But to Americans, I fear, we Arabs are all alike. You read about us in your National Geographic and watch us on the news."

"You're wrong. I'm not Mrs. Majdi. Not until Saturday, at least," she finished in a tone of superiority.

"My apologies." Again, the show of teeth. "I forgot that so many American women these days are unmarried."

"I'm not *unmarried*. I'm betrothed. We delayed the wedding for a reason." Then the final shot: "We wanted to be married on native soil."

"*Ya salaam!* A traditionalist!" The smile gave his face an unexpected glow, as if *he* were the betrothed. "How do you find Lebanon?"

"Difficult. The truth sounds undiplomatic, I know." From the corner of her eye, she observed Khalil's expression of disapproval. "But so many people look and dress like me, I expect them to *think* like me. They don't."

Again Marwan seemed startled, then oddly amused. "*Bil-lahi,* we are not an easy people to study from afar. We are primitives. But *not* the sort of primitives you see, breasts bared, in National Geographic!"

"*Tfudduli.*" Khalil, looking uncomfortable, motioned to the food.

He had ordered the traditional Lebanese *mezze*. Camellia recognized the dish, or rather dishes, if only because the famous Lebanese spread was so widely photographed; perhaps she had even seen it in National Geographic. The *mezze* consisted of literally dozens of tiny dishes, each filled with strips or pieces of this delicacy or that. Tiny plates crowded the tabletop. They were filled with tomatoes and white cheeses and black olives, potato salad, marinated cucumbers, pickled eggplant, even small, whole redfish in tomato sauce. There was *hummos*, of course, and *tabbouleh*. And gelid lamb's brain and tongue — all laid out in a fantastic and appetizing array. It mattered not that this was an Italian restaurant whose main entree was lasagna. Many things in Lebanon weren't what they superficially seemed.

The Italian decor, the atmosphere, the obsequious service — all became irrelevant. The strong ethnicity of the food overpowered everything. The smell of lemon seeping through garlic ... the sight of chopped parsley sprinkled on tiny new potatoes ... the elongation of green onions as garnish — the food appealed to the senses. Straw baskets cradled golden rounds of Arabic bread. The bread was a paradox: flat, but not unleavened. Its yeasty aroma obliterated the scent of the roses.

Camellia folded her hands dreamily. "To *completely* answer your question, Dr. Marwan — I find Lebanon wonderful. I've been trying to convince Khalil to take me everywhere. What I wouldn't give to visit Byblos!"

Marwan nodded, seemingly sympathetic, which inspired her. She continued somewhat breathlessly: "Byblos! The city that gave name to the bible."

"It is called Jebeil now." Khalil held his bread like a scimitar. He used it to scoop up a turnip, pink and pickled.

Undeterred, Camellia pulled a dog-eared guidebook from her purse. "And Baalbek. Baalbek! Did you know the Temple of Jupiter was the largest temple in the Roman Empire? And Baalbek's 'little temple' is larger than the Parthenon?" She ate a stuffed grape leaf.

Khalil cut in, hurried and curt. "You have been to the Beirut National Museum. You have seen the jewelry and the mosaics." Growing confident: "The Egyptian display is better and more complete than Cairo's...."

She ate another stuffed grape leaf. Marwan was attentive. "And south to Sidon," she said, continuing her prologue to travel, "that Phoenician stronghold. Sidon! With its gold coins of Alexander the Great ... the magnificent sarcophagi now on display in Istanbul, or is it Paris...?"

Khalil again: "What is left of Sidon if all its treasures are in the Louvre?"

Her voice faltered. She dearly loved Khalil, but she also admired him to a point where she sometimes had to remind herself that he was, after all, an engineer, to keep from being overwhelmed by his occasional lack of imagination. She continued with new energy: "If not antiquities, then think of the Castle by the Sea! Imagine walking barefoot in the sand, collecting purple Murex shells — the Phoenician dye of kings!"

Marwan stopped eating. "Twenty-two people were killed in Sidon last month," he said, almost in a whisper.

"Are you making small talk?" she asked, startled.

"Welcome to Lebanon."

Embarrassed, Camellia almost choked on a piece of parsley. Dr. Marwan was, after all, a stranger to her. And Khalil's original plan had been to meet him alone. She was the intruder.

"*Sahtein.*" In the pause, Khalil saluted the doctor's health. Khalil himself had eaten little. The sun flooded his pale complexion, giving it a washed-out cast. "The Lebanese *mezze* is unequaled in all the world. It can be eaten quickly ... or one can linger over it for hours."

The restaurant seemed filled with lingerers. Patrons' comings and goings there were barely noticeable. At one table, a woman, her shiny wing of black hair caught back by a headband, stared into the eyes of her companion. At another, four men chain-smoked and exchanged boisterous jibes. The restaurant clearly was a place for lovers or old friends.

"Food and ceremony." Camellia put away her guidebook. She munched on a forkful of *tabbouleh*. "You know, I've never understood where anyone in Lebanon finds time to fight. The national pastime is socializing!"

Khalil blinked. He had been waiting. "That is exactly why we must fight. To preserve our culture." Then, intense, "We Christians *made* Lebanon. We are its strength, its brains, its enlightenment."

Marwan raised an eyebrow. "I did not realize you had been back in Lebanon long enough to have joined the Guardians of the Cedars."

"Why not?" Khalil shrugged. His expression grew soft and bitter, and he made the motion of spitting. "Colonel Qadhafi says the Christians have two choices. Convert to Islam. Or hand Lebanon over to Arab-Moslem rule. I will die before I submit to either."

"What does Qadhafi have to do with Lebanon? Libya is nothing. And Qadhafi is mad." Marwan looked amused. "Are you so sure we are the enlightened ones? We Christians — by keeping the upper hand — cling desperately to the status quo. Lebanon's last census was in the '30s. And *it* was taken by the French. Enlightened? We can't even count heads!"

White-knuckled, Khalil gripped his fork. "The Palestinians —"

"Ah! Now we come to the source of your discomfort. Would you exterminate them? Would you, like the Israelis, call them 'two-legged animals,' say they do not exist?"

Khalil flipped his hands palms upward, indicating question without answer. "The government cannot control the fedayeen. The army cannot control them. They are unbearable."

Marwan clucked his tongue wearily, a Levantine gesture of ambiguity and regret. "Why does everyone feel free to fight his proxy war in Lebanon?" The question seemed rhetorical. Marwan, suddenly indifferent, dug his spoon into a cluster of tiny golden eggs. Tasting them, holding out a sample on his spoon for Camellia, he regained energy. "'Pearls of the Caspian.'" He licked his lips appreciatively as she swallowed. "Iranian caviar is still the best in the world. It is extracted from fish as it lives."

"Some sacrifices are necessary," Khalil muttered. Then he ordered more wine.

Camellia blinked in disbelief as the waiters replaced the tiny, empty dishes with full platters and plates. The *mezze* had been only a prelude to the entrees: stuffed peppers and squash, shish kebab, grilled vegetables on skewers, Moroccan couscous, chicken on blackened onions, rice with *snobar* — which were, Marwan explained, the seeds of the umbrella pine. And more whole fish and birds....

"Quite literally, 'birds.'" Marwan ate one, deftly removing its meat. He seemed determined to enjoy himself. Though Camellia suspected that his exchange with Khalil reflected, in microcosm, the political dimensions of Lebanon itself, Marwan had lost interest in argument. In fact, he all but ignored Khalil, like a good Moslem avoiding Scotch.

He became expansive, drinking Turkish coffee. Khalil ordered a *nargeila*, a water pipe, and Marwan sat puffing on it. He spoke to Camellia as if the two of them were alone.

They had known each other since boyhood, he told her: Khalil the Maronite, graduating and leaving for America; Marwan the Greek Orthodox, off to Oxford. "A man in two cultures will never be happy in either," he asserted almost casually; then he drifted into reminiscence, speaking wistfully of his days at Oxford. He spoke exclusively in English, flawless English, with diction Camellia found mildly irritating. Marwan's language was natural, yet more precise than her own.

He worked half-time at Barbir Hospital in Beirut, half-time in a mountain clinic in the south Lebanon town of Beaufort.

Behind him, triangles of white light or water or both danced on the Mediterranean. The infinity beyond, the misty horizon, swirled into nothingness.

Marwan smiled, hands aloft, demonstrating some angle, some plane of Beaufort. His grandmother had grown up in the mountains. So had he. He had trailed her as she, a midwife, scoured the hardscrabble hills for healing wildflowers. "Hills fed by the Litani ... land fed by legend and history, by the blood of Adonis and Aphrodite's tears."

More comfortable with tourism than lover's tears, Camellia asked: "Isn't there a castle there?"

His nod was almost imperceptible. "Beaufort Castle. The incline of the cliffs facing Israel, the impassable valley — all make Beaufort militarily strategic. The castle itself has a line-of-sight view of the Galilee. It is a depressing place, overrun by soldiers. Still, the fedayeen manage to break through. They lob random shots over the cliff. The Israelis retaliate ... swiftly and without fail."

His voice grew dispassionate. Frequently he performed surgeries back-to-back. The injuries were the senseless, ghastly injuries of undeclared war. Sometimes the fedayeen returned from bungled suicide missions half alive. Other times victims were civilians caught by stray bullets or caught up in indiscriminate revenge dealt from the air.

"Still you choose to live there."

"In Beaufort, the myths become believable."

Arab style, he passed the water pipe to Khalil. Khalil puffed sourly.

"At least there's no war," Camellia said.

"Intermittent shelling is worse than war. My mother fled to Beirut after ... after my wife was killed. Her cottage sits vacant on a hill." Sighing, he looked at his watch. "I must go."

Khalil, alert, stiffened. "Stay, my brother. We will stroll along the Corniche."

"Sorry." Unrepentant apology. "I'm needed ... at the hospital." Even so, he lingered, nipping toucan-like on dried pumpkin seeds. "Camellia," he began, "the French tell this story: God created the world, beginning with the great nations. But somehow He forgot Lebanon. At last realizing his mistake, He sighed, more in sorrow than anger. Then He formed Lebanon — of the land He had planned to keep for Himself."

"Ohhh. What a beautiful story."

Khalil blinked. The glint of interest in his eyes had faded, leaving him looking bereft. For once he resembled a proud and glorious Phoenician — one whose ship was filled with off-color silks.

Camellia, protective, turned on Marwan.

"Why aren't you concerned about Lebanon — the way Khalil is?"

"And choose sides?" Marwan's laugh seemed to erupt from his belly. The sun caught his hair, reflecting reds and golds. "*Wallah* — why do you look disappointed? Forlorn as a Moslem girl told plucking her eyebrows violates Islam."

"Did you know that in America, men who speak patronizingly to women are referred to openly as male chauvinist pigs?"

At first the silence was her answer. Marwan's face held tension. Tiny lines rimmed fixed eyes, rigid mouth, taut lips. But then he exhaled, the mouth relaxed, and words flowed smoothly as an unrolling prayer rug.

"Lebanon is run by whim — by warring clans, by the corrupt *zu'ama* and fanatics of every faith. All propped up by confessionalism. The Gemayels, the Franjiehs, the Jumblatts.... The warlords!" There was passion in Marwan, too. He paused, then finished gruffly, "More killing won't help."

He nodded and stood up. But there was another battle to be fought.

Before Camellia knew what was happening — she had missed the cue, the simultaneous reaching for the check — he and Khalil were fighting to pay. Marwan, instinctively, had snatched up the check; simultaneously, Khalil dived for it; now the two men all but grappled for it. Why aren't other people looking? Camellia wondered, but no heads turned. How ordinary, here: two men fighting for the honor of paying. Their outraged grunting was like that of rams. Their gestures approached violence; their expressions, anger if not outright hostility. "Be ashamed of yourself!" Camellia could understand some of what they said in rapid-fire Arabic, in voices that grew suddenly high-pitched. There was a question of obligation and honor. Khalil had earned the right to pay by inviting Marwan. Marwan was obligated by Khalil's return, doubly so because of the presence of his fiance. Each man knew his claim and defended it with equal vigor.

Camellia tensed and leaned away from their pushing hands, admiring the competition. No matter what momentary anarchy might seize the political system, laws that governed individual behavior were immutable.

Neither willingly gave in. They were like Lebanon's commodity dealers, who took fierce joy in economic fight, forcing prices down to the lowest point consistent with survival, selling imported grain at cost — with only the jute bags for profit.

At last Marwan curled his fingers decisively around the check, signaling firm intention. Khalil retreated gracefully. He murmured the ritual of thanks.

Marwan bowed slightly toward Camellia. "It is my pleasure."

"I certainly hope so."

"My pleasure," he repeated. "*Diameh.*" Always.

Awkward, at a loss for words, she shrugged.

"How sad!" she said to Khalil. "Did you hear him say his wife had died? Oh, look! The roses have begun to wilt."

Outside, the taxi drivers slouched against their taxis like street-weary whores. They were the long-distance drivers. They bellowed destinations in flat voices:

"Byblos!" "Baalbek!" "Sidon!" "Tyre!"

Ignoring them, Khalil maneuvered the red Mercedes into the honking traffic.

"The way you two fought! Lebanon needs an Emily Post."

"Lebanon could never sustain one. Rules of behavior are written down only when they have become largely unobserved."

"What did you want from Marwan?"

Khalil, his face a mask of aristocratic neutrality, said nothing.

She sighed. Another silence. Marwan — his was a face that could never conceal. Gaiety, tempered with a hint of grief, gave him an ironic beauty. If only Khalil were so easily read, vulnerable of expression, lyric as shifting sands!

Khalil was cool and hard, unknowable, like the eerie gleam of the moon on ruins just before dawn.

****

They left the waterfront in silence. Khalil drove with exaggerated concentration.

I botched whatever he came here to do, Camellia thought. Khalil suggested no further entertainment or tour, and neither did she. She assumed he was heading straight back to Ain Rumaneh.

All the major thoroughfares were thick with cars — Datsuns, Mercedeses, American cars and painted Volkswagen bugs. Strangely, the traffic in the city's heart was subdued. No one cursed or shook his fist; few drivers broke at breakneck speeds. Low clouds scudded in a gray sky. The sunny afternoon had been eclipsed. The odd atmosphere, the silence — Camellia wrote them off as an extension of her private attitudes.

She leaned her head against the half-open window. Memories. Sunshine and friends. Lebanon promised both. Two days ago, half a dozen friends had piled into someone's new Peugeot. They drove to an orchard and spread out a blanket under the fruit trees. Wine, lamb-and-garlic sandwiches, crusty French bread and pliable flat Arabic loaves, dates from the trees.... Yasmina was there, and her fiance, young, frank-faced. His eyes were wide and ingenuous, shaped like almonds; his nose was jutting and aquiline. A shaggy mustache gave him the look of a peasant. Yasmina, her skin dewy and cream-white, leaned across the picnic hamper to kiss him.

"Tell me about Yasmina."

She didn't think Khalil would answer. But he did. "What is there to tell?"

"Her boyfriend. You said he is a Phalangist. He looked perfectly ordinary to me."

"Did you expect a scimitar between his teeth?"

"Something like that."

He gripped the wheel harder. His voice came in an undertone, absurdly gentle. "I love you," he said. "I love all your faults."

"I am so happy." Oddly embarrassed, adding quickly, "Do you remember, at your uncle's place, in the mountains, where I was running and fell?"

It had been nearly dusk, but at such heights the sun fell piercingly before waning, and family and friends up from the city sat, rimmed in mystical light. It was a summer home — bare walls, little more. No refrigerator, no stove. Stuffed squash and cabbage leaves were steamed in an iron pot over an open fire. The beer was hoisted up from storage at the bottom of a well. Amstel — so cold it snapped. The young boys had dashed off in search of figs; Camellia, on a whim, followed. The hard-packed dirt of the slopes scuffed her loafers. She wished, as their slippery soles struck the loose white stones, that she had brought her jogging shoes. The view of the city below was spectacular. Momentarily distracted, she misjudged the height of a terrace and tripped, rolling and laughing as she tumbled. Finally, several yards down, she came to a stop against a large flat rock. She lay there, winded.

Khalil's shadow fell, and she opened her eyes to his expression of reproof. His breath came hard. "Do you want everyone to think you're *majnooneh*?"

But she had only laughed harder. "You said they all know that Americans are crazy. I'm just living up to their expectations."

A motorcycle cop screeched past.

"American flakiness? Are you asking me to become accustomed to this, an excuse for abnormal behavior?"

"Well, you certainly do all manner of strange things in the name of being Lebanese."

She wondered again, as she had wondered often, how he had wrested himself from Lebanon in the first place, even temporarily. Khalil was a creature of Beirut: beautiful, fashionable and vain, so utterly unself-conscious the superficiality was forgivable. She grew close to him only to be repeatedly cut off. So many others — so much else — laid claim to his time and attention.

"That is exactly the point. Dr. Marwan misunderstands me. You misunderstand me. Kamel — Yasmina's fiance — will go underground when the time comes. She understands. No one can claim to be a man in Lebanon and do less."

The atmosphere changed. Camellia grew sensitive to the environment, the oppression of weather and wind. The hulk of a wrecked car littered the side of the two-lane highway. At the base of the mountain, at the dangerous point where road met shoulder, sheep ambled, herded by a shepherd.

"Will *you* go underground?"

Why had she been daydreaming in class when she should have been alert? Why hadn't she absorbed the information needed to understand and perhaps even to dispute the things Khalil said? Dr. Elias had suggested she read the writings of historian Albert Hourani. At first she thought the recommendation came because Dr. Elias shared Hourani's dark and cynical viewpoint. Now she realized he had wanted her to understand that to be a Levantine "is to live in two worlds or more at once, without belonging to either...." Death wasn't challenge. It was reality.

Khalil veered sharply onto a narrow dirt road. Camellia had not been here before. Alleys. Houses jammed near the street angled strangely to guard privacy. High walls. Small flower gardens. Children doing chores.

"Where are we going?"

"You wanted to see Lebanon. Perhaps it is time you saw what they have done to Lebanon."

"What who has done?"

A donkey stood tethered. Children ran in groups. A woman chased chickens ... a man grinned, showing bad teeth ... it was a street scene from the Bible.

Farther on, with finality, the character of the neighborhood changed. The roads were desolate and flat. Dust covered the wash that fluttered on clothes-lines. Camellia's tongue grew thick with it.

Khalil stopped suddenly.

"There," he said. "We're in the midst of refugees. Get out if you like."

She looked around in wonderment. Slowly she got out of the car and was relieved to see that Khalil was following. What was he trying to prove?

The colors of the camp were beige and brown and dark blue. Roads, clothes, walls. A blue truck generated spirals of dust. It had large initials on it: UNWRA.

"United Nations relief," Khalil said, observing her gaze. "Bringing in parcels of food. Perhaps medicine. There is said to be an outbreak of cholera."

Women, heads shrouded in scarves, stood in line, waiting for their children's turn to be vaccinated. The doctor inside the clinic was prematurely gray. He ordered tea for Camellia and Khalil. He seemed glad of visitors.

The doctor's laugh was rich and cynical. "I keep hoping things will change. They never do." He glanced at Camellia. "Are you a spy for Israel?" Then, shrugging, "What does it matter? Even the Eastern Bloc countries cannot help us."

The tea was the color of tiger's-eye, its taste bitter.

"Why do the women have so many children?"

He rubbed a child's upper arm with alcohol, preparing the site for injection. "I have explained to them everything — about birth control. 'It is too much,' I tell them, 'to have six or eight or nine children.' They listen. They agree. But if they are healthy, they have more babies. They hope for boys. 'It is for our future,' they say. *Wallah*, as long as we have war it will be like this."

"And the cholera?"

"It is impossible to maintain a standard of public health when conditions are unsanitary."

The floor was cracked concrete. Even the hard-packed roads outside were cracked. There were pathways and wire fences around the hovels where water pooled in gutters. The cloth roof of an open-air storefront sagged like the face of the man who sat beneath it.

Twenty minutes later they left. "*Wallah*," called the doctor as they passed. "After almost thirty years, we still call them *emergency* camps."

****

"How could you do that to me?"

In the Mercedes, at 85 kilometers an hour, the wind washed over them in purifying waves.

"You wanted to see a camp. Now you've seen one."

"I felt like a keyhole-peeper."

"I offered to take you inside their homes."

"They were hovels."

"You romanticize the refugees."

She closed her eyes against the wind. "Maybe I should have gone inside. I had no energy."

A siren sounded in the distance. Its shriek made noticeable the dead hush of the traffic. Camellia, apprehensive, chewed on a hangnail. Khalil put a tape into the cassette. It was Fayrouz.

Moslem West Beirut. The suburbs. The dome of a mosque gleamed above tiered balconies. For the first time, Camellia saw the Moslem sanctuary as Khalil saw it: alien and threatening, forbidden.

"You haven't told me what you wanted from the doctor — Dr. Marwan. What business did you have on a Sunday?"

"Sunday is a working day — like any other."

She giggled. "You'd think with the world's major religions all jammed together on the same few square kilometers — they'd at least agree on a common Sabbath!"

A raindrop penetrated the sodden air. It moistened her lip. She rolled down the window, hoping for more. But only dryness followed it. The sky was dark, distended, withholding rain.

Traffic slowed further. The pedestrians moved faster.

A woman ran past, clutching a sack of vegetables. A chicken dangled from her arms. A man ducked into an alley. The children were gone. Out of sight, at least. A car swerved off the road into a private drive. A grilled iron gate slapped shut behind it.

East. The roads converged in the center of Beirut. A rounded corner, and the street was a mass of black Mercedeses and beige Datsuns, grayed Volkswagens, horns stilled, moving not in the normal anarchy but as if in procession. Closer to the Christian suburbs, the lanes became clogged. Khalil, forehead furrowed, braked. Camellia could see only the blank faces of other drivers. Still ahead: the last major intersection before Ain Rumaneh. The demarcation, not shown on any map, separating West Beirut from East.

Khalil cut the Fayrouz tape. He clicked on the radio. Urgent voices crackled against the static.

Another siren. This time it wailed against scattered gunlike bursts.

"Khalil — what's happening?"

He revved the Mercedes as the cars ahead began to crawl. For once he did not equivocate.

"This morning, in Ain Rumaneh. Some sort of incident —"

"Ain Rumaneh! That's where we live!"

The traffic moved slowly now, steadily.

"Let me listen. Two of Pierre Gemayel's men — shot. Gemayel inside the church — "

"The church? Our church?"

"No one knows who shot them. Two men sped away. Were they Palestinian commandos? Or just common thugs? No one knows. After the shooting, Gemayel's sharpshooters crawled to the roof of the church. They clung to the steeples. They fanned out over the church yard. A bus of refugees happened by. It never had a chance."

The hangnail broke clear. She tasted the blood of its root. "Who was killed? How many?"

"Two dozen Palestinians, they say."

Brakes screeched. The driver behind made a decisive U-turn and sped back to the West.

"Sons-of-bitches." Khalil's knuckles whitened on the wheel.

The cause of the delay was clear. The roadblock. But it was bigger now. Piled obstacles ... an acrid smell ... boys, roughly the age of Samir, waving cars through... the glint of gun-metal....

"Maybe we should turn around. Like the car in back of us."

"Do you think *anyone* can keep me from my home?"

Closer. The boys formed a quasi-military grouping. They looked oddly Scout-like in khaki uniforms. They stood clustered around a makeshift blockade, among strewn tires. Parked cars and pick-up trucks loaded with metal formed a perimeter.

Young men — senior statesmen? — sat atop them, perched on their roofs. They smoked casually.

The boys were surprisingly officious. They sliced the air with rifle butts, waving to the cars, signaling them to slow, then to pass. Their economy of motion was graceful, riveting.

"Khalil! Are you insane? Let's go back."

"Their pride is wounded," Khalil said sardonically. "Their honor violated. They will show us they are tough!"

"Palestinians?"

"Look at that Land Rover." Khalil's exhalation was a snort. "Probably stolen. And the Kalashnikovs — displayed for their shock value, not their power of recoil."

"Khalil...."

The red Mercedes was now two car-lengths from the blockade of tires. A fist pummeled the windshield. Khalil rolled down the window to the smells of sulfur and sweat.

A press of faces. Like boy-kings they gathered around, eyes dark and flickering, mindful of martyrs. She could not understand their Arabic; nor could she fathom Khalil: suave, polite. He surrendered his identity card without protest. One of the boys plucked it from Khalil's palm. Khalil looked straight ahead, declining to meet their eyes.

A voice that had not yet found its adult pitch inquired: "*Amerikee?*"

"Ah," Khalil assented. He stretched out his hand to Camellia. "Give me your passport."

"My ... my passport? I don't have it with me. Why would I?"

Khalil's fingers curled as if they had been burned. "I told you to carry it — always!"

"But I — "

"*Ma'alesh.*" A man bent down to peer in the window. His eyes were pleasantly wrinkled beneath a solid line of eyebrow. He wore the slightly hunted expression of a man past forty. His eyes gleamed with empathy. She didn't have her passport! The universal thoughtlessness of women!

Tranquilly, he waved his rifle. They were to proceed.

Khalil slipped the Mercedes into gear. Camellia relaxed slightly. Her hands and shoulders, rigid, tingled with release.

Then everything began to happen in slow motion.

One of the young men began to shout. It was a long-drawn-out syllable, like the death cry of someone falling from a great height. Like a swimmer completing a graceful arc, he grabbed at Khalil with an overhand motion. The attack escalated to became combat as Khalil, imprisoned in tight-lipped silence, clawed back.

Something small — envelope? parcel? — was withdrawn from Khalil's shirt pocket. The young man held it high. His eyes were deep-set and full of joy and scorn. His hair was bristly and black and grew in a beautiful counter-clockwise swirl. Camellia was close enough to touch him.

Khalil thrust himself chest-high through the window. He snatched at the package, but the young man lifted it beyond reach. It was long and flat and brown. It jutted from between bony fingers. Camellia saw spidery Arabic script. And block lettering: "Dr. Marwan Attiyeh. Avenue de L'Independence."

"Give it back!" For a confused moment she realized she had shrieked the wrong command to the wrong person. "Khalil, let him have it. Give it *up*!"

But Khalil lunged upward like an arrow, which was a mistake because it enabled the boys to work as a team, pinning him against the roof. He — straight-legged, half-in, half-out, chest thrust through the cranked-down window — completed the only maneuver open to him. He stomped on the pedal. He floored it. Boys, young men, slightly older and weary men, de facto leaders — all were now mobilized. Maybe a dozen of them pressed against chassis and windshield. They jerked Khalil upward by exerting pressure under his arms. The Mercedes jolted like a roller coaster caught repeatedly in power surges, jumping forward, stopping, jumping forward, trailing boys like streamers. After fifty yards, someone had the presence of mind to shoot its tires out.

Khalil was dragged from the car.

Camellia, disheveled and bruised, spilled out after him. Disoriented, she took a step in one direction only to stop short, deciding to stagger off in another. She shouted "Wait!" and "You can't" and "I'm an American!" as they took Khalil away from her. None of what she yelled made any sense. She was transported by a traumatic memory of childhood. Once, at dusk, she had climbed a large oak tree only to become stuck, and it seemed like hours during which she cried every plaintive appeal she had ever heard on any cartoon, specifically Olive Oyl's, "Help! Please! Somebody! Anybody! Help me, please!" before a neighbor responded by calling Angela and instigating a rescue.

Khalil did not look back. They took him to the Land Rover, which roared to life. So, at that moment, did the loudspeakers of a nearby mosque, erupting into the *muezzin's* call to prayer.

Radials spinning, the Land Rover rammed stacked tires as the driver made a clumsy, violent three-point turn. Then it careened into alleys that stretched out, endless and impassable.

Dazed, Camellia took a step backward.

The young men encircled the abandoned red Mercedes. They poked and prodded it. Camellia almost gave in to hysterical laughter. They reminded her of lost tribes picking at a whirlybird.

Then, like high priests abandoning the sacrifice, all backed off but one. He was small and sturdy as a jockey. Momentarily, he crouched beside the frame and seemed to peer beneath it. Only then did Camellia realize the Mercedes had been set afire.

No one seemed to notice her. Was this intentional? She was disoriented, and rational thought escaped her. She realized, in one point of high ridiculous detail, that she was still clinging to her purse.

Escape. Escape seemed prudent. She wheeled around. The traffic was still backed up, of course; it had nowhere to go. She looked at the white-faced drivers in their gridlocked cars and saw no hope of rescue there. Deserted side streets, tire-blocked alleys ... They led — angled, unplotted and unmapped — to wherever Khalil was now.

The sky cleared. The storm passed without release. Only the bitter sparkle of a winter-spring sun remained. Her mind cleared also. Unthinkingly, she took another step backward, then turned and ran: away from the conflagration and murmuring of the crowd of men and boys like frenzied flying insects. Where to seek refuge? In the oasis of tall buildings, mirage of shelter and life? She fell once, hearing the slap of her palms against the grit, the pebbles, but she jumped up and brushed her hands together as she ran, fueled by urgency and despair. If only the road would take her to Khalil! Faster, harder....

There was a silence then, desolate as the keening wail that would not quit: he's gone.

****

Silence. An end to the running. She sat in someone's faded parlor. The children had all been shooed away. Women brought bitter, sugared Turkish coffee. Men sat shaking their heads and speaking in somber tones, as if someone they knew had died. How quickly they had come to her aid! Beirut was, after all, not New York, and the people whose neighborhoods she had streaked through with tear-stained face had emerged from their modest flats like Bedouins offering hospitality to a desert traveler. They drew her gently inside.

How foolish she had been! Khalil promised enchantment without danger, and she, forgetting he was five years removed from his home and out of touch....

Home. Beirut. Throughout its neighborhoods of lyric name — Ashrafieh, Badaro, Furn al-Chebbak, Shiyaih and Hadath — there burst sounds that belonged on soundtracks or in movie houses. Spasmodic rocket fire and grenades. Blasts of machine guns. The random rat-a-tat of snipers.

These people, this middle-class Arab family sitting in their parlor — already they knew what had happened. Not through radio or television. Official communications had been cut off for hours. Rather, the news had carried from one to one, traveling by that mystical, peculiar osmosis that censorship or incompetent journalism couldn't suppress. They were calling it the "Ain Rumaneh incident." Not Khalil's abduction. *That* was far too insignificant and unimpressive an event to command attention on the neighborhood political scene. "Incident" referred to the slaughter outside the church where Pierre Gemayel was presiding over a family baptism or dedicating a church or simply attending Mass, depending on which rumor one chose to believe. The victims were Palestinians, it had been established. Refugees from Tel Zataar. Twenty-seven deaths. Camellia no longer cared about the death toll or the carnage at the church or the whispers of the horrible revenge the Palestinians were sure to extract. One thought blasted through her brain and cleared it of all matter: Khalil is gone.

"We thought the government had rid us of the Palestinian problem ... even in 1973." One of the women, a mother, was a young widow dressed in the customary black of mourning. As other women admonished the children or refilled dishes with pistachio nuts, the young widow sat beside Camellia, keeping company or standing guard, Camellia didn't know which. Camellia had wanted to return to Ain Rumaneh at once, but had been persuaded to stay until the fighting elsewhere played itself out.

The widow, Jamila, crossed her legs; nylon-encased thighs swished beneath the black polyester dress. Jamila apparently had shopped for fabric from the European-import stores, not the shops that offered rough black cotton from Damascus. She nibbled pistachios from her cupped hand; her blood-red fingernails waved like the innards of a flower. "We watched the bomb attack from our balconies," she continued dreamily, "the jets gliding over Bourj al-Barajneh."

Listless, Camellia leafed through the two-week-old copy of Newsweek on her lap. Why hadn't she listened to Dr. Elias? "Lebanon is a mosaic. A society of fragments," he had said. Further, the government was corrupt, the system hypocritical, the social order beyond reform. No one was loyal to Lebanon. Other allegiances beckoned. Internecine warfare kept ancient hatreds fresh. "Kiss the hand you cannot bite, then ask God to break it." Such was the logic of Lebanon, where each new killing justified the one that came before.

Images of Vietnam dominated the Newsweek cover. The world was busy with America's retreat from Saigon. But the Middle East had never left the headlines. Not even for a day. Why hadn't she seen? Why, for example, hadn't she read Newsweek in Ann Arbor? Even the wire news in her own paper. In Egypt, a domestic crisis roiled. In Iran, the Shah repressed riots and put down opponents. In Israel, the military unveiled the Kfir, a neat little jet which could fly at twice the speed of sound. And in Lebanon....

She *knew* these things. She had listened at the feet of Dr. Elias. She had absorbed Khalil's monologues. Black September ... the Palestinians crushed in Jordan ... commandos tightly reined in Syria. All such events conspired to leave only one country free: the least qualified, the country whose political fragility could least tolerate armed outsiders, was most vulnerable to the shock of repeated Israeli reprisals: Lebanon.

Lebanon. Where Israeli commandos had invaded by sea and assassinated three Palestinians in their Beirut apartments, while their families, forced to watch, looked on; one, Kamal Nasser, a poet, dying in his pajamas.

"Seven people were killed near here — only last July," said the widow. "Last month, a Phalangist leader was cut down as he filled his car with gas." Her tone was almost gleeful. She did not say which side her husband had been on or how he had died. Camellia did not ask.

Just yesterday, Camellia had met the Maronite priest who was to have performed her marriage ceremony — hers and Khalil's. He lowered his lumpy body onto the divan where Yasmina had been sitting. (She had jumped up to offer the prelate the most comfortable seat.) His odor of wine, incense and sacramental unguent obliterated any other fragrance.

Camellia had expected him to brief her on the meaning of the Maronite marriage ceremony, which she understood to be elaborate. But he spoke not of religion but of political imperatives. Time and again, he said, the Christians had nearly wrested Lebanon from the Moslems. One day they would succeed. "I agree with Pierre Gemayel's theory of the Christian 'psychosis of fear'." The cleric's coffee grew cold in its cup. "We cannot resist madness unless the Moslems reassure us, once, and then again, a thousand times, that Lebanon is ours."

His words stimulated Khalil.

"What's happening to you?" she demanded after the priest had gone. Sunset filled the bedroom with rose-gray slivers of waning light. But Khalil was full of energy and preparing to leave.

His laugh was harsh, his eyes an opaque gleam. "Do I advocate anything others do not?"

She leaned against the balcony, inhaling the suffocating jasmine-scented dust of evening. "And what is it you advocate? Violence in the name of God?"

"Camellia." His breath raised gooseflesh on her neck. "The poet says, 'I, Man, have no ending.'"

She tossed her head furiously at his violation of Gibran's tender sentiment and of the memory of them sitting cross-legged under the oaks, savoring it.

"You're corrupting Gibran! He wrote of love, not death."

His kiss was a stinging slap, breath-snatching and debasing, and she responded like a bartered soul, enduring fierce kisses and clawings; Khalil took her savagely, barely loose of his clothes, in sweaty thrusts, his discharge chilling her like dirty rain.

Later, as she left the faded parlor, Jamila said good-by decisively, her eyes brimming with unbearable sweetness. Two of her dead husband's relatives walked Camellia home alongside deserted shops on empty streets. They wove through arches. They hugged buildings grayed in the twilight. They smelled the cloying stink of urban battle: rubber and asphalt and acridness. No sound occurred but the nocturnal cries of insects, occasional distant shots, the efficient swish of women on the rebound, hurriedly retrieving their wash.

On the landing, she turned to shake hands with the two men. They did not speak. She did not ask their names. Were they Christian or Moslem?

Perhaps, by that time, it no longer mattered, not even to the men themselves.

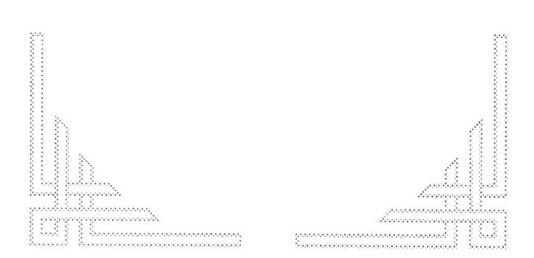

5

The Embassy

Beirut was the scene of monstrous crime.

The city was like a brain-dead body whose lungs still processed air as limbs grew idle, then rigid. Fighting spread from quarter to quarter, raging here, subsiding there, like infection. For a time, the fighting would recede, putrid bubbles on a dead lake. But no one was safe. The streets were a battleground, rooftops the front line. When organized fighting stopped, snipers started.

Camellia had been dimly aware that Khalil's apartment building had a basement. Until this moment, she had no idea what it looked like. Now she sat huddled there, driven there by people whose extravagant hatreds had been allowed to fester, then overrun the city. Khalil's family sat alongside a dozen other families, all caught in a collective quarantine, able to do little but hunker down among the furniture of pillows, jerry cans and sandbags. They listened to the guns.

Tayta slept, enveloped by the merciful exhaustion of the aged whose world has changed beyond all recognition. Her fingers did not relax. They clutched the mother-of-pearl worry beads, which lay against her black dress. Her fingers were the same unearthly shade of white as the beads.

Abu Mousa looked physically ill. Om Mousa was somewhere beyond reach of pain or illness, stranded on a plateau of grief. Camellia dreaded the moment Om Mousa emerged from that plateau. There would be agitation. Wailing. Catharsis. Grief. But later. Now Om Mousa looked stunned. Her eyes held stoicism, an emotion or attitude Camellia had never understood.

And me? she thought. How do I feel? What is my place in this dreadful universe of waiting and pain?

Voices sounded around her. But they didn't touch her. Two of Khalil's aunts and a neighbor murmured words of resentment and solace. They spoke to Om Mousa, who seemed to absorb the phrases as if they were medicine. Camellia felt a sudden, sharp loss. Not only for Khalil, but also for the extended family that was not hers:

the blood-link, the earthy, primeval cohesion; the aunts and cousins she would never have.

Her thoughts raced. Her mind grew panicked, groping for connections.

She stared at the palm of her hand. Pebbles had scraped it raw. Did her face look as gray as the white underside of her arm now looked? Scrapes and cuts were ashen tracks, the color of the walls. The air was exhausted, heavy and stagnant. The silence was punctuated by nasal breathing and coughs.

Samir brought a wet cloth. He wrapped her hand with it.

"Who would do this — ?" she asked. "Why would anyone — ? Why Khalil — ?"

Samir's response was a recitation. "The Palestinians take their revenge." He had learned the futility of questioning irrational acts.

But Camellia was not prepared to let the questions drop. "I know a massacre occurred. What is Khalil's fault in that?" She adopted his syntax without conscious effort. "What did *he* ever do to Palestinians?"

"What is anybody's fault?" Samir shrugged. His expression was neutral. She wanted to shake him.

"How can you be so indifferent?"

He looked genuinely puzzled. "Indifferent?"

"Or fatalistic? Or stoic? Or whatever it is that allows you to sit here and ... and *wait*!"

Samir removed the cloth from her arm, exposing raw skin to the air. He waited patiently for a question he could understand.

"To hell with philosophy," she said. "To hell with logic. Just tell me: number one, who is shooting, and, number two, when are they going to stop?"

Samir now looked genuinely baffled. He turned hands palms upward in a gesture of innocence. "*Wallah*, I don't know what you are asking. You know the Palestinians are Moslem. You know the Phalangists are Christian."

"It can't be that simple."

"You want to know why they kill each other? They have always killed each other. For as long as anyone can remember. And, of course, the Shi'ites and the Druze...."

"Israel supports the Phalange," she said, more to herself than to Samir. "And Syria the leftists. Even so, some part of the explanation is missing. There must be something more to understand. A key element that makes everything make sense...."

("Everyone is on someone's payroll," Dr. Elias had said. "Who knows at any given moment who is shooting — or why?")

"What does the radio say? Where's the governor? Doesn't Lebanon have a president? Where's the army?"

Samir gave her the same unwavering, puzzled look. "What can we do but wait?"

From time to time, missives arrived from outside. A rumor brought by someone's cousin, who had run from building to building, risking being shot. Or a bulletin bursting through the static of the radio someone held:

"The cabinet is meeting in emergency session. Security forces are besieging the street of Mar Maroun in Chia."

A rumor had spread that the army was about to take over Ain Rumaneh. Just enough artillery noise lingered in the air to give it credence. Between news bulletins, the station played march music and patriotic songs.

"If this were America, we'd be *doing* something." Camellia chewed her finger disconsolately.

"What?"

Samir was strangely eager. Her mood had infected him. His English was better than she had realized. He had never spoken much to her when Khalil was around. "What would we do?" he repeated.

"Uhh...." When it came time to name an action that would accomplish something, she was at a loss. Do what? She sighed. Fatalists were a pain in the ass. But maybe they had a point.

Samir noticed the failure of will. "In the morning, my father takes you to the airport."

"He does *what*?"

"To the airport. You go home."

"What on earth for?"

"My father has spoken." Samir was more ingenuous than Khalil. Also more straightforward. "He wishes me to say ... truly, we are sorry for what has happened. We will not rest until we are sure of your safety. We cannot be sure of your safety until you leave Beirut."

Briefly, she considered it. Ann Arbor. A newspaper reporter again. An air of mystery would attend her, since fate had plunged her into an exotic world, where she had suffered loss. Young, she would recover. She would file away the experience, in a part of her mind labeled "foreign adventures."

"You must be out of your mind if you think I'm going to abandon Khalil. Who will find him?"

At the mention of his name, Om Mousa lifted her head like a wounded animal. She lowered it when she realized no further insight or clue into Khalil's disappearance was being offered.

"The Moslems will release him," Samir suggested passionately.

"I can't live with faint hopes. I've got to make it happen."

"You must leave. Before the airport closes."

"Don't be preposterous. Airports don't *close*."

"This is Beirut."

"Oh." Of course. The airport did close — predictably. Dr. Elias had used that fact to sorely irritate Khalil one evening. Dr. Elias was discussing the Lebanese army, in particular, its ineffectiveness. He had told this anecdote: After a PFLP attack on an El Al airliner in Athens, the Israelis retaliated by destroying 13 aircraft on the ground in Beirut. An outcry arose over the army's utter failure to protect the airport. Now, during times of trouble, the army simply closed it.

The man with the radio, weary of straining for details through static, switched from station to station. Seeking an uncluttered transmission, he skipped across a station playing music.

Fayrouz echoed in a sweet lament.

"Oh!" Camellia's reaction was almost involuntary. "Please bring it back."

The man obliged. Losing interest in the radio, he leaned against the cool stone wall, lowering his chin to his chest in a prelude to sleep.

Camellia knew this song. Dr. Elias had translated it for her in Ann Arbor.

Take me and plant me in the land of Lebanon
Take me to the house that is guarding the hill
Where I shall open the door and kiss the walls
And kneel under the loveliest sky,
And pray and pray....

How different Fayrouz sounded here, in context. Like seeing antiquities on the ground in Tyre, rather than viewing them encased in glass in London. Maybe it was just that Camellia now knew what to listen for. Diminished sevenths. Tragedy in E-minor scales. The voice lingered, finding power in subject. Fayrouz sang of treachery, lost love. Hope denied. Truth revealed.

Lebanon. A fragile political entity now in the hands of what Dr. Elias called "uncontrolled elements." Health, spirit, body, mind: "Uncontrolled elements" now controlled them all.

You'll need more than love to survive in Lebanon.

When at last it was too obscene to be underground another moment, to be suffocating, closeted in air that reeked of rosewater and garlic and impotent sweat, at last it was time to go upstairs.

The smoke of candles quickly extinguished. The wafting and clinging of their smell. Imprisoned sound echoed.

Upstairs. She could remember again that Beirut was a city of scented air, sculpted streets, graceful balconies, crowded bazaars, elegant skyscrapers. Families stood up. The old were assisted. The young were carried. The women rode on bitter chatter to their rooms. Someone led Om Mousa to her bed.

In her room, Camellia opened a can of 7-Up. Room temperature. Gritty carbonation dried out her mouth.

The window drew her. In contrast to the spent air of the basement, the outside air seemed fresh and cold. It wasn't. It had a dirty quality. Each inhalation brought a powdery clinging substance into her lungs.

But she continued to drink the air. It energized her. The night wore on. She did not sleep. She sat by the window. No thought made sense juxtaposed with any other thought. Why did her mind seemed filled with static? Every few minutes she leaned over the counterpane to scan the surroundings.

The moon glittered on broken shards in the street where they lay as if the buildings had vomited glass.

Once, a car whipped around the corner, made a panic stop, screeched through a U-turn and pulled away.

The night was remarkable by its absence of sound. There was nothing to hear. No nocturnal wing-rubbing of insects. No furtive scuffle of running feet. No abrupt shutting of a window.

Where was Khalil?

Nothing. Until dawn and the astonishing sunrise. A few tentative notes by birds.... Then they sang shrilly, as after a storm. Camellia came awake without experiencing the sensation of having been asleep. She swiveled her head, as if she were capable of hearing sounds beyond human range.

She thought she heard voices in the parlor. Was Om Mousa well or ill? Was Tayta awake — ?

Camellia grabbed a flimsy silken wrapper off the hook and flung it around her shoulders. Something sounded strange. Off key. The silence carried a curious distinctiveness — which had nothing to do with sounds of fighting, or its aftermath.

All the bedroom doors were closed. At the end of the hallway — a light. A large obstruction on the floor.

Camellia stopped short as the obstruction took shape and form. An ornate trunk came into focus. She knew this trunk.

She laughed giddily. "Surely not visitors." Then, tentatively, "Anyone home?"

As her senses absorbed the evidence, suspicion evolved to become recognition. Then outrageous realization. Camellia blinked and walked closer, and the details of the trunk became unmistakable and clear. There it sat, embossed with three brass initials, bound with rope and festooned with sleeves and scarves caught in its crack: Angela's trunk. It was grand, like Pigeon Rock. It announced Angela like a loyal butler. Knowing Angela, it was stuffed with medicines and books. Butterfly wings and botanical paraphernalia. A box of Bisquick for making breakfast pancakes. Angela packed a trunk as if to demonstrate Yankee ingenuity to anyone who might paw through its contents.

"Mother?"

"Good morning," grunted Abu Mousa. He had been standing next to the trunk. Now he lowered himself to sit on its edge. He grunted as he wiped at his forehead with a handkerchief.

Camellia wondered what the Arab word was for "hernia."

"Mother?" Where was Angela? Camellia stretched out her hand to steady herself against the wall. She had spent half the night in the basement, cramped, surrounded by strangers, unable to comfort either herself or her stunned, grieving mother-in-law-to-be, and the other half alone in her room, listening for sniper fire and watching the pale glint of the moon on asphalt. Now — Angela, like a grand dame on safari.... With growing dismay, "Mother?"

Tayta came awake. She raised up on her elbows. She had been sleeping in the living room. She always came to the living room when she couldn't sleep or when there was trouble of any sort.

Head cocked in alert bewilderment, she swiveled for a clearer view of the stairs.

Cork-soled shoes thumped against a background warble of little oaths.

"Camellia!" Angela's voice, a rich maternal sing-song, shot ahead of her. Imperative, like a general's. "How do they *live* without elevators?"

"Awk!" Camellia struggled to produce some sort of welcoming sound. All that came out were cries of consternation. "Awk! Awk!"

"Well! Don't just stand there gaping." Angela emerged on the landing. She had dressed for the natives: wrap-around skirt, ceramic earrings, cashmere jacket, feathered hat. "Nobody here speaks English!"

Camellia, who prided herself on quick thinking in tight situations, could only respond: "What did you expect?"

Panting from exertion, murmuring gracious thanks to Abu Mousa, Angela stepped over the trunk to get into the parlor.

Abu Mousa leaped up, apologizing, and — to clear the path — heaved the trunk several inches out of the way, almost to the wall.

Now Om Mousa was standing in the hall. Her eyes, red-rimmed, widened as she peered into the parlor. She made eye contact with Camellia, who shrugged.

Angela settled on the divan, patting Tayta's gnarled hand as if they were old friends.

"All those hours on the plane!" she began. "I thought we'd never get here."

Unaware of, or at any rate unaffected by the incredulous silence, Angela removed her hat. Its pink feathers rustled as though the bird lived.

Camellia marched to the center of the room. "What do you mean — *we?*"

Seeming not to have heard, Angela looked from Abu Mousa to Tayta. "Is this some sort of Lebanese national holiday? I keep hearing explosions."

"Mother — there's been fighting. Perhaps even the start of a civil war!"

"Ah, I remember! From your father's day. Domestic politics is always unpredictable in these little countries." Astonishingly, Angela seemed relieved. "That explains it! My driver huffed off without a word. For a minute I thought I'd shorted him on the tip."

Footsteps on the staircase ... a blur of motion ... a tangle of fringe and leather straps and limbs.... Violet took the trunk at a leap. She skidded to a stop in the center of the room. The fringe of her jacket and moccasins continued to sway. "Alas! Lebanon!"

"Don't you mean, 'Alas, Babylon'?" Angela asked.

"Muzz! Take your things before I drop them."

Two parachute bags, a camera case and one large purse, impelled by momentum, now dangled perilously from Violet's extended arms.

Camellia closed her eyes, waiting for the crash.

Tayta sat fascinated. She stopped clacking her mother-of-pearl worry beads.

"You — too?" Camellia opened one eye.

"Smooch. Smooch." Violet pursed her lips in an exaggerated kiss. "We came for the wedding, sister dear. I *hope* we're in time." She looked pointedly at Angela. She wore the martyred air of one whose fine timing is frequently sabotaged by others.

Deliberately, she slumped her shoulders. Purses, bags and camera case cascaded to the floor.

The camera landed near Angela's feet.

"Dad's camera!" Camellia cried.

"Well, I told you I couldn't keep holding that stuff."

"That Nikon belonged to your father," Angela intoned as she bent to retrieve it.

"Don't worry. I padded the lens with tissue paper."

"Tissue?" Camellia asked. "Tissue?" she repeated. Her voice became a shriek. She began to laugh. Great, uncontrol-lable, snorting heaves. "But...." She lost the power to articulate. She hugged her ribs against the clawing glee. "But tissue will scratch the lens!" she finally gasped.

"You're spoiling my vacation," said Violet. "Already."

Camellia sagged against the couch. She seemed to have no control over the muscles of her face. A stuck smile was pasted on her face. "I'm glad to see you. Really. But under the circumstances, I'll be thrilled to see you go."

"But we just got here!" Violet, of course, in the way of teen-age girls, could look utterly forlorn at will. Fluttering her eyelashes, she surveyed the pile of parcels and purses she would have to shoulder again if everyone agreed on departure.

"But what about the Tour?" Angela asked.

Camellia retreated to the wall. She leaned against it. "The tour?"

"Holy Land Visits Inc." Violet looked hopeful.

"We've come with a group." Angela, accepting a pillow from Tayta, burrowed more thoroughly into the divan.

Violet cast her eyes heavenward. "Bunch of holy rollers. It's enough to try the patience of St. Paul."

Ignoring Violet, Angela continued. "After your telegram, we just got to talking, and we thought, 'Wouldn't it be wonderful if we could surprise everyone by showing up?'" she explained. "Then I saw an ad for this tour. Two members had canceled, two seats were available — "

"It seemed like fate," Violet said.

"And going with a group of fellow travelers seemed the safest way."

"Yeah," Violet interjected. "All you have to do is beat back the attempts on your soul. You learn to recognize the avid glint in their eyes. If you're smart, you either escape or create a diversion. Otherwise you get asked: 'Do you know Jesus Christ as your personal savior?'"

"Haven't you heard about any trouble? Didn't anyone warn you about the fighting?" Camellia asked. Domestic turmoil in a small foreign country wouldn't rate much air time or many column inches in America. But surely the dateline "Beirut" would have been accompanied by at least a body count.

"How could we have? We've been traveling for 24 hours!" Angela exclaimed.

Time enough, in Lebanon, to start a civil war.

"Yeah," Violet confirmed. "The entire trip was nonviolent. Except for the in-flight movie: 'Jaws'."

A crackle of far-off gunfire punctuated the discussion. Angela gasped. It was a whoosh of partial comprehension.

The silence returned. The import of the gunfire apparently escaped Violet.

She giggled. "Besides, even if we'd had access to television news, what makes you think we'd know what's going on? I don't know Saudi Arabia from Shangri La. And Muzz's been known to look for your face in crowd shots of *Cairo*."

Om Mousa, having donned a black skirt and sweater, hastened to the kitchen to join Bahija. Bless her, Camellia thought. Ready to cook for the crowd.

By contrast, Abu Mousa, already introduced, sat picking at his neat black mustache as if it were a scab. Perhaps for the first time ever, events occurring under his roof were beyond his power to control or even influence.

"Egypt. Now *there's* a country." Angela lifted her chin, gazing at the ceiling, scaling mental pyramids. Dreamily, she caressed the lip of her hat. "Even now we could be floating down the Nile. Perusing papyrus scrolls — "

"Raiding Tut's tomb," Violet suggested.

" — if only Khalil had been born *west* of the Euphrates...."

It sounded like cannons now, and closer.

"Where is that Arab hunk, anyway?" Violet asked.

"Khalil?"

"Three points for remembering his name. What's wrong? Has he gone off into the desert to acquire a harem? Or, better yet, dumped you in favor of me?"

"He's been kidnapped."

"By Moslem slave-traders? By — " Violet sputtered to a stop.

"Whatever for?" Angela's lips pursed to form a circle of horror.

"I didn't hang around waiting for explanations." Camellia gripped her sides against painful laughter threatening to return.

"You were with him?" Angela's expression escalated from apprehension to panic. "Were you harmed?"

"No. But they torched Abu Mousa's car." She drew in a breath to steady herself. "Look. You've got to take Violet and go home. Not two miles from here, more than twenty Palestinians were massacred. In a *church*yard. Now the Palestinians are on a rampage and, to counter them, every two-bit Christian militia in Beirut has taken to the streets. It's nothing like Ann Arbor."

"But not so very different from Detroit the first two weeks of school," Violet said. "Okay — so I'll shut up."

In Angela's lap, the hat all but collapsed under the pressure of two nervous, picking hands. The pink feathers quivered. "After the wedding, we're to meet the tour in Sidon." Her expression grew pinched and absent. She seemed to be talking to herself. "We'll call in the FBI. The American Embassy. The Marines! Khalil will return. You'll get married" — her voice grew stronger " — and Violet and I won't have missed anything but the Cedars!" she finished triumphantly.

"But who's got him?" Trust Violet to get to the point. A child of television, she had been weaned on a diet of problems solved in 30 minutes.

"Moslems. The PLO. Maybe even the Israelis."

"Barbarians!" Angela's throat reddened to the color of a lizard's.

With great effort Camellia kept her voice calm. "The FBI doesn't operate in Lebanon. The Embassy isn't equipped to do police work. And what makes you think the Marines will go charging in at the drop of a hat?"

"But we're all U.S. citizens!"

"Khalil isn't. And even if he were — "

The sound of feet thudding on the stairs ... Samir bounding, taking the steps two at a time....

"Watch it!" Camellia called.

Too late. Samir crashed into the trunk. He sprawled over it. The sack in his arms tore open. Bread, tomatoes and goat cheese spilled out onto the floor.

"*Isma'allah!*" Tayta exclaimed. "What in the name of God —"

"*Shu beek?*" roared Abu Mousa. What do you think you're doing?

Breathless and dirty, Samir met the gaze of his elders, including his mother, who stood at the door of the kitchen. Raw egg dripped from the spatula in her hands.

He made a respectful reply.

Then he turned, grinning, toward Camellia and the American visitors.

"Abu Yehya was selling out of the back of his shop. A militiaman chased me, but not before I got these." He held up a ripe tomato as if it were a trophy.

Violet, down on one knee, picked up the flat bread and turned it over and over in her hands. "Pita pockets!" she exclaimed. "Just like from Haddad's Bakery in Detroit. But these are flatter and more brown...."

"Violet!" Color rose in Angela's cheeks. "We mustn't insult them with comparisons!"

A gurgling sound emanated from near the kitchen.

"Ha ha." Om Mousa covered her mouth with her hand; the spatula then dripped from a higher elevation.

"Ha ha ha," burbled Tayta.

"Ha harumph! Ha ha," Abu Mousa echoed.

Soon Angela, Violet and Camellia joined in, not quite understanding why their Lebanese hosts were laughing, or even how much they'd understood, but nevertheless grateful for the momentary hilarity and the unself-conscious bond it created between them. Violet's lilting bark ... Angela's soprano trill ... their chortles mingled with the guffaws of the others, creating a joyous convulsion of sound to drown out distant guns; it hardly mattered whether true merriment inspired the laughter or everyone was merely gripped by awful mirth-like spasms of despair.

Introductions followed, and a cordial clash of languages. Then the universal warmth of handshakes and hugs as Arab tradition was allowed to run its course like springs feeding rivers that coursed to the sea. Abu Mousa reclaimed his home and the home its language.

How the old ways lived, even during crisis! Perhaps especially during crisis. Gentle manners born in the harsh heart of the desert stood the modern Lebanese family in good stead as the country progressed from upheaval to upheaval. How she missed Khalil! When she found him, they would talk for hours! (Never for a moment did she doubt he was alive.) He rejected the old ways; she would bring him back to them by challenging the rejection.

Angela and Violet blinked incredulously and nodded graciously, ad libbing, as though they were completely conversant with Arab hospitality. Despite the family misfortune, Angela and Violet were greeted with all the respect due the family of the bride-to-be. They were kissed soundly, offered refreshment and led to the bathroom for hand-washing. Om Mousa profusely apologized for the flickering lights even as she pointed to the jerry cans filled with water. Soon, no doubt, the electricity would quit altogether.

By the time Bahija, the maid, had returned lugging more water-filled jugs, Om Mousa was filling the table with food. Over a gas flame, she fried potatoes and made an omelet. She grated Samir's fresh tomatoes into a spicy puree heated and amplified with reconstituted dried beef. The Lebanese weren't big on canned goods. But most were resourceful enough not to suffer during a crisis — unless, of course, they were unfortunate enough to live in a sector of the city whose enemies had put it under total blockade. This happened occasionally, in periods of particular strife.

Camellia set the table while Bahija boiled sugar water for coffee.

Soon it was time to eat. Violet looked tentatively at the food. Then she dipped her pinkie into the *hummos*, licked it and made a face. Camellia elbowed her discreetly.

Violet knew body language. She wrinkled her nose in injured reply.

Angela nibbled at a piece of goat cheese.

Om Mousa, listless, ate a piece of bread.

Distant weapons rumbled.

Again the dynamics changed and English became the dominant language.

"This part of the world defeats understanding." Angela had finished the cheese. She tasted the coffee; she swallowed, looking slightly astonished at the taste, but drinking more. "Exactly who is doing what — and to whom?" she asked.

Camellia stifled a giggle. Angela apparently was unaware her phraseology echoed a bawdy limerick whose vulgarity, upon reflection, seemed oddly appropriate.

"I'll tell you what. My exposure to international relations at the university never prepared me for Lebanon. You need a Ph.D. just to understand the cast of characters. Beirut is a roll call of the disenchanted, the disenfranchised, the despairing. Palestinian refugees. Moslems of various sects. Christians for whom going to church is a far greater political act than casting a ballot. And everyone's on someone's payroll. Israel supports the Phalange, Syria the leftists...."

"Wait a minute. Wait a minute." Violet choked on the coffee but refrained from commenting on it. "Who are the white hats?"

"They're *all* barbarians." Angela laid down her fork. Then, atwitter with embarrassment when it occurred that Khalil's family might have understood and taken offense: "Of course, I don't mean that literally..."

"Don't worry." Camellia, confident with the seniority limited experience grants, took a sip of coffee, welcoming its bitterness. Awed and somewhat startled by her new prominence in the household, she was nevertheless empowered by it. Arriving in Lebanon auxiliary to Khalil, she now flew solo. Being the link between his family and hers gave her a free hand at the controls.

"I'm going after Khalil," she announced, draining the coffee. "Alone."

Simultaneous Arabic and English exhortations washed over her like baptismal waters from a font. Bahija crossed herself.

"What do you mean — going *after* him?" Violet asked.

"I suppose I mean I'm going underground."

Underground. How grand and reverberant a word! Black slaves went underground to escape servitude. So did Catholic clergy fleeing Cold-War communism in East Europe.

So did hostage negotiators in Lebanon.

So did lovers.

"Do you think that's wise? I know you care about Khalil." Angela frowned. Motherly disapproval was evident in the furrowed brow, the tight, bowed lips. "You'd be exposed to needless danger."

"As opposed to needful danger," Violet chimed in. "Okay. Okay — I'll shut up."

"Please." Camellia slid her fingers into her hair and kept them buried there against her scalp, palms to temples. "Please let's not discuss it. Romeo and Juliet indulged in discussion — and look where discussion got *them*."

How could she convey — to anyone — the depth of her ends-of-the-earth love for Khalil? Or his for her? Or the sweet torment of missing him, the urgency of the need to find him?

Imploring, she looked at Angela, then at Om Mousa and Tayta.

"Will everyone just forget about me?" She placed her fingers across Angela's freckled hand. "Nothing is as it was. Not for me, anyway. Take Violet. Get out before the airport closes."

"Airports don't close," said Violet, for once responding logically.

Though Camellia had said the very same thing, hearing it from Violet was distinctly unbearable.

"They do here," she snapped. "Just *go*. Don't worry about where. Paris. Amsterdam. It doesn't matter. You can make connections from anywhere."

Abu Mousa had understood enough to grunt in assent.

Tayta, hands fluttering, said something equally emphatic. Her slurred, lilting diction seemed to convey great distress. Her body language expressed vehement agreement.

Trading on what she hoped might be Angela's sense of inferiority in the face of unknown local custom, Camellia offered: "You know, Tayta is the last word in the family. Most people think Arab women are treated as inferiors. But in reality they're revered and respected. Especially when they get old."

"Ummm."

"Pack it in, Muzz. It's bye, bye Beirut." Violet, giving up on the food, was munching bread. Samir was watching her in abject fascination.

Angela took Camellia's hand in both her own. "What are you going to do?"

Camellia's answering sigh became a shriek that was lost in a blast. Fighting.

The walls shook like paper calendars. Glass broke so close by they heard it shatter. Reverberations echoed and ceased and echoed until the tinkle and thud of the bomb quivered into a strange sort of harmony and the shelling's aftermath gave way to an equally explosive domestic din of shrill yelps and gasps.

"Oh, my God!" moaned Violet. "Ohhh...."

"Shush, will you? It's *over*." The air was as suffocating as chewed food.

Samir put his ear to the radio. "Security forces are — how do you say? The siege continues in Chia. The cabinet is in session..."

"Turn that blasted thing off, will you?" Camellia said. "Or at least find something we can all listen to."

Instantly, Camellia was ashamed of herself. But Samir, unspeaking, handed her the radio.

She fiddled with the tuner, then stopped it, recognizing the sound of Omar

Khorshid's electric piano. His sad gavotte-like melodies and rousing repetition masked the noise of cleanup and other unpleasant tasks.

Violet had recovered her aplomb. "Is there a Richter scale for bomb attacks in Lebanon?" She surveyed the table with its upended plates of uneaten food. "I'll bet this was only a 3."

"Just don't hang around waiting for aftershocks."

"Look, if you don't at least play-act at being sweet, you're going to forget how. And where will that leave you when you find Khalil? He'll be ripe for me to steal away from you."

"Shush, will you!"

The dynamics of work and routine and actuality came into play, and exchanges of Arabic once again filled the air. The Americans fell silent. Even so, Om Mousa and Abu Mousa spoke in hushed tones, as if *they* were the intruders.

Camellia carried a platter to the kitchen. She brushed against Bahija at the door. On the way out, she stubbed her toe against a jerry can.

Om Mousa was working efficiently and single-mindedly. Abu Mousa looked trapped.

Samir had been waiting. He leaned close, speaking guardedly above the music. "Did you mean what you said? Will you go? Will you look for Khalil?"

"How else do you expect me to find him?"

"Why should you go — an American, alone? Even my father is staying here."

"I'm sorry. I just can't understand your *or* his capacity for doing nothing." She crossed her arms with dramatic flourish.

"Do you think my father is a coward?" Distressed, Samir screwed up his face. But the right words, in English, would not come. At last he shrugged. "You are wrong. When the kidnappers are found my father will kill them. By hand."

"Fine. And in the meantime, will we all just wait until 'they are found'? Until 'Khalil is found'? I just can't be passive. Anyway, what's to be accomplished by staying put?"

"My father is needed here. My mother and my grandmother — " Samir rubbed his nose thoughtfully. "Perhaps my father believes he'll be around to *really* help if later he is needed...."

"I'm not asking you for anything." Camellia chewed on her fingernail.

Samir's voice dropped to a whisper. "An *imam* has arranged a cease-fire to clear out wounded. Until two hours."

Khalil never got his prepositions right, either. "You mean, two hours from now?"

He nodded, and she read kinship in his eyes: a hint of brashness, of rebellion. She touched his shoulder. "Are you with me, then?"

"*Wallah* I am with you. But —" He put a finger to his lips.

In the kitchen, Angela had taken charge. She was giving little chirps as she stumbled onto one unfamiliar thing after another. Efficiently, she stacked cups where the plates should be. That completed, she searched for another job. Between tasks, she collided with Bahija and Om Mousa in the kitchen or the adjoining hallway. They did their best to work around her.

Tayta had gone off to the balcony.

Abu Mousa ranged from window to window, peering at the streets below. Every now and then he issued observation or warning. The threat of sniper fire was always present.

Violet, bored, had rummaged inside her knapsack and pulled out an electronic toy.

Camellia stood over her. "Can you learn enough Arabic — quick — to get the two of you out of here safely? With my luck, mother will order a cab to West Beirut and end up in Jerusalem."

"No sweat." She waved the electronic instrument in Camellia's face. The thing actually *spoke*, in English, in a nasal, obnoxious tone.

"I'm busy programming it in Arabic," Violet explained. "It can repeat any number of foreign phrases."

"Can it say, _Get me to the jet on time?_"

"Of course. It was designed for travelers. How do you think we got here from the airport in the first place?" She held it aloft again, wanting to demonstrate.

"Oh, Violet. I'll just have to trust you." Implying weariness, Camellia pushed the thing away. "I need to think."

Abu Mousa, groaning, dragged Angela's trunk to the bedroom. There would be no forays, not even to the airport, before the next morning.

Tayta had come in from the balcony. She sat dozing.

Camellia drew a breath and let it out slowly. Time to pack. Already mentally ticking off the things she would need, she resolved to travel light, unencumbered by excess baggage. She would wear her suede jacket and Hush Puppies loafers. Carry a hairbrush and change of clothes.

Absently, on her way out of the living room, she noticed a gleam of white on the coffee table. She stopped short at the sight of Tayta's mother-of-pearl worry beads. They lay, momentarily beyond Tayta's grasp, on the marble-top.

Camellia scooped up the beads.

"Forgive me, Tayta," she whispered. She would stash them in her red-and-black leather shoulder bag, the one from the *souq*, embossed with golf-leaf Nefertitis in profile. The one Khalil had bought her. "I need your *baraka*."

****

A row of hibiscus bushes ringed the courtyard garden. A breeze blew softly. It delivered the scent of spring, which settled like ash in the heart of the garden.

Yasmina wore a white pantsuit, either because white was fashionable or because it showed off her tanned, exquisite skin. Samir was in the kitchen with Yasmina's black-robed grandmother, being fed cookies and sweets. Neither Yasmina's brothers nor her fiance were in evidence. Yasmina, mysterious or protective or both, was evasive. She didn't know where any of them were.

"It seems bloodthirsty to be sitting here like society ladies, drinking tea. People are dying out there."

The tea, steeped with mint, steamed in glasses too hot to touch.

Yasmina, impatient, flicked her glossy hair behind her shoulders. She strode over to the edge of the courtyard. Her home was a villa. Pillars framed a view of the spread city. "No one is dying this afternoon."

"So we sit in our silk dresses and pretend nothing happens."

"How else can we live? We sit and drink tea and think of the future."

"How can you plan for the future when you don't know where Kamel is, much less when he is coming back?"

Kamel, a member of the Phalangist militia, was beyond doubt engaged in active duty. He might be building fortifications on a mountain outside Beirut. Or manning a roadblock at the entrance to a Christian suburb of downtown. Or, in some lawless way, seeking retribution for Khalil's abduction. Militias worked like that. They waited for a chink in the overall stability and order of Beirut. Then they overran the city like scorpions in an empty house.

"Suppose he doesn't come back. Suppose none of them do." Yasmina's voice was husky, autumnal. Her tone conveyed the dull flatness of truth. "We are not important. Lebanon is."

"I thought nobody cared about Lebanon. I thought that was the whole problem. Tribal allegiances supersede everything, even loyalty to a country."

"That is only part of the explanation. The Moslems — "

"I'm sick of hearing you blame the Moslems. I'm not going to sit here and wait for some two-bit kidnappers to decide my happiness. I'm going to make things happen."

Yasmina whirled back around, surprised. "Do you think nothing is happening? The entire family is mobilized. Khalil's uncles are negotiating with every tribal chieftain within a ten-mile radius of Beirut. They've bribed a sympathetic cabinet member and the chief of police. There's a Majdi in the prime minister's office. He's been put on alert. It's a well-connected family. Behind the scenes — that's how things get done in Lebanon."

Suddenly Camellia was cold and tired, though the wind spread warm flower-scent like a balm. She had hoped for an ally in Yasmina. But Yasmina was an agent of the status quo.

She drank the tea.

She should have known Yasmina would be of little help. But, Yasmina or no,

Camellia wasn't about to rethink her plan of action. Actually, there wasn't a plan. What propelled Camellia was more of a primitive, emotional forward-going momentum to which she submitted without thought.

She collected Samir from the kitchen and said good-by. That was the first stop. Now for the second. The driver was waiting.

Yasmina's part of town was quiet. The driver napped at the wheel, his car parked against the white curb.

Yasmina's kiss was still warm on her cheek when they reached the urban core of Beirut. The streets were ghastly, like a recurrent dream. Traffic consisted of one or two cabs moving furtively from street to street. The lone pedestrian scurried.

The only noise was of spotty gunfire and the sound of the driver's tongue. He clucked it continually, in reproof, as if Camellia and Samir were somehow to blame for the scattered bursts which still erupted somewhere north of the city.

Soon the hotels loomed, near the university, near the waterfront cafes. The driver deposited them on the street with its arcing vista of the shoreline. This would be the end of the line, he said before departing. He declined to set a rate of payment. Camellia counted out five bills. Unceremoniously, he accepted them. At the sound of fresh shots, he jerked the cab into gear, jolted forward to the traffic light, careened around the corner and sped decisively out of West Beirut.

The U.S. Embassy had the ambiance of a fly-by-night business and the smell of the first day of school. In the public waiting room, cigarette butts smoldered on the floor. Tattered, gray-lined computer printouts papered the walls. Fascinated, Camellia read one of the messages:

"The U.S. government can no longer ensure the safety of Americans traveling to Addis Ababa...." Other worlds. Other kinds of turmoil.

Camellia shifted her weight from foot to foot. Samir left to recruit another driver. Deserted, she stood leaning against the wall, hands clasped behind her back. She began to shake. Violently. An errant shell ... a sniper's bullet.... How vulnerable they had been! The cab had driven through Beirut like a roach seeking crevices. And there was no way back but the way they came.

"Wait for me!" There, before Samir got out the door.

She followed him to the sidewalk. She had changed her mind. She wouldn't go it alone. Even if Samir disagreed with this particular part of the mission, she would force him to accompany her.

"Go on. Get it over with," was his cynical reply. "You will not be long."

She returned to the public waiting room. The door shut behind her.

The room was positively claustrophobic. Can this be the *U.S.* embassy? Why no palatial foyer? No polished columns, marble tabletops, glistening floors? Where were the ambassadors? The people in *authority*?

A clerk handed her a number. And a form.

Lord, she thought. Khalil could be halfway to Baghdad, and she'd still be sitting here, waiting her turn among the beleaguered Lebanese. Dark-haired and desperate-eyed, they huddled on vinyl-covered seats, awaiting the beneficence of the United States. They sat like convicts. They smoked jerkily or tended to their fat-cheeked children. Awaiting summons, they seemed driven by a herd instinct, drawn to democracy. The clerk called them barber-shop style, one by one. A representative family member would approach the desk and present his case.

Enough was enough. Camellia rapped on the clerk's desk.

After a moment he looked up.

"Don't you have a line or a person assigned to U.S. citizens?"

"You are American?"

She nodded eagerly.

The clerk's smile was a display of teeth. "So are half the people in this room."

Americans? "Oh. Well, yes, but —" She swallowed. "Is this how you handle kidnappings?"

"Kidnappings?"

"My fiance," she began eagerly. "We were crossing into East Beirut — "

He held up two fingers. "This is how we handle every-thing." He shrugged, palms upward, a gesture of helplessness. "Requests for political asylum. Americans in local jails. Lebanese relatives of Americans who wish to make a claim to citizenship. The naturalized Americans are bad enough. The tourists make me crazy. Over Christmas a group became stranded in Bisharre. They wanted us to send helicopters! To deploy the Marines! This week is hardly better. The airport is closing. If it has not closed already."

Camellia thought fleetingly of Angela and Violet.

The clerk held out his hand. "Your form — is it ready?"

"Name. Social Security Number. And this time I brought my passport." She handed it over. "Does the ambassador also need to know my shoe size?"

(Insufferable, I know. But later I'll tell Khalil how I pounded on tables and...)

"Please follow. The vice consul should be free."

"I hope you're taking me to someone with authority."

The vice consul was James Thurgood III. He had prominence if not authority. His office was on the fourth floor with a window framing a still-life of the Mediterranean. The waters sloshed, gray and lifeless.

Beneath a presidential photograph of Jerry Ford, the vice consul sat smiling. A strapping, sandy-haired all-American, he looked impressive but overgrown as he stood up to shake her hand. Startled, Camellia realized how accustomed she had become to small men. Because she, herself, was short, Lebanese men seemed especially endearing, human, a race of equals. Khalil, tall and thin, was the exception.

The vice consul smiled faintly. What a diplomatic expression, Camellia thought. How artfully it conveyed regret and concern and hinted at intractability. How hard she would have to work to get through to him!

Thurgood's name and numeral were engraved on a desk-top plaque. She wondered how it had come to sit on a desk in Beirut.

"I'm Camellia Kessler. My fiance has been kidnapped."

"Oh?"

"Khalil Majdi. A Michigan graduate. An engineer."

Thurgood seized at once on the only point that mattered. "But ... not a U.S. citizen?" He had been trained to read omissions. His tone matched his expression: aloof and measured.

"We're getting married."

He perused the form; finally, he sighed.

"But you're not married yet."

"No."

"Clearly a domestic matter. In Lebanon, kidnappings fall neatly under one heading. 'Politics as usual.'"

"Even when a U.S. citizen is involved? Namely, me?"

"On any other continent, in any other country, I'd direct you to the local authorities." Again, the faint smile. "In Lebanon, there *are* no local authorities. To speak of," he immediately added in qualification.

"Why can't the Embassy —"

"Send out the troops?"

"It's an abduction. A kidnapping. A *crime*."

"One of half a dozen in the last 24 hours." He glanced again at the form. "You've just come from Ain Rumaneh. What's it look like?"

She straightened her shoulders, contemplating. She had grown up reading Helen MacInnes spy novels. She remembered nothing but the plots, and that the ability to observe and recall detail could never be underestimated. Perhaps from her description Thurgood could derive some clue —

"Well, the soft drink factory's been gutted. Cars are crumpled on the streets. Lots of acrid smoke, like a poker game after midnight. And children playing in the rubble." And all the while the driver's tongue clucking in reproof.

He laughed derisively. "'Scattered clashes,' the Washington Post calls it. Newspapers report other people's tragedy as if it were football. Palestinian vs. Lebanese ... machine guns vs. rocket-propelled grenades ... Meanwhile, in Beirut, the Red Crescent runs out of blood. The death toll is 60 — and rising. First down."

He leaned forward, fingers entwined. "The average American..." He considered briefly, then gave up the generality. "We who would like to encourage stability and order in Lebanon suffer from underfunding and neglect. Shuttle diplomacy has its good points. But even Dr. K. can't handle more than one hot spot at a time. And everyone's hung up on Saigon. Good Lord, the Commies are three miles from Phnom Penh! So— " His exhalation, short and emphatic, signaled a change of subject. His mannerisms were part stilted British, part Oriental Worldly Old

Gentleman. Acquiring continental airs was apparently an occupational hazard. "Did your fiance have enemies?"

"Of course not. Khalil was not political."

Thurgood's mouth puckered like a rabbit's; his pinched nostrils flared with repressed amusement. "A Lebanese without an enemy?"

"None I knew of."

"In Lebanon, *everyone* is political. Even the military. Hell, *especially* the military. The country is in absolute turmoil. Blood is being shed. Weapons carried openly. All hell's breaking loose. And the army won't act — without *written* orders from the government."

"And in the fourth quarter? Anarchy? Revolution?"

"God help us if the Israelis get restive." He looked at her. "How'd you get across the Green Line, anyway?"

"Would you please stop talking football?"

"Oh, God. Innocents abroad!"

All semblance of poised control vanished in wounded pride as she reminded him: "I've been here barely a week!"

"You couldn't have gotten here without crossing the Green Line. Sniper's paradise. No-man's land. Most kidnappings happen there."

He pointed to a line on a map; it stripped diagonally across Beirut, bisecting neighborhoods in a line perpendicular to the sea. It ran perilously close to Ain Rumaneh.

"That's it! But Green Line, red line — who cares? It's like knowing how much heart muscle withers during a fatal heart attack. Doctors care. But for the victim, it doesn't matter."

"In Lebanon, territory is crucial." Had he read MacInnes, too?

In a rush, "Do you think Khalil is in danger? Who would want him? The PLO?"

Thurgood tapped his fingertips together. "We can probably rule out the Maronites, though God knows they're perfectly capable of mayhem. Sounds like your Khalil has run afoul of Moslems. The PLO ... maybe. But it could also be George Habash's PFLP or Ibrahim Qulayat's *al-Murabitun*. Either one of them makes Yasir Arafat look like Mister Rogers."

"How reassuring," Camellia answered.

He had moved to the window. Arms crossed, he stood watching the steady slap of the waves. He could have been a quarterback planning strategy. "Yesterday the chief of American security stood right here. Looking down, he saw a stolen car. Here, under our noses. A $50,000 limo. One of *ours*. 'And not a goddam thing we can do about it,' he said."

"Are we from the same U.S.A.? I mean, I sort of thought you guys were John Waynes with diplomas."

But he was talking more to himself than to her. "Oh, I write incisive memos to

Washington." He flexed his knees with rapid little jerks. The quarterback warming up. "I describe — poetically, at times — the 'shifting mixture of violent elements' in Beirut. What could America do? We could use whatever influence we have left in this part of the world to reassert stability."

"What do they think of your memos in Washington?"

A look of beleaguered resignation crossed his face. "Lebanon's integrity is not our problem."

Camellia was still thinking spy stories, maybe even tempting some ambitious D.C. undersecretary with the possibility of intrigue. "Suppose my fiance is involved in something I don't know about. Something big. I know he's pro-America! That would make him an ally, right?"

"Ummm." Noncommittal agreement.

"And if you just happened to mention in one of your cables that armed hooligans have abducted a highly trained engineer with U.S. leanings and sympathies...?"

Thurgood sighed. "Look. I've worked in Europe and North Africa. I've got seniority. I'm in Beirut because I *want* to be. I love the chaos, the marvelous complexity..." He had turned away from the Mediterranean. The waters tossed and churned. The gulls had fled. "Once, early in my career, I briefed an admiral on an obscure but vital country I won't name. I described undercurrents. I analyzed motives. I detailed the clash of competing interests and the effect of superpower interference. After ten minutes, his eyes began to glaze. 'Yes, yes,' he said. 'You've been wonderfully analytical. But now tell me — *who* are the good guys?'"

****

Barbir Hospital echoed. Between soundproofed shrieks, even the silence reverberated.

People, relatives — only their eyes darted freely, red-rimmed and expectant. Women in head scarves and men in ankle-length *gumbaz* were clustered, in corners, on benches filled with quiet children. Unnaturally quiet. Instinctively, people repressed anxiety and grief. They avoided the urge to weep, which would reveal them as Bedouin. Loud lamentations had no place in a hospital.

Urgent antiseptic business.

Orderlies whose slapping footfalls trailed squeaking stretchers. The dead weight of blank-faced cargo. Doctors whose heels on polished floors made harsh thuds as they pushed past, unseeing, to new emergencies. On urban battlegrounds, the hospital becomes the front line.

For Camellia, stop three.

She stood in the hallway. Artificial light gave everyone a blanched look. The hall stretched ahead. The scale of the place dwarfed her. The hall was very bright, fuzzy, like the tunnel described by people who register out-of-body experiences — people who have died but returned to life.

She stood still for a moment, disheveled in her jeans, fringed suede jacket and scuffed shoes. Then, with a shake of her head, she pressed on. If she stood too long, people in white coats would descend, she thought, like antibodies to a germ.

At last she found the office cubicle that was Marwan's. Two orderlies or clerks or interns, whatever they were, ushered her inside. They invited her to sit. They even brought tea. They must have figured Marwan knew her. Or maybe Marwan held such authority, they did not dare to cross him, question him, or interfere with his plans. And, of course, nothing ever happened in the life of a doctor which was not planned.

But why should tea surprise her? Even the most meager merchant at the *souq* closed the most minor deal with tea — why should not the eminent surgeon routinely do the same?

The room was empty, filled only with his books. They were piled, stacked, massed — on desk, on shelves, on the tweedy upholstered chair she cleared of them so she could sit. Some in Arabic, but mostly English.

There were voices. Announcements over intercoms. Footsteps suddenly, stopping at the threshold ...

Flustered, she set the small glass down sharply, spilling the tea. She stood up.

"I did not expect you again, so soon."

Marwan was too big for the room. He bumped into the corners of end tables and brushed past the edges of books. He mopped the spill with his handkerchief, then stopped to shake her hand. Formally. He moved efficiently but with concentration, as if he were very tired.

"Khalil is gone. Someone has kidnapped him. They took something from him — a package. A package addressed to you."

He stood rigidly behind his desk. He did not sit down. His posture became stiff, though his expression still reflected ambiguity if not indecision. His muscles seemed aligned by conscious effort. He was clearly exhausted. How large he was — not tall and reedy like Khalil, but compact and muscled. Why did she automatically compare him to Khalil? A sweet acrid smell clung to his clothes, like a vine heavy with fruit.

She grew angry with him. And he hadn't said a word.

"Please," she said again. "Khalil was bringing you a letter of some sort..."

His eyes were unfocused. They stared past her, through windowed double doors. Either he had not heard her, or he chose not to understand.

"Please..." She touched the back of his hand, but — as if it were not part of him, the hand recoiled. A movement too quick to have been voluntary.

"The shifts are back to back. I must leave for Beaufort. There's fighting in the south. More casualties...."

"But can't you ... Khalil ... I've got to find him!"
"Then why don't you ask someone who can be of real help?"
She looked at him.
He gave a slight shake of the head.
"I'm needed elsewhere."

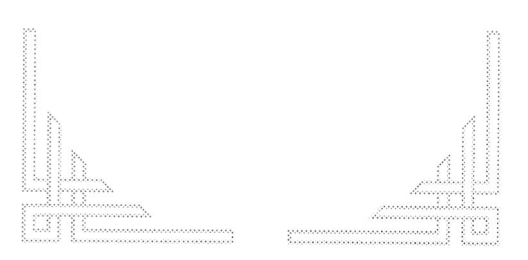

6

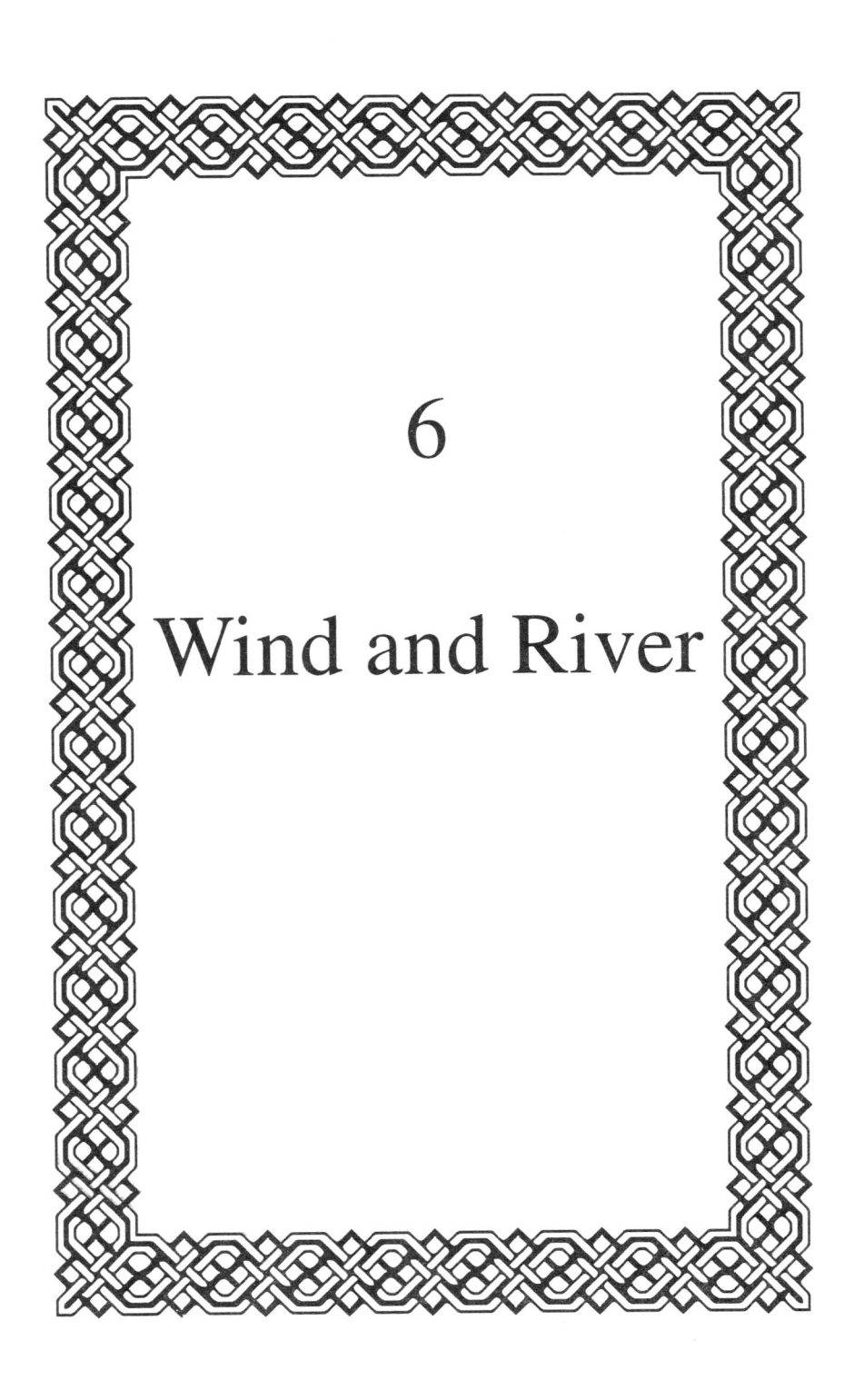

Wind and River

*C*all it instinct, intuition, reflexes of a trained news reporter, Camellia was on the phone trying to get through to her colleague and friend at the Ann Arbor News. After three frantic hours she heard the husky voice of Myra Wendt. In a torrent of words and tears she blurted out the sorry story, ending with her pathetic vow to somehow go after Khalil. Even to her, especially now, it sounded absurd.

If she had expected reassuring tones, kind words from Myra she was due for a dash of ice water in the face. "What is his family doing about it?" were her first words. Camellia had to mention what Yasmina had told her of the connections, the inquiries, possibly bribes. Myra was not impressed.

"That figures," she said; "Arab greasing Arab palms. It won't help anything. Despite their claims, their politesse, they have all the finesse of a one-eyed camel driver."

"I can't help you from here, Camellia," she rasped, "and probably I'd be no better there, Jewish and all. You need a confidant and a contact, someone from back home you could relate to. I know only one in Beirut — Jerry Hurst, who teaches classes in reporting of public affairs at American University there. Find him, tell him I sicced you on him."

"How can he — ?" Camellia's question was cut short by Myra.

"Jerry was a gunner's mate on a U.S. destroyer in the Pacific in World War II," she said. "He got the Navy Cross for shooting down two kamikaze planes off Okinawa, then dragging three wounded sailors out of a burning gun turret while trailing a shattered leg behind him. I knew him at the Herald Tribune where he was a reporter. He helped cover the Korean War with Homer Bigart and Maggie Higgins for the Trib. In the '60s he drifted to the Middle East and landed the faculty job. He knows the territory. If anyone can help you find Khalil or what happened to him, he can."

She gave Camellia a local number. "Let me know what he says," she said, "and for God's sake can the heroics. Just be a good reporter. Please."

****

Hurst answered his own phone. Camellia mentioned Myra, then told her story again without a single question from him. Camellia was thrilled when he said, "I know of your fiance and of Dr. Marwan but it is nothing we can discuss on the phone." His flat tone sent a chill through her.

They met at a cafe near Khalil's home. Hurst was a man of indeterminate age. There was nothing distinguishing about him except for his cane and a decided limp — from his Navy Cross heroics, Camellia supposed.

"I never know about safe phones," he apologized, "so it is better we talk in a place such as this. Both Khalil and the doctor have been trailed by terrorists but I'd guess it was pure accident they got him with that package, whatever it was ... do you know?"

Camellia could only look at him in wonderment. Hurst could see she knew nothing about any of this.

"Look," he began. "Khalil is a known militant in the Christian sectors here. His hatred for the Palestinians and their cause is well known throughout Beirut and in the camps. Dr. Marwan is an enigma: he seems to work both sides of the street helping the wounded but both Moslems and Christians are suspicious of him. He is a good doctor — and fearless."

Oh, my God! Camellia thought. This helps explain so many of Khalil's mysteries. But how could he have asked me here — blind, and knowing none of this? Doubt, rage and love for the man washed over her in waves, each emotion leaving telltale signs on her anguished face.

"Will they torture him — or kill him?" she finally got out in a tiny voice.

"Nothing is certain," he said. "I would guess he is a blue chip for whatever bargaining they fancy. They know his value. If ransom is not their game they can get invaluable information from him, as long as they keep him alive."

Hurst rose to go. "I'm sorry for you," he said. "None of this looks good now, but you never know. I will make inquiries." And with that and a slight bow, he limped away.

****

They drove too fast on roads that were too rough. After leaving the city, they veered south along the coast. The gritty urban landscape transformed gradually to become a seascape of coastal flats and fruited grades. But Camellia could still smell Beirut. Its odors permeated the cab, clinging to the vinyl, mingling with Beirut cab-smells: the essence of sweat, dung, rotting vegetables and smoke, a choking blend that included the ripe Moroccan leather of her shoulder bag.

In less than the twenty minutes Camellia had spent with Thurgood at the U.S. Embassy, Samir had found and recruited a politically neutral and geographically suited driver: one Ahmed, a Shi'ite Moslem from the south.

He was ready to go when they were: immediately following the meeting with Hurst. Ahmed smoked. Incessantly. His ragged black hair fell across his forehead, and smoke curled up to meet it. Ash dripped from the end of his cigarette. Pitted skin and opaque eyes completed the Mediterranean Gypsy look. Busy with his cigarette, he drove carelessly. Camellia didn't object. Speed and motion combined nicely to obliterate rational thought — at this point, a relief. How long could she live on nerves, pure emotion and nonstop thought? Ahmed's fast lurching gave significance only to forward momentum.

Samir, quiet, stared westward at the Mediterranean. The waters churned with a wild sparkle.

Camellia couldn't be quiet. "I'm almost afraid to look back." She crossed her arms and looked at Samir. "We might be turned to stone."

"Like Lot's wife?"

Surprised: "You know the story?"

"My people wrote it."

How much he was like Khalil at that moment! Aloof. Insouciant. Superior. Never for a moment forgetting his place in the world, or allowing anyone to preempt it.

She blinked rapidly. Impulsively, she put her hand on his arm. "Maybe it's just as well you *haven't* read the Hardy Boys. You're smart-mouthed enough as it is. Damn! Dust in my eye."

"The Harrrd-ee boys?" Only a Semite could have said it that way: all aspiration, rolled R's and vowels.

"I can't *wait* until this is all over. I'll corrupt you with American adolescent detective fiction. Lord knows you've got instinct. But for now..."

Actually, Samir would have done Frank Hardy proud. In short order, he had committed Ahmed to a week's hire, no questions asked; negotiated the pay; then whittled it down so low Camellia wondered where the profit was. She, reduced to observer, watched Samir pay Ahmed for half the week, then promise him the balance, and a bonus, at week's end.

Ahmed knew the roads. He knew the curve of the mountains as it receded from the sea. He knew the dirt tracks that ran off into nowhere, and the paved ribbons of roads that rounded the hilly bases and circled the distant crests like scattered bits of peel. He drove so fast the cab vibrated as if it were a single-engine plane above the clouds, beyond those crests. From the rear-view mirror hung baubles — dangling suspended gewgaws — which shook and jounced with every revolution of the wheels. They made a gaudy frame for his reflected eyes.

"Tell him to slow *down*." Suddenly the jerks and bumps were inordinately jarring.

"*Ma'alesh*. Look — the Evil Eye protects us." Samir pointed to the plastic purple triangle hanging from the rear-view mirror. Premier among the gewgaws, it was a blue iris, a blue unblinking eye.

"*You* believe in the Evil Eye? A minute ago you were upholding Christianity."

"What does it matter whether I believe — if *Ahmed* does?"

She bit her lip. But this time she couldn't hold back tears. Are we born to speak a certain way? *What is one night ... in the land of a thousand and one nights*?

Mount Lebanon trailed them, its shadow sometimes touching them, its sheer incline nearly abutting the water in places. No wonder the Phoenicians had taken to the sea. The land had squeezed them. Yet ... how wanton and abundant was that strip of fertile land, where fig trees arched to the sun. Grape vines clutched at latticed trellises. Tomatoes and eggplant ripened on terraces.

Cliffside villas hung like pearls on bronzed necks.

She plunged her hand into the shoulder bag, feeling for the sandwiches. Khalil had been right about the bag: "Middle Eastern kitsch," he had said, feigning contempt, but had bought it for her anyway, pleased that she valued things Arabic, even ostentatious things. The bag was gaudy, red and black, and to examine it was to get a whiff of barnyard-ripe leather. It was embossed in gold with Nefertiti in profile. It was totally unfashionable by American standards of 1975. Annie Hall layers were in, and so were skinny chain belts and bow ties. Accessories were small and matching. They did not stink like Moroccan leather.

Deep inside the bag, her fingers met the cool orbs of Tayta's worry beads. She passed over them, groping for the sandwiches, made from lamb, hacked rather than sliced, in Om Mousa's kitchen.

Samir split his sandwich with Ahmed, reserving the whole for Camellia, then ate hungrily with the unself-consciousness that overtakes traveling teen-age males of any culture, whether or not they have been exposed to detective fiction.

She couldn't eat. After a bite or two, she gave her sandwich to Samir.

Samir. The little brother. His face was child-grimy, framed by hair in matted ringlets. Khalil would have been cool as a *kheyarah*.

She closed her eyes against the brilliance of the pain.

She had only the *thought* of Khalil to carry her now: Khalil in Ann Arbor: Mussing Violet's hair. Kissing Angela's hand. Khalil with his contemporaries: Talking politics. Becoming so indignant she sometimes had to dig her nails into palms to keep from smiling. Khalil in bed with her, loving her, then sleeping, then waking up to talk. Quoting the wisdom of the ages, in lilting Arabic, attributing all grand thoughts to Tayta, who could not possibly have produced so many grand thoughts even if she had spent her life doing nothing but thinking. Sometimes the lilting Arabic turned out to be nonsense, or at least became so in English.

Translated, the parable might sound silly but profound, as in: "The horses were to be shod, and the mouse stretched out his foot." This he recited when Camellia said self-important things.

Memories replayed, relentless as images of a dancer's undulating belly when the dance is done. The memories fueled her, like the anger of someone wronged.

Beirut. Khalil belonging. She could smell the smoke of the *nargeila*, hear the trilingual babel, taste the spices of *felafel* washed down by the treacle of Seven-Up. Khalil, provoked, pulling her away from the disreputable, the dangerous, away from clustered hovels, from camps, away from the martyr's cemetery, where wildflowers grew on graves... "Don't ever come here." Then, an instant later, laughing, showing her *his* Beirut, enamored of its glitter, its enchantment ... its eroticism. He had been her confrere. Protector. Talisman.

Now, alone. It was time for her to act. She *must* create her own luck. Her own *baraka*.

Dusk threw a haze on the landscape as afternoon melted into twilight. Abandoned, now, by sea, the slopes dimmed until one contour was indistinguishable from the next. Vivid purples grayed. Deep in the mountain terrain of hairpin turns and plummeting cliffs, the land was eerie, empty. The engine slowed to match the whine of an oncoming Mercedes truck. There was the steady flick of Ahmed's cigarette.

Camellia came fully awake.

A new element. A fresh scent — water. Savoring it produced a sense of euphoria and heightened perception. It made her sit up and say to herself: I will remember this always, this twilight chill, this crepuscular journey through mountains, on roads that shadow rivers.

At Beaufort the noises stopped, and she heard nothing but the gentle rush of the Litani.

****

Thank goodness Samir's English was schoolboy at best; one iota more of sophistication or fluency and he'd argue her to death. Here they were in Beaufort, and already he opposed her plan to confront Marwan. Samir objected on several grounds, none of which he could articulate effectively in English.

Granted, he was far more proficient in her language than she in his. But he couldn't philosophize. And it was inconceivable that an argument could be won in this part of the world without philosophy or at least some damned impressive poetic underpinnings. Samir lost not because he was wrong, but because he was incapable of communicating nuances and complexities — the only defense against the headstrong. Nor did Camellia try to understand his side of it. If she could comprehend the unwritten rules of Arab society, she would be forced to abide by them.

Oblivious, willful, free — she plunged ahead.

What else could she do but pursue her only lead?

Was Marwan at home? They had found his house. They could detect neither sound nor movement. The front door to Marwan's modest home was unlocked. Indeed, it stood ajar.

Camellia and Samir stood half-hidden in the shadows, peering through the breach.

They had left Ahmed at the town's center, then hiked up this dirt road, asking directions as they went. People answered their queries readily and without suspicion. A plump aproned woman guided them around a corner. A man in a gray burnoose directed them down the lane. Either Camellia and Samir looked innocent, or Marwan was so much in demand the inquiry attracted little notice. Typical. An Arab M.D. might work in the most modern of hospitals. He might be professionally involved in state-of-the-art technology. Yet he would never turn a patient away from his home.

Most doctors had anterooms in their homes, set aside for patients. It would be mandatory for Marwan, here, in this small town. The door that stood ajar no doubt led to this anteroom.

Samir tapped lightly on the door.

Waiting, Camellia leaned against the wide, cream-colored arch of the doorway. Arab homes were a paradox. They were thick-walled and boxy. Cannon shot couldn't penetrate their stone-and-concrete construction. Yet locks were a rarity and doors were left unlatched to be pushed open by friends.

The anteroom was empty.

"Suppose I were hurt? I'd have to screech to wake the dead to get his attention."

She tiptoed to the middle of the anteroom. It contained a shabby wooden desk and chair, an ashtray, a cot. Beyond was the home's interior. Small, plain rooms. Rose sailcloth curtains fluttering in the kitchen.

A few more steps, and she penetrated further. Bulbs cast shadows on torn lampshades and stained formica. Battered pans were clean but upended. Crystal glasses, empty beside a half-full liter of Scotch.

Marwan. Looking like a pasha whose servants have fled, he sat cross-legged on a faded Persian rug. Muttering curses, he struggled to light a water pipe.

"He will not succeed. The tobacco is damp," Samir whispered.

Marwan sucked rapidly, pressing live charcoal into the mounded tobacco. Air passed through the water, bubbling dramatically. But the tobacco would not catch fire.

"*Ya kelb!*" An ember burned on his shirt as coal slid through tongs. Clenching the mouthpiece between his teeth, Marwan batted the burning lump off the rug. The coal skittered to a corner, where it continued to glow.

"*Isma'allah!*"

The mouthpiece fell from his lips. It snagged on his shirtsleeve, where it held, stem swaying like a cobra, as he surveyed the pursuing pair. "My home invaded?"

Caustically: "Am I a criminal? To be followed? Pursued even to my home?"

"*Doktor Marwan*," Samir said respectfully, his voice gliding, "*Bitreed hadherlak nafas tombac?*"

"'*Nafas tombac?*'" Incredulous, Marwan shook his head. "You offer me a 'breath of tobacco' — from my own pipe?"

Samir, murmuring placatingly, moved into action. He deftly molded fresh tobacco around the tip of his finger, then tamped it atop the pipe's wooden basin. He blew the coal back to life and pressed its red heat into dry leaf.

Marwan watched, incredulous. Then he shook his head slightly. "Son of a bitch." His tone grew gentle, even awe-struck. He tossed Camellia a cushion.

"Bedouin hospitality, if you don't object to sitting like a Bedouin. I gave my mother my furniture when she moved to Beirut."

"Didn't she have any furniture of her own?"

He lit the stove. "She had possessions. But no chairs. Nor even glass in her windows. In the mountains, one needs little to survive."

"I always wanted to sit with a Bedouin. In his tent," she finished dreamily. Then, because Marwan had begun to poke around in cabinets and lift the lids on jars: "Please — don't worry about fixing food or drink. This is business."

She sensed, rather than saw, the imperceptible break in his rhythm.

"You offend the Bedouin by refusing his coffee," he said lightly.

His coffee-making method was identical to Yasmina's. The same heating of the water in a small-lipped pot. The same heaping dose of sugar. The constant stirring. By the time the coffee came to its third boiling, Samir had readied the pipe.

"I wish I could offer dinner. I have only bread and goat cheese. You are welcome to it — I have no time to eat, except on the run."

"At the clinic — "

"Things are under control. There were people in the halls, on the steps. The worst cases we have sent to Sidon and Marjayoun. Still..."

Squatting, Marwan set down the tray. The fragrance of cardamom rose from the cups.

When she had begun to drink her coffee, he leaned back on his heels, accepting from Samir the stem of the *nargeila*. When he inhaled — deeply — the water gurgled. The essence of tobacco sprang free. Marwan breathed, lazily, in clouds of scented smoke.

Camellia downed her bitter coffee in one gulp. "Look, forgive me for rushing the sheik part of the Bedouin ritual but I've got something important to ask."

He looked at her reflectively.

She rushed on: "Look — can't we just for once do it the American way? In America it's called getting to the point. Khalil is gone. Gone! I think you are a friend. His package was labeled with your name, which they confiscated — the package, I mean. Maybe if you think about it you can remember some-thing that will help me find him."

"*Yakhti*... My sister..." He looked startled, then amused. "It has been so long since I tried to do anything British style, and, I regret to say, I have even less experience with Americans...."

But instead of finishing with something flippant, he took another draw on the pipe. "Before I left Beirut, the Phalangists had sealed off Ashrafiya. I am astonished that you broke through the lines. I barely got out myself. Riots have spread to Tripoli and Sidon. Maybe a hundred people have died. Vengeance ... reprisals ... the killing is far from finished."

"So what's one kidnapping, more or less?" she asked heatedly.

"That's one way to view it."

"Do you think I've come this far only to give up? Do you think I'll go away just because the authorities won't help and *you* don't care?"

"Care? Do you think *I* would be here if I didn't — " He squinted, eyes like a guttering flame. But he abandoned the argument as quickly as he began it. More slowly: "Some kidnappings are random, the work of hooligans. *Political* kidnappings are far more common. In that case, the victim himself has a history."

"History?" She had no hard information documenting Khalil's innocence to offer in contradiction. It would be up to Khalil, later, to vindicate himself. "The ... the vice consul at the Embassy said kidnap victims are sometimes released. Unexpectedly. Or, their release is secured, through person-to-person contact — "

"Then let the vice consul negotiate on your behalf. You're a U.S. citizen, aren't you?"

"And you're Greek Orthodox, aren't you? Neutral? Unaligned? Isn't that a valuable asset in Lebanon?"

"How much would neutrality be worth if I violated it by taking sides?"

"I'm not asking for much. If you won't ask questions, can't you at least tell me *who* to ask — "

Impulsively, she lunged forward and took hold of his arms, trying to force eye contact.

He stared beyond her, into the night of barking dogs and ephemera locked in the throes of brief existence. Night sounds. The thrum of insects masked the cascading march of the Litani.

Bitterly: "I gave everything I had. Before you came. There is nothing left."

He dropped the pipe stem. The wooden mouthpiece clattered to the floor.

Samir, sensing defeat, shut his eyes.

"Wait — please..." Her arms hung limply at her sides.

Marwan pulled the sailcloth curtain back from the sill, where linen was piled atop a wide ledge. Foam mattresses. Thick quilts. He grappled with fabric wedged beneath the false window's arch.

"They are waiting for me. At the clinic."

The bedding fell in a heap at her feet.

Formal, distant, almost affectionate: "I hope you sleep well."

He left her sneezing in the dust.

****

"What nerve!" Hands on hips. "He can't just leave us here like this."

Samir was arranging the bedding on the floor. Deliberately, he kept his eyes at counterpane level or below.

"Where's Ahmed?"

Samir, down on one knee, but alert to the peremptory tone of her voice, refolded the blanket he had begun to spread out. "Gone to his cousins in Marjayyoun."

"Gone? Never mind. We'll walk."

Samir knew better than to argue or philosophize.

Beaufort. A compact mountain town, river-fed and rugged. Homes, buildings and churches bore close relation to the human scale. Intricate gardens, ceramic pottery, arched doorways and decorative iron grillwork established Arab identity; in the Arab world, art is woven into the fabric of everyday life; it is not an unrelated thread. Never isolated. Never called "art," categorized, and separately displayed.

Her fury subsiding in degree but not quality, Camellia strode rather than walked. Her gait was ungraceful. Dust swirled on the dirt road, even though the speed of passing cars reached no more than 15 kilometers per hour. White-wall tires packed down the gravel kicked up by donkey hooves. A boy astride yelled, "Hiyah!" to his reluctant mount, then whistled to his friends.

At this elevation, the Litani was no more than misty scent, soft gurgle, spitting roil. Down the road a pace, a small wooden bridge spanned a gully. It was picture-perfect, with wooden planks leading to a grassy knoll. The gorge was a grassy chasm.

"What a bridge! All it needs is a troll." Though the bridge did not seem new, wood and stones were stacked nearby, as though building had occurred. Patches of upturned earth, metal and debris hinted at construction in progress. "Why doesn't someone clean it up?"

"Probably they are waiting. Or they have given up. Certain spots, hit from the air, are rebuilt only to be hit again."

Momentarily, she paused and looked at the surroundings: forbidding inclines, groomed terraced stretches, subtle slopes, a haze of cloud at the mountain tops. Much of Lebanon was the product of the goat and the ax, of small uprootings and deforestation. Here some spots were bare, others lush. In the distance, a small herd of goats danced home. But the sun had receded, and the black ones were impossible to pick out, blending with the dusky land.

I'm developing Oriental patience, she thought. I'm able to absorb and focus, though all I *want* to think about is how to deal with that *infuriating* man....

With Khalil, she was an equal. With Marwan ... The rules changed. The worst of it was, she didn't understand why or how. She knew only that she wasn't used to someone else being in control....

Daylight passed to evening, and the town square came alive, like town squares all over Lebanon, awash with fluorescent and neon lighting. Recorded Arabic music played to an audience-at-large. Folk tunes evolved to become the music of the '70s as electronic instruments took up the melodies, and added rock's insistent four-four beat. Stores, cafes and a butcher shop at the town's heart.... Farther north, set into a clearing bounded by vineyards surrounded by hills, stood the Orthodox church. Still farther north vegetation and vineyards gave way to stony plots and hard trails. Cars stood parked in clusters of weed and grass. The misjointed ambulance seemed an assembly of cannibalized parts, painted red and white and topped with a jerry-rigged bubble-light.

Here sat the clinic. The Red Crescent symbol clearly identified the small square building's mission. But any resemblance to hospital ended at the front door. Tattered posters and indecipherable graffiti covered the walls.

The heavy wooden door creaked. A man, exiting, gripped a cigarette in the hand that was not bandaged. He glanced at Camellia, flicked his cigarette into the dirt and strode briskly away.

Quitting time? She and Samir walked inside.

No receptionist waited behind the front desk. The doors were not locked or even firmly closed. The swishing of mops ... the clang of trash cans tapped against metal ... unmistakable sounds of clean-up.

Grayed walls and cracked countertops combined to create an impression of people too busy or too demoralized to care. The clinic looked clean, however, and strong antiseptic smells spread from the rear of the building to the front as end-of-the-day activities intensified.

It was about the size of a wing of a modest U.S. hospital.

Camellia whispered to Samir, "I'm experienced about hospitals. All you have to do is look like you know where you're going. Nobody will stop you." She added confidently, "Especially in a small and informal place like this — ."

At that point two vigilant nurses caught sight of Camellia.

Their faces tightened in alarm. They rode on twitterings of Arabic, staccato and emphatic, down the hallway. They confronted Camellia and Samir, stopping short when they realized no counter or desktop made a barrier to separate nurse and outsider. Their white caps and uniforms contrasted with the walls and ceilings, grayed either by twilight or by the day's work.

Samir's choir-boy looks were often an asset. Camellia pushed him out in front.

But the nurses easily drowned out his soprano. Camellia's attempts to explain, in English, also were decisively overpowered.

Drawn by the commotion, Marwan emerged. He stood alone in the hallway. The nurses changed direction, charging toward him. His expression, which had been merely quizzical, changed to consternation — and when he saw Camellia, defeat.

He spoke to them in Arabic. Then, when they seemed only slightly mollified, he switched to English, perhaps to forestall their further comment: "Relax, my sisters. Do you think they are commandoes? It's only a woman and a boy."

Then he turned to Camellia. With a gentlemen's reflexive courtesy, he welcomed her. In Arabic, in timeless phrases repeated in their ritual order.

Then in English: "*Wallah* they are tired. I cannot blame them for being edgy. A morning of treating people with bronchitis and colds, abdominal pains, pneumonia. Then an afternoon of shrapnel wounds and head injuries. Arranging for evacuation — for transfer to hospitals. They should have gone home hours ago."

The nurses, unconvinced, nevertheless retreated to the reception area. They made no effort to mute their continuing dialogue. Every syllable disclosed disapproval. Nor did they attempt to soften the thud of the front door being shut and decisively locked.

Samir had a way of disappearing, of blending in without seeming to slink away; he did so now.

"Are you set up to treat the wounds of war?"

"Usually, no. But occasionally we treat Palestinian guerrillas on failed suicide missions. We have learned to mobilize."

"Are you the night shift?" she asked.

Marwan had only one foot in the hallway. The other remained planted in the treatment room; he stood at the threshold.

"Only out-patients today. The last one is on his way out."

Camellia pushed ahead, deliberately ignoring the way he stood with his arms crossed. She tried to close the distance between them without seeming to close in. In the room behind him, two men knelt beside a gas flame. The boy who sat on the examination table looked older than 5 but younger than 10. His father, clutching worry beads, wordlessly watched.

"If there's a bed filled, the nurses stay. Last year, in May and June, during heavy raids, we had people in the halls."

"Terrorist raids?"

"That depends on who you believe is a terrorist. If, in your vocabulary, Israeli fighter pilots are terrorists, the raids were terrorist raids. I suspect Khalil would call them commandos."

"Ummm."

"There's not a village in southern Lebanon, not a single refugee camp, that has escaped assault or scorching."

"But — what about what's happening in Beirut? The Moslem-Christian stuff? So close to Israel, I expected to find you in a MASH unit, sorting out incoming wounded."

"Sometimes it's like that. South Lebanon suffers from intermittent terrorism, which can be worse than outright war. Last month in Marjayyoun — there's a hospital there — a young goatherd was shot by an Israeli foot patrol. 'I was frightened. I ran. They shot,' he said. He didn't live long. Half his back was gone." Marwan reached for a cigarette but didn't light it. Ironically, talk relaxed him, even talk that recounted horrors. "It's quiet now."

"Who's the current casualty?" She looked over his shoulder, into the examination room.

"A kid. He was climbing a tree, fell, and broke his arm."

She couldn't help laughing. "You see," she said. "There is hope. When children are allowed to fall from trees and break their arms, there's normalcy in the world."

Briefly, Marwan closed his eyes. "Near the town of Rashaya Fuqhar, my cousin's son found a shell. Intact. He was young, maybe 7, and he and his friends had collected other shells and sold them for lamps. This time a jelly-like substance trickled down his arm. He was badly burned." Marwan looked at her. "Napalm. The old ways are gone. If anyone claims to understand the transformation, he is pretending. If anyone claims to welcome it, he is lying."

The light waned. The clinic began to seem cavernous. Voices echoed. The boy's arm was now bent across his chest in the rigid line of the cast. Shy, he hid his face against his father's chest. Wrapping. Drying. More wrapping. The process unfolded rapidly and soon was done.

Camellia was astonished. The boy's father and Marwan began to replay the scene Marwan and Khalil had acted out in the restaurant beside the Mediterranean. A blustery exchange. The father thanking Marwan and the technicians profusely. Pressing money into their hands. They, vehemently, refusing it.

"He is the *mukhtar* — sort of like the mayor," Marwan explained when man and boy had left. "Of course we would not take money from him."

Camellia, laughing again: "And you wouldn't take money from the village priest. Or from charity cases. Or from anyone related to an important personage. Or from a relative. Or someone you owed a favor to. How do any of the Arabs stay solvent? How do you keep your books?"

"We don't *think* that way." He became aware of her again. "Don't be fooled. The system is based on reciprocity. You would be surprised, how well things balance out."

He stood relaxed, arms at his sides. The nurses had gone. The technicians were packing up. They were small men, thin and dark like Pakistanis, with large mustaches. They wore oversized white uniforms whose bagginess accentuated their dark, lean aspect.

Marwan picked up a section of surgical gauze and began to mop his forehead.

"Are you going to banish me again?"

"Why shouldn't I?"

The wheedling quality had left her voice. The harsh quality had left his.

It was possible to take stock of the situation, realistically, she thought. She could not force Marwan into the role of negotiator or, as the Lebanese might call it, *wasita*. If he were prepared to help in only a perfunctory way, out of duty or guilt, he would be of little use. But might he not willingly become her friend?

She did not allow herself to consider that truly he might know nothing.

"If you send me away again, I will go."

A smile. He half-sat on a desk. "How worried you look! Maybe I *should* send you away. But not just yet." The gleam in his eyes could have been resolution.

"I could approach a Druze chieftain. I could go underground."

Underground. The word no longer held romance. Not when she stopped to realize how strange it felt to be adrift, cut off. No one knew where she was.

"If underground means being grubby, set apart from the familiar, and totally on one's own — then I would say you already are underground."

Then he was energized again. "Samir! *Wallah*, where are you? Let's go to the mountains. I'm going to show you a mountain wedding."

He took her by the arm and bounded for the door.

He was a careful driver. He drove a vintage VW bug, burnt-orange with not a speck of rust. He negotiated the stiff incline of the mountain with practiced ease. Samir was in the back. Camellia sat up front; she could see, when Marwan veered close to the cliff, the shimmering streak of the Litani. For the first time since Khalil's abduction, she was calm. She was exhausted, of course — but it was the dreamy tiredness that comes at the end of a day spent in the open. The only outstanding emotion was an almost palpable ache that lay on her chest. Marwan, representing security, made it easier to bear.

The sequence of events that had brought her to be in Marwan's car spiraling upward at a 45-degree angle was so improbable that, momentarily, she forgot the ache. Just as it had never occurred to her that Khalil might not be alive, it had never occurred to her that Marwan might not help. How lucky she was that he had not refused!

And how shaky the assumptions which were the under-pinnings of her ambitious journey. It was faith that had got her here — faith and Yankee ingenuity, or at least a mundane, step-by-step process of arrangement and detail. How ordinary it was, to drop by the U.S. Embassy. How ordinary to hire a cab for an excursion south. But how extraordinary the outcome — to have thrust herself into the domain of a virtual stranger. A stranger not easily understood, one whose outlook was shaped by equal parts British college and Lebanese cottage, by European thought and Oriental emotion, and whose days and nights were girded by the healing arts and by violence.

Only once before had she been this close to plummeting: as a child, she had piled into a dune buggy with her crazy uncle in northern Michigan; he had powered the vehicle perilously close to sandy edge. Then, she had been too young to imagine fear.

A Peugeot overtook them and, engine racing, passed; the driver was a woman. Her hair streamed up and out like a fox's brush. She left the Volkswagen in a plume of dust.

Marwan grinned. "If anything, the farm and mountain backwoods are bastions of fashion. Worse, even, than Beirut."

"And you — you are not hip?"

"I try to be at least ten years behind the times."

Stifled laughter. Samir. She swiveled to glare at him. "What are you cackling at?"

"Nothing. Just — as you say in America — minding my own business."

"How on earth would you know what we say in America?"

Marwan answered for him. "Probably by watching 'The Six Million Dollar Man.' Imported television has done more to undermine Arab social structure than years of urbanization and the collapse of the extended family."

"Are American values and ideas so destructive?"

"No...." he said slowly. "Mostly, it's not content, but the very *fact* of the program. People rush home at a set hour, intent on watching a show — when once they would have stayed late in the company of friends. Grown men cut short games of Seven-and-a-Half, apologizing, all the while looking at their watches, timing their travel so they don't miss more than five minutes of 'Mannix.' Listen — do you hear the drums?"

The sound reverberated, faint at first. Then pulsing and repetitive, with such force Camellia could sense, rather than hear, the vibrations.

"Good heavens! Are we going to a wedding? Or a sacrifice?"

"Isn't marriage," Marwan asked, "something of both?"

Camellia settled down in her seat for the remainder of the drive. It was possible to relax; Marwan drove sedately, unlike Khalil, who drove aggressively and fast. Marwan reminded her of a definition she had once read. Happiness: not a destination, but a means of travel.

The night air was pungent with balsam and pine. Bright lights flickered in clustered homes. Traffic intensified. Soon they were part of a caravan, led by two cars and trailed by one. Alongside the road, people trudged or sallied forth on foot. A woman and three daughters tottered two abreast, clutching shiny purses as they walked. Their high heels dug into the road's shoulder; their filmy dresses swirled around their ankles. They picked their way among cars parallel-parked up and down the winding streets and in yards blocking alleys. Marwan pulled up beside a house, and the beetle's engine, backfiring twice, shuddered to a stop.

People walked in various directions, with seeming aimlessness. But the atmosphere was tense and purposeful. People shouted the Arabic salutations of evening, in voices categorical and crisp. The drums had ceased and now recorded music spilled from the open windows of a two-story house with opened doors and people showing in the darkened windows.

"This looks like the reception, not the wedding."

"Actually, it's an engagement. The engagement, to Moslems, is by far the more significant and momentous occasion. The wedding ceremony is merely a detail. In fact, the bride is not even present."

"You mean we're with *Moslems*?" Somewhat alarmed, she wondered if she had acquired something of Yasmina's unthinking hysteria.

Marwan whistled as he walked and was accosted every several yards. Three people stopped him on his way to the front door: A man in a turtleneck, slouching and regarding Camellia with speculative interest; a middle-aged woman whose girth was fashionably ensconced in patterned silk; and, last, the bearded and berobed imam. A few exchanges of pleasantries. Then what seemed like short bursts of intense personal gossip, punctuated by tongue-cluckings and gestures of innocence or dismay. Camellia stood dumbly by his side, and though each person pumped her hand in energetic welcome, she might as well have had "American dilettante" tattooed on her forehead. She wished, now, that she had developed a reason for being in Lebanon. Conducting anthropological research. Or perhaps gathering material for Sunday newsmagazine pieces. She had settled for being auxiliary to Khalil, and she — who hailed from a country self-consciously enlightened, she who had come of age in an era of rebellious liberation — was possibly the only female in Lebanon who had no purpose beyond locating her fiance and marrying him.

By day the wildflowers bloomed. By night the air was full of the essence of pine. She blew her nose.

The house was packed. The size of the crowd created a sense of anonymity. Like the Arab Americans of Ann Arbor, these Lebanese of the mountainous south sparkled with jewels and exuded the pleasant scent of well chosen oils and perfumes. They bloomed like exotica against the shabby walls and on furniture covered with faded throws. Italian shoe leather gleamed. Serpentine chains adorned necks, and earrings as wispy as filament cascaded from ear lobes.

"Do they still show the bloodstained sheets?"

Marwan laughed, head thrown back and mouth open to reveal white, even teeth. "No, but sometimes a crowd will gather around the house to encourage the groom to his task. The pressure is tremendous. One night, a stammering husband showed up at my house after midnight. He had slipped out his own back door!"

"What did *you* do?"

"At first I was confounded. I didn't want to pose as a psychiatrist, especially among people who are skeptical about anything but the purest intuition or science. Finally I gave him an aspirin."

"An aspirin? Did you tell him what it was?"

"Of course not. I insisted he swallow it, then and there. '*Sah*,' I said. 'Go back to Safeya.' The next time he saw me he grinned and winked but did not elaborate."

"And now they have a passel of brats. One named after you."

"Let Samir take care of you." The energy had gone out of Marwan's voice. As quickly as he had become exuberant escort, he now became detached. "I'm going upstairs to the men. If you get claustrophobic, go outside."

"To the — ?" Camellia's voice trailed off, its comparative softness overwhelmed by the animated chatter of others, as she watched him leave the room. She surveyed the composition of the crowd — why hadn't she noticed it before? There were only one or two men here. Of course. The men must be somewhere else. Segregated sexes.

"Have a pistachio." Samir, too young to be segregated, held out a handful of nuts.

She extracted one from the shell and munched. None of the women were veiled. But some wore enormous silken scarves, an integral part of their costume, wrapped to cover their hair. It created the appearance of a room full of madonnas.

These were Moslems. No champagne or beer, of course; only society and language and music and the capability of waves of thought and dance to transport them to a higher plane of reality. The music changed now, again; the melodies vanished; there were only drums. The women began clapping and singing, their song steady of rhythm and strong of beat. A little girl, maybe 5, with glistening braids and tiny jewels in her pierced ears stood to one side, hugging a rag doll. Lebanese children were *different*, somehow, from American children, in indefinable ways; they were at once more knowing and more delicate, and infinitely more plump.

One woman, now lost in a cappella song, rose and swayed with the mesmerizing force of words that seemed forced from her lips; was this the bride poetry? Lebanese women were different, too; perhaps it was a matter of style: the harsh look of hair pulled straight back, the inescapable contrasts vivid make-up creates, the heavy value of gold. Or did Arab women weather time in some different way? Lines on faces seemed deeper, harsher, fewer — like men's. Bodies did not run to fat but grew sturdy and thick. The woman sang, and the others fell into respectful silence as her expression grew childlike, unreachable, as if a light had gone off.

A sudden stillness. The women moved toward the doors. Camellia moved or was pulled along with them, to the outside, where the drumbeats were loud. She gasped. The bride: White and pearled and veiled. People threw rice. She was like a vision. Two young men in white shirts each played derbekis, exhibiting the singers' same other-worldly concentration, each transported by the rhythm he created until it seemed to absorb him. Was this the state of *taksim* said to overtake any artist performing exquisitely? Faded drumskins glowed.

In the cool breeze, pine needles rustled, and young women tied sashes around their hips and danced.

Camellia had never been more alone. It was physical — an aching aloneness — not psychological. Not the alienation she had experienced from time to time on the Ann Arbor campus or on SEMTA buses or in shopping malls. Until now, she had seen Lebanon from within the circle of Khalil's family. She had been grateful for the intimacy and the vantage point. What security! Khalil always there to translate, interpret, explain. Or explain away. Now, on the mountaintop, let loose and isolated, she had only her few words of Arabic, the insights of cultural immersion, and the knowledge that Marwan was somewhere close by. These three elements were enough, somehow, to bolster her. Strength consolidated in a way she could almost measure, like the fullness of a meal.

The drumbeat stopped. The young men sat, hands stilled. Into the silence came a woman's throaty voice. Half singing. Half chanting. One of Camellia's best friends had become a Jesus freak, and Camellia had once heard her speaking in tongues. An unhesitating profusion of words. The same unself-conscious delivery. A woman stood trance-like, dressed in a black skirt and silver sweater, hands clasped in front of her. The words kept coming, rhythmic and inspired.

This was the bride's poetry. A hymn of praise. Her sweetness! Her strength! Her beauty! Her utter desirability as a young woman and suitability as a wife. One extemporaneous compliment followed another, each adjective intensifying the meaning of the last. The bride — one white arm came up to push at the veil; Camellia imagined the sultana eyes fringed by fluttering lashes, the half-embarrassed smile.

Inexplicably, as if seized or chilled, Camellia began to shiver. She tried to resist, but she was fatigued, her facial muscles overdrawn; she began to cry. After a long while Marwan came and took her arm; she and Samir accompanied him in silence to the car. On the moonlit drive back down the mountain the cleansing wind washed over her face. She didn't ask Marwan where he had been, or what he had found out.

****

She woke to the cry of a rooster and a rhythmic pounding just outside.

She rubbed her temples. Was the wedding celebration still going full force? Had the revelers stayed up all night like Saudis to greet the dawn? Groggy, she sat up. Village drums with their primitive throb had pounded through the night. She had slept hearing them. And women's voices, swelling in primeval ululation.

Actually, she could not remember sleeping. She remembered only being sleepless on the rough stone floor, fighting the buzz, hum and static of her overtired brain.

The room, awash in light, was empty.

The rooster sputtered, finishing its call. Somewhere a baby cried.

The pounding was coming from just outside the door.

Marwan, squatting, was crushing coffee beans. The percussive instrument was an ordinary pestle.

She leaned against the doorway, watching.

"My grandmother used to do this," he said without looking up.

Encircling breezes captured the scent of the battered beans. Other beans, whole, roasted over a flame.

In the fig tree, a sparrow flitted from branch to branch.

"Where's Samir?"

"Gone for Ahmed."

Camellia stood awkwardly, conscious of how she must look: with her hair wildly out of control and her purple polish chipped. She was happy for Marwan's lack of a mirror. He was a gentleman; his glance betrayed nothing. "If there is time before Samir returns, may I show you something of my part of Lebanon?"

"I'm too worried about Khalil to think about enjoying myself."

"And yet — " He rubbed the coffee-powder between his fingers, inspecting the grind. "It would be sad if ... if you didn't see something of the land." His tone was oddly formal, curiously warm. He poured coffee from a copper samovar into one of the handleless cups.

" — while it is still beautiful," he finished.

The cup fitted her palm, warming it.

"Won't the land always be beautiful?"

He shook his head slightly.

"I mean," she pressed, "won't south Lebanon stay just as it is, no matter what happens in Beirut?"

"Nothing stays as it is. Israel may take the land — 'north to the Litani,' is the political battle-cry. Or, relinquishing that land, may leave it scorched." The sparrow's cries had become raucous. "The south may soon be uninhabitable ... as it is now, for the birds of prey."

Why did he always lead the subject down unproductive byways? Impatience and anxiety made her heart beat faster. "Birds?"

"Eagles and raptors on their 6,000-mile migration down the Syrian-African rift. Men shoot at them."

"Who shoots?"

He didn't answer. Instead he picked figs from the tree and brought them to her, adding bread, cheese and olives: a traditional Lebanese mountain breakfast, offered without apology.

Chewing, she gazed at the pink-hued hills. Beaufort Castle crowned a nearby mountain, guarding the pass to Sidon. "...with its line-of-sight view of the Galilee," Marwan had said in Beirut, "depressingly overrun by soldiers." Now she understood its strategic importance. The cliff was a sheer incline facing Israel. It was impassable. A fatal plummet.

Above the Litani, swollen with melted snow, shepherds with fat black goats dodged terraces of sun-washed stone.

"Are there cedars here?" she asked despite her vow not to give Marwan an opening.

"Lebanon is a casualty of the builder's ax and the hunger of goats. Mostly the cedars are in Bisharre — you know Bisharre, because you know Kahlil Gibran is buried there."

"Gibran." She exhaled dreamily. "'...the first love and the first kiss ...the first magic note plucked on the silver string of the heart.'"

"Did you ever read C.S. Lewis? He knew the difference between love and lust."

"No cedars here?" She looked at him hard.

"Just pines and junipers. But look — " He pointed to a distant cottage. Beside it stood the blackened stump of a sycamore. "Look what happens to the trees."

"Lightning?"

This time his body language was Arab. Sound and movement signaled firm negation: a thrusting upward of the chin, a cluck of the tongue. "You have heard of Rashaya Fuqhar? A village Israel destroyed? One of my patients couldn't stop talking about his olives. Shattered. Some burned by phosphorus. 'Every week I see more,' he said, 'sleeping like women on their sides.'"

"What became of your mother's cottage?" she asked quickly.

"It sits vacant on a hill. I couldn't stand the thought of selling it. I couldn't sell land."

A degree of intimacy was forming between them; it was not only uncomfortable, but also counterproductive. The fire had died under the coffee bean. Breakfast was over; it was time to move on.

"Oh, aren't these bugloss?" she asked in a voice of controlled disdain. The bugloss was unmistakable. Its top-heavy pink-mauve petals dangled from a spiny gray stalk. "*Echium horridum.*"

He seemed not to notice the abrupt shift of subject or mood. "A flower of the desert," he told her. Then, a note of admiration warming his voice: "You know its scientific name."

Noncommittal, Camellia shrugged. "My mother: the botanist. While other kids were riding tricycles, we were feeding Venus's flytraps."

"Then you will know this blossom."

A crazy-quilt of wildflowers bounded his house. He picked his way through them, stooping to examine a cluster in the patch.

"*Ke'hil.*" He cradled it under her nose. "Forget-me-not."

She inhaled its fragrance. His fingers grazed her cheek.

"*Ke'hil* can break a fever."

"You couldn't have learned that at Oxford."

Rumbling laughter seemed to emanate from his belly. "You forget. Western scientists derive hundreds of medicines from plants. Cyclosporin was discovered in Kenya in the mud. But you are right. In the West, medicine is a science, not art. Body, not soul."

How deft he was with an insult. Frustrated, unable to refute him: "You don't even *look* like an Arab."

"Oh? What does an Arab look like?"

It was too late. The conversation had run away from them both.

"You know; brown-eyed and skin the color of cinnamon bark."

"Hawk-nosed? Shifty-eyed? A 'desert nigger'?"

"That's not fair. Khalil is none of those things."

Maddeningly, Marwan seemed invigorated by any comparison between him and Khalil. "Maybe I'm descended from a Crusader. The Crusaders — your ancestors, and possibly mine — planted more than just spiritual enthusiasms in these hills. They also planted — "

"I'm trying to find my fiance and you're talking about the Crusades?"

Impassioned, she stood up.

At the same moment, Marwan released the bloom. The petals fluttered to the ground like shriveled leaves. He turned away from her, toward the lush verdant hills. On the opposing slope, a herd of clumsy sheep had unloosed an avalanche of pebbles. All at once Marwan turned back and gripped her by the shoulders.

"Khalil lied. He's a Phalangist. He's in dirt up to his *kaffiyeh*."

Her hand flew out as if empowered by some outside force. The sound echoed in the valley like a rifle shot on a Sunday morning; the slap left a two-pronged stripe across his cheek, wider than her fingers.

There was silence. Then, from Marwan:

"I have not yet told you of my wife."

Marwan stood with his hands behind his back. He had turned again to face the castle. Sun glinted on the rubble, the rubble newly occupied and pressed into service for modern aims, the fort resurrected and manned anew, in unending cycles of violence.

"Your wife?" Tone unrepentant. But voice spent, thin and soft.

He stood looking at the castle. From time to time he blinked. "She died by her own hands."

"Suicide?"

Again the response was Western, a slight shake of the head, a shedding of unacceptable ideas. "She drove a car loaded with explosives into an enemy checkpoint."

"Who was the enemy? Was she Moslem? Palestinian? Lebanese?"

"What does it matter? For all that, she could have been Israeli."

"Why didn't you stop her? Why didn't you ..."

"She wanted babies." His voice was dry, devoid of sentiment. "In this part of the world, babies are the martyrs of tomorrow. You raise children only to watch them — " His jaw tightened and he finished, "In the end she couldn't make the sacrifice."

Abruptly, he unclasped his hands to touch Camellia's shoulder, turning her gently toward the winding, foam-flecked river disappearing north. It wound into the mountains, north to Mount Hermon, a forbidding rise on the most distant horizon. Ice was clinging to its peak.

"Look — wildflowers bloom on slopes capped by ice. There — that is Baalbek, and spring has settled on the temples."

"I must ask Khalil to take me there."

The absent quality vanished. His voice became ironic: "You'll resume your *programme* of sightseeing."

"Actually, no. I'm not a total idiot." She put their empty cups back on the tray, effectuating an efficient clean-up. China clattered against china and the copper of the pot. "We're going back to Ann Arbor. Where it's safe."

"Where you will be absolutely assured of never being exposed to any disturbing idea, thing or person."

With startling *deja vu*, she felt again that time would not erode this moment. Her eyes and her skin and her senses absorbed detail, emblazoned on her memory. Smell or sound would trigger it, and conjure up the ripe fragrance of the coffee, the wing-rub of crickets, the earthy silence, the silken breeze. The aliveness of Marwan, arrogant and sensual, earthy, eyes like uncut fire-opals reflecting sun.

This time the urge to slap him was willful rather than involuntary. She resisted it all the same. Strangely, a voice came — it wasn't Marwan's. A shadow fell between them.

The voice again. A harsh, guttural laugh.

Then, suddenly, inexplicably, Camellia could no longer see or know or remember. She could only fall like a lost soul into swirling blackness, dizzyingly, until, head throbbing, she woke and breathed stale air that smelled of oranges.

****

She came fully awake. Which meant she had been asleep.

She lay prone in a dark room. She was dimly aware of time. The passage of time. Of hurt. Her head hurt.

Out of the corner of her eye, she saw forms and patterns. The outline of a table. Orange rinds and tea glasses — all came gradually into focus. The air, heavy with kerosene. It defiled the room. The atmosphere was subterranean, pungent with the smell and chill of earth.

She had the impression of being in a cave.

Soft voices. Harsh murmurs. Echoes. Marwan's raspy bass. Distinguished from the rest, it was loud, deep, with a commanding edge.

Fury gave her voice an edge, too. "Where the hell am I?"

He made some reply. In Arabic. Whatever he said caused other men to laugh.

She propped herself up on one elbow, repeating the question, this time loud and strident. And adding, "What the hell are you doing? *Doctor*?"

"No harm, I hope. That would violate the Hippocratic oath."

She swung her legs over the bench. "Bastard."

"I must teach you Arabic — if only to put poetry in your curses."

"'A Lebanese without a cause,' hunh? That's what you called yourself in Beirut. Aloof, rare, Augustinian ... leaving the tawdry fighting to others — " Then, freshly irritated, the meaning of his words having registered: "I'll tell you where you can put your poetry — "

"As they say in America, Whoa!" Marwan's eyes gleamed like spiders. He sighed windily, but kept wrapping a bandage.

Darkness shrouded the patient; three men looked on. They wore the black-and-white *kaffiyeh* of the commando. Or terrorist. Or *fedayeen*. Suddenly she forgot which.

Her head still ached, but her vision cleared. Camellia watched the outline of Marwan at work. White flashes of bandage circumscribing armpit and chest. More bandages, heavy with liquid, dabbed at a head wound.

"It is difficult being Greek Orthodox in Lebanon. It is even harder to be a doctor."

"Spare me." She sat up. Her arms were stiff and prickly; her legs just numb. "What did you do? Tie me to a donkey? My head hurts."

"I will give you aspirin."

"You're damned good at dispensing aspirin. Where are we?"

"Deep in the land. An excellent place to be in Lebanon. Didn't I once overhear you trying to persuade Khalil of that?"

"You know that's not — " Contradiction faltered; she ran out of words. She fingered the goose egg at the nape of her neck.

"I've been knocked out," she said, feeling pleasantly scandalized. "Did you just *hit* me?"

"Not without pretext."

"Funny. I don't remember any great debate."

"You wouldn't. Losing consciousness somehow erases short-term memory."

"Will I *ever* know what happened?" How awful — to have the most exciting part of her adventure purged like eighteen minutes on a tape.

"Hard to tell. Some people hit head-on in traffic never remember the accident."

Savoring that information, she wondered how long had she been unconscious.

Long enough to have traveled far? To another city? Somewhere near the border? The smell of oranges — where *were* the groves in Lebanon? Damn her memory, and damn Marwan. He was disagreeably evasive and flippant. She would ask him nothing further in this mood.

In the absence of hard information, her imagination supplied other possibilities. Could they have descended into the rumored terrorists' network of caves?

"Why didn't you convince them to leave me behind?" she cried. "I would have waited for you."

No longer flippant, he spoke in a somber way. In a low voice, almost a whisper. "Has it occurred to you how much easier to would have been to leave you? That I might have *insisted* you come? For a reason?"

"You mean — "

Perverse, he returned to her first question, answering it comprehensively. "We are in Nabatiye. At least the residents call it Nabatiye. The Israelis call it Fatahland."

He was putting the finishing touches on his patient. Winding, adjusting, taping. He should have signed the work, like a canvas.

"Nabatiye is one of the ironies of the Arabs' war with Israel. Nabatiye, repeatedly smashed, is hopelessly devastated, like any number of small European towns liberated by the Allies. Yet this is a war like no other. Not a single soldier has ever set foot in the city. Nor is likely to. Listen — "

Too low to hear. A vibration, no more. A dry rattle of the tea glasses.

"Mirages. Perhaps a mile away."

She leaned her head against the wall. With no motive but her own immediate security: "Will they come here?"

Marwan, done, straightened. A look of inquiry at the men gave them carte blanche to answer her question. Silent too long, they needed no further invitation. (Astonishing, how respectfully they deferred to Marwan.) Replies erupted simultaneously, a swell of Arabic which then died off, demanding translation.

Marwan obliged but gave their words his rhythm. "'And if they come here, and we are killed, others will take our place.'"

Marwan's mummified patient, overcome with patriotism or bravado or hopelessness, burst forth in English. "We will fight until they are finished!"

"*You*, my son, are finished," Marwan said lightly, retaping a bandage which had become unglued.

And then the mummy told a joke in Arabic.

Camellia, at the sound of the uproarious laughter when the punch line came: "Are you all absolutely insane?" Of course it was not theirs but her voice rising, tinged with hysteria.

"It recalls Israel's defeat of the Arabs in '67."

"Sounds hilarious." Then, curious in spite of herself: "Tell me the joke."

"Why not? Egypt has exhausted every possible strategy of war, and still the

Israelis are demolishing them and Syria, largely because their armies are inept. 'I have a plan to defeat the Israelis!' an eager peasant tells Egyptian President Nasser. 'Station the Syrian army on the Egyptian front line. Station the Egyptian army on the Syrian front line. It is foolproof! When each army retreats, to get home it must cross Israel!'"

"So the Arabs defeat Israel by bumbling," said Camellia, still curious. "That sounds like a joke made in Tel Aviv. And yet the Palestinians are repeating it. Strange world."

Fingers entwined, Marwan stretched, then sighed. Like a horse approaching a rickety bridge, he sauntered over to her. She, a minor emergency, like a patient on crisp white paper, could wait.

He lifted her lanky hair. He felt the lump at the base of her skull. His fingers grazed her neck.

The air became humid, pungent with tea. One of the men squatted over the glass flame of a portable burner.

Blood rushed to her head and settled in her cheeks. She finally understood. These men could help find Khalil

"You'll live," he said crisply, dropping her hair.

"Marwan! Would you — could you ask them — ?"

He smiled unhappily.

"Could — "

She bit her bottom lip. Would the vibrations never stop? Noiseless waves of unpleasant sound. She, of course, could associate them only with regular things: dog whistles, or tuning forks, or electronic surveillance in a department store. Sounds outside the range of human hearing, nevertheless as insistent as that which is audible. Especially when it signals threat.

"Marwan." His hands were square and strong. She squeezed them till it hurt and her fingernails left indentations in his flesh. She had been wrong about so many things. Clearly, whatever strange mix of religious and patriotic fervor had motivated Khalil, whatever the nature of his political dalliances, it all had nothing to do with Marwan. Still —

"They accept you — don't they? They trust you — *everyone* trusts you — because you're Greek Orthodox?"

His smile became a tight, compressed line.

"And that's how kidnap victims are ransomed, isn't it? By neutral third parties? That's how *everything* works here, doesn't it? Behind the scenes, through connections ... never, in Lebanon, by full frontal assault. I could spend a dozen years demanding answers and getting nowhere — "

Drawn by her intensity, the men in the black-and-white *kaffiyehs* bit off their own talk. Politely, the resumed their conversations, but in low tones.

She knew, instinctively, how to hurt Marwan. There didn't seem to be another way.

"You let your wife go, didn't you? She was liberated, and *you* were liberated, careful not to try to influence her. You didn't stop her. She died alone. Well, sometimes a woman *wants* a man to take a stand, and loves him better for it...."

The atmosphere was sodden, still. The vibrations slackened, retreated on waves of sound along with the jets; the air, no longer a receptacle but merely itself, returning to its origins: and the atmosphere became a dying symphony, an ode to nothingness.

Marwan removed his hand from hers. His eyes were vacant of expression. "What are you asking of me?"

She dug her nails into her palms. Dammit, I've won, she thought. I've won an ally. I pitted his Oxford side against his Arab side, and the Arab won. The Arab hopelessly in love with history, and chivalry, and his own idea of himself.

"My approach is wrong for Lebanon, I realize. But I've come too far to give up now. My first mistake was refusing to admit, even to myself, that Khalil was involved with the Christian Phalange." In fact, she had unsubtly, and illogically, been holding Marwan accountable for Khalil's disappearance. "But he *must* be." She had it all worked out. The truth was an ally, too. "OK — so we're in south Lebanon. In Fatahland. I want to talk to the head of the PLO." Again blood rushed to her cheeks, this time in the triumph of brashness over ignorance. "Yasir Arafat himself — if that's who it is!"

This time her appeal was to the Oxford man. The student of the West who had replaced his grandmother's folk arts with hard science, whose first rude shock at Oxford had been the intuitive, cultivated contempt of the English toward his people — for all their contribution to language, history. To civilization. In whom a lifetime of rationality could never obliterate racial memory.

In the end it was his Arab side that prevailed, perhaps because of the audience of Arab men.

He nodded assent, then quickly turned away.

Was she more observant now? Or hyper-sensitive? Had admitting certain basic truths given her the power of insight? Marwan could no more have refused her than he could have dragged his wife from the wired car. Such would have entailed compromise, and "compromise," Dr. Elias had once remarked, "in English, is a word with many meanings. In Arabic, it has but one — as in, 'He accepted the bribe and was compromised.'"

One of the *fedayeen* climbed from the shelter; a moment later he returned and, like a deer who has sniffed the wind, pronounced the silence consistent.

They could "return back," he said, to Beaufort.

He drove a nondescript vehicle, top down, which Camellia naturally did not recognize but assumed was the same car which had carried them here.

He stopped once to inspect a rut where a Jeep had piled into a Peugeot. He swerved to avoid a sheep's carcass which lay as if tossed, blocking the road. Mostly he overtook other cars, all going north. An exodus. They were family vehicles: farm trucks and boxy sedans. Heavily laden with household goods. Filled with family whose arms hung out windows, giving the impression of insects with antennae or jointed legs. Their chassis scraped the ground.

The road was hilly, and the driver took it at great speed, in a smooth ride, and Camellia settled back, refusing his repeated offer of a cigarette. She was oddly unaware of Marwan, of what he might be thinking; she only rested her head against his shoulder and contemplated how glorious it was to have shifted some of the burden, the responsibility — and, with it, the anxiety! — to him. She half-closed her eyes against the whipping wind, the heavy sun.

She laughed unself-consciously as the driver glanced over his shoulder and forced the engine to greater speed.

"Slow down, my brother." Marwan's voice, no longer amused and cynical, was flat with weariness, but strangely buoyant, almost devil-may-care. "Slow down, my brother," he repeated. "You cannot outrun a jet."

****

The sounds of Beaufort and the smell of the Litani carried her awake. The driver had not angled through town. Rather, he had chosen rural backroads, dusty shortcuts to the mountain shelf where Marwan's home sat.

She spotted two people on the white-dirt road a thousand feet from Marwan's front door. A whole day had been lost. It made her think of Samir. And Ahmed. Perhaps Ahmed had abandoned them.

"I'm starving," she said. Then, remembering priorities: "Samir will be out of his mind with worry."

"That's not Samir."

A certain terseness of his voice caused Camellia to look up. She had assumed the people on the road were locals. Fat women in aprons. Housewives carrying bunches of grapes or balancing baskets of laundry on their heads.

She stared, fascinated, at the figures, hazy in the dust but familiar, like a dream that recurs so frequently there is no sense dreading it.

Unwillingly, she recognized detail. The indolent gait. The broad-brimmed hat. Bangle bracelets like uranic rings encircling wrists. Gold huaraches, sparkling in the sun, making objets d'art of feet. A butterfly net propped in silhouette.

"Oh, my God." Camellia felt her mouth go slack. A sparrow screeched into the sleepy late-day silence, heralding the rural bustle of evening.

"It's my mother. It's Angela ... and Violet."

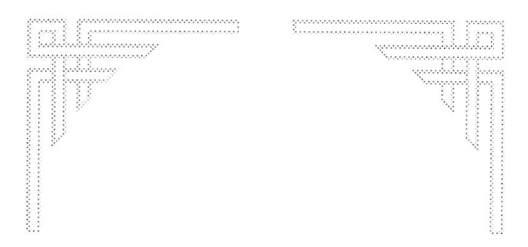

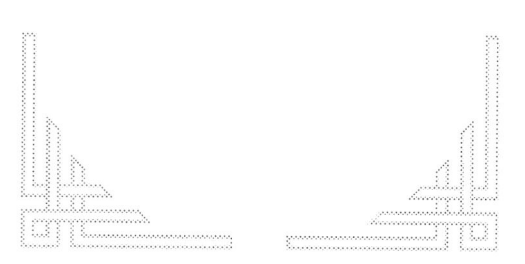

7

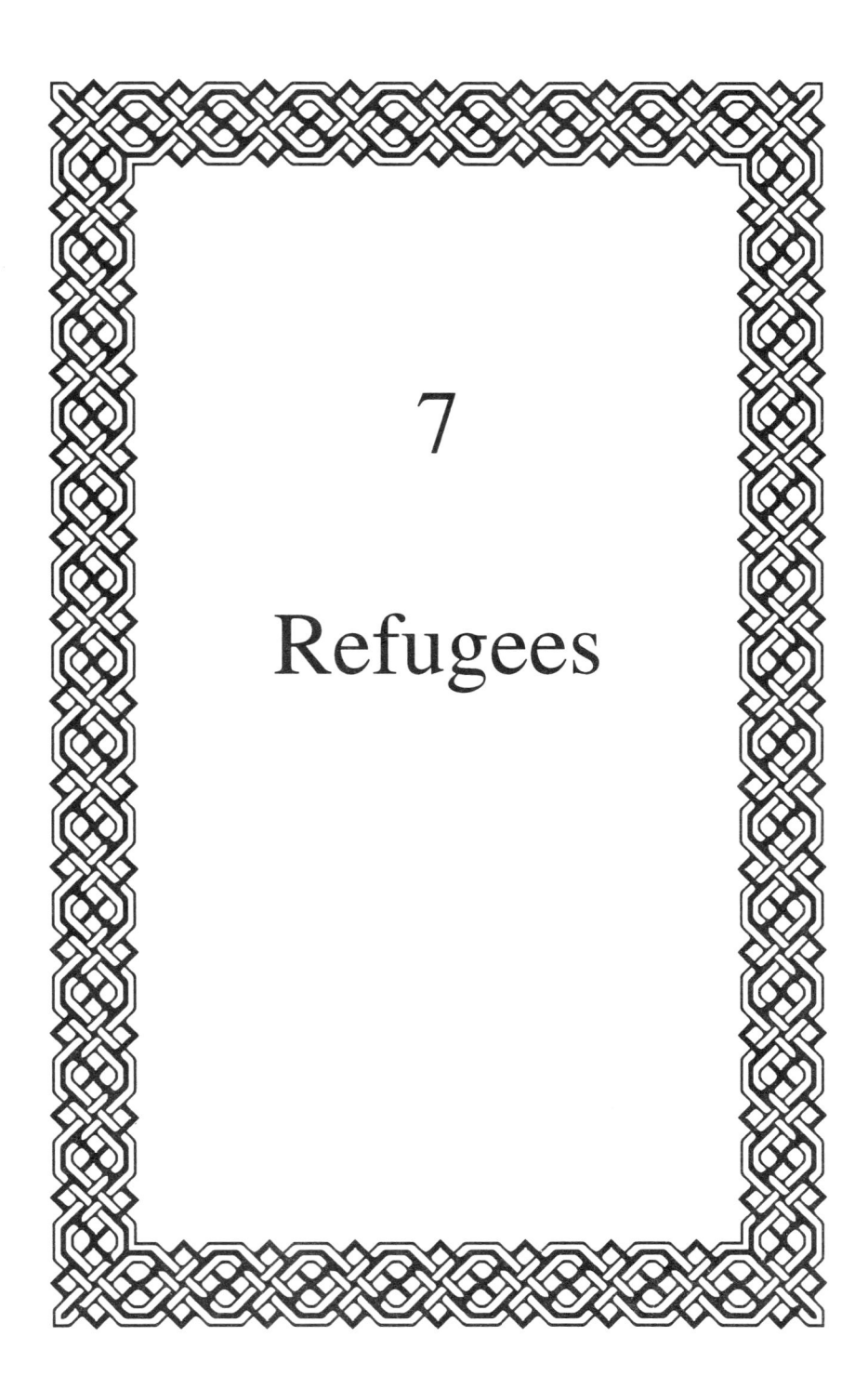

Refugees

"What serendipity! To meet a white man in this Godforsaken place!"

Angela, florid as always in speech, had warmed immediately to Marwan. She sat cross-legged on the Persian rug, luxuriating under the hospitality he offered effortlessly. With coffee, he had made her welcome.

At the same time, Marwan became formal if not cool toward Camellia, circumspect, as if suddenly he remembered himself. Almost as soon as her mother had entered the house, Marwan excused himself. He had driven off in the rust-colored VW to the butcher's and grocer's. Bread and cheese wouldn't do.

Angela adjusted her ruffled skirt, which stretched across her knees like the goatskin of a drum. Angela began to project nervous enthusiasm, as she always did when one of her creative impulses landed her in what Marshall, her late husband, called a "fix." She added, for good measure: "And these mountains — they're positively alpine!"

"*All* the Lebanese are white, Muzz," Violet objected. Her mouth was full of crackers. "They're Asians. Not Africans. Right, Camellia?"

Though she was tolerant in the extreme, Angela had no patience for analysis. "East of Ypsilanti, they're all the same to me." She gave an airy wave of her hand before turning her attention to the landscape, visible through the decorative iron grille.

Camellia had been pacing. She stopped in the center of the room. "Here we are in Lebanon, just miles from the border with Israel, and you two sit here making like Margaret Mead? I need a smoke. Damn! Where is Samir when I need him?"

She would have to light the pipe herself. It was surprisingly easy.

She found matches in a drawer near the enamel stove. She pushed aside the curtain and removed the *nargeila* from the thick windowsill. She carried it gingerly, afraid of dropping and shattering the glass. She balanced the cord on her arm.

Fortunately Marwan had left the tobacco in a dry place. It ignited instantly. Camellia inhaled. The water bubbled. Scented smoke misted in front of her eyes and clung to her hair. A rush of blood warmed her face and extended to her fingers and toes. Her voice, almost level, seemed to come from a far place:

"I thought you two were on a plane."

"Muzz!" Violet was aghast. "I thought neither of us was allowed to smoke."

"Oh, hush." Camellia pursed her lips like a beginner at the clarinet. She drew deeply and choked. "This isn't Virginia Slims. This is *nafas tombac*. A breath of tobacco."

The infusion of nicotine did not relax her. It made her lightheaded.

"A breath of fresh air," Angela said. "That's what I need." She strode to the window and lazily inhaled the warm spring air.

Puffs of smoke. Camellia released them in short, jagged bursts like an erratic heartbeat. "What the hell are you doing here?"

"Smoking — " Violet again " — *and* cussing?"

"I thought you two were winging your way to Europe."

"Aren't you happy to see us?" Violet fluttered her lashes, curled to perfection and coated, no matter the continent or time zone.

"Did you really think we'd go and leave you alone?" Angela tucked her skirt more securely around her legs.

"Hah! Tell the truth, Muzz." Violet sat in a corner among heaped bags and purses. "She lost our passports."

Eager to revive the quarrel, Angela said, "Only because I made the mistake of entrusting them to *you*."

A scrape of shoes on the threshold ... the creak of the heavy front door. Marwan laden with packages, white plastic bags imprinted with a black scrawl of Arabic. Plastic reached to every corner of the world, even corner groceries in Lebanese villages.

He registered no flicker of emotion at the sight of Camellia drawing noisily on his pipe.

Unpacking in the kitchen, he said, "Angela, Violet — you must be tired from your travel. What would you like to drink?"

Angela never needed an invitation to enter a kitchen. Instinctively she offered help. Marwan made room for her in cramped quarters; they moved without awkwardness in the small space. Camellia, by contrast, would have been bumping or elbowing him.

She had worked so hard to gain Marwan's sympathy! It piqued her that Angela had established immediate rapport.

"Yes. I want Coke. No — wait!" Violet dived for her parachute bag. She pawed through it. "Here it is! I'll tell you exactly what I want."

It was the tape-recorder-like device she'd fiddled with at the Beirut flat.

"I've got it programmed." She punched a few buttons. The machine emitted a command in nasal Arabic. The English translation followed. Both Arabic and

English were articulated with the same robotic intonation:

"I would like some tea."

"The damn thing talks?"

"It got us here. It gave flawless directions to the taxi driver." Violet patted the machine with the admiration Americans reserve for technology which can be operated without being understood. "It can repeat a string of up to eight phrases. Now that I know how it works, I'm going to add seven more."

"Oh? Did the machine tell you where I was?" Camellia asked.

"No, silly. The Embassy did."

Angela was engrossed in learning to make perfect Turkish coffee. She snatched the copper pot from the stove, just as the black liquid was beginning to boil over. Marwan looked on in a proprietary way.

"What made you think of going to the Embassy?" Camellia asked.

"You were right about the airport," Angela said distractedly. "It was closed. By the time we found our passports, the Tour had gone on to Byblos. Lebanon seemed perfectly safe."

"But the Embassy?"

"You left the phone number lying around. Besides, where else would a U.S. citizen go?"

"I loved the waterfront!" Violet exclaimed. "And the marines!"

"Thurgood! I should never have told him anything."

"Thurgood?" Marwan stopped spooning sugar into the coffee. "Who is Thurgood?"

"Some idiot vice consul. Last thing before I left Barbir Hospital, I managed to get a live phone line. I gave Thurgood my itinerary. Dad taught me — " Marshall, her father, a pilot, always filed a flight plan, even when he was going no farther than Ann Arbor. "I thought ... it seemed.... more legitimate, *safer*, if someone knew where I was...."

"So you did not trust me ... entirely," Marwan said.

"Thurgood told me the most amazing story," Angela said. "A couple of years ago, a party of American tourists went up to Bisharre — to see the cedars. They were promptly snowed in. Who did they telegraph but the Embassy! They expected to be airlifted out!"

"So I heard," Camellia said dourly.

"No one can match the Americans for zany charm." Marwan held out the tray. "Coffee?"

The coffee, steamy, fragrant, and bitter, went well with the *nargeila*.

Marwan apologized to Violet. "We have only Pepsi, not Coke. No Coke in all the Arab Middle East." Coke was on the list of products Arabs boycotted because of Israel. Or were supposed to boycott. Charlie perfume was on the list, too, but Camellia had seen it on every dressing table in every bedroom she had been privileged to see. Including Yasmina's.

Marwan returned with another tray, filled with white cookies, *k'ak*. Marwan lowered it before each guest individually, as was the custom. He was gracious, natural, the opposite of subservient even as he served. Even so, he was pensive, as if meeting Angela somehow reminded him of something.

Marwan took the tray back to the kitchen, dusted off the crumbs and loaded it with meat and cheese. He and Angela had made an omelet, she whipping it and he chopping up the parsley and onion.

Camellia continued to keep the water pipe alive. Her tongue felt like cotton. The coffee wetted it. "Did you hear anything on the radio?"

"Sons of bitches." Marwan shook his head. He added Arabic bread to the tray. "Beirut's a battleground. Al-Fatah has the upper hand, with Arafat's men smashing the neighborhoods. Pierre Gemayel wants the army in on the Phalangist side. But it was *he* who caused the massacre."

Violet shuddered. "There's too much violence in Lebanon." She licked her finger. "Let's go back to Detroit."

"We're safer here," Angela said firmly, absent-mindedly.

"You *are* safer here, in the south, than in Beirut," Marwan said. "At least for now."

"I can corroborate that, on good authority," Angela said. She had settled back on the rug. She spoke between bites. "I met the loveliest man at the Embassy. A Lt. Col. Humphries, I believe. On his way to Pensacola — or to retirement, I forget which. He recognized me. Can you believe it? Marshall and I knew him briefly in Frankfurt. Anyway, he described Beaufort as only a military man could. The 'impenetrable line of the cliffs ... line-of-sight view of the Galilee ... ' Who but a military man would see it that way? He talked about the Litani River as if it were a perimeter, not a lovely gushing stream." Her voice trailed off romantically. "Marwan, I adore your hometown. *This* is travel."

"But we're not staying here." Camellia's fingers tightened around the stem of the *nargeila*. "There's nothing more to be accomplished in Beaufort. Marwan promised —"

"Nothing at all?" Angela asked. "I understand there's a historic castle."

"I'm talking about finding Khalil."

Marwan's jaw tightened; the fluid expressiveness drained from his face. He spoke to Angela. "We must visit Ein el Hilweh: a refugee camp near Sidon. I know some Palestinians there; they may know where Khalil is."

"Why didn't you tell me?" Camellia asked. Why did he spring this news now, without warning, in front of Angela and Violet, giving her no time to contemplate or consider? Gratitude softened her tone as she finished: "You left me to worry all day."

"Refugees?" Angela looked horrified, befuddled and somewhat stimulated.

"What have refugees to do with us?"

"I haven't told you about my trip to Fatahland."

Marwan interrupted. "There's a possibility Khalil is a member of the Christian Phalange. Many people would be motivated to kidnap such a person."

Camellia picked up the tray of cups and set it, clattering, on the countertop.

Violet was chewing bread. "Phalange? Sounds like a disease. Is it fatal?"

"Only to Moslems and Palestinians," Marwan said softly.

Angela, puzzled: "But I thought the enemies of Arabs were Israelis."

"*Wallah*, it is complicated." Marwan squatted by the round platter of food. Holding a triangle of bread like a dipper, he deftly scooped up a bite-sized piece of the omelet. He showed Angela how to do the same.

"Israel gives weapons, money and protection to the Phalangists," he continued. "They, in return, give substance to the Israeli dream, which is, put simply, to supplant Lebanon with a Christian state. A state indebted, of course, to Israel."

"Just like the Leopard butterfly!" Angela's eyes shone with comprehension. "*Apharitis*," she added. She set aside her bread to rummage in her bag for a tattered reference; speaking from fond memory, she laid the book, unopened, on her lap. "Discovered in the Empty Quarter of Arabia. By Harry St. John Philby and Bertram Thomas. In the '30s."

"Oh, Mother! Insects and plants! Can't you keep on point?"

But Marwan, innocently: "How does a butterfly live in the desert, deprived of nectar?"

Angela smiled eagerly. Her face lit up like an ingenue's. Butterflies were a thing she knew well. "By — as a caterpillar — excreting honey to fascinate the predatory ants. Even the ferocious *Oecophylla*, a natural enemy, nurtures the eggs. Not to devour them, but rather to carry the tiny caterpillars to its nest, caress them and drink from their glands. Risking its own life, the ant drives off the caterpillar's natural enemies — assassin bugs and wasps."

"Hmph. All for the sake of nectar," Camellia said.

Marwan brushed crumbs from his lips. "Have you ever tasted nectar?"

Angrily, "Of course I have."

"More coffee, Angela?"

"I'd love some."

But, before the stove could be lit, Samir and Ahmed arrived. Driving too fast to stop, Ahmed made a pass. The cab was a black blur across the front windows. Then it was a black blur, across the windows in reverse. A sweeping U-turn in the dust. Wheel-spun gravel spattering on the house. Ahmed tapped the horn as if it were a telegraph key and he the bearer of urgent code. Samir added a rebel yell to the din.

"Your ride's here," Marwan said. "Your mother and your sister can ride with me."

He steered Angela and Violet toward his burnt-orange VW. Violet exclaimed over it. A beetle — in Lebanon! Especially impressing Violet was the lamb's-wool upholstery. She and Angela piled into the bug. Violet was nothing if not easily impressed.

Before taking the driver's seat, Marwan explained to Ahmed the way. Eloquent hand gestures and much repetition helped cement Ahmed's understanding of the route.

Watching from inside the house, Camellia dumped out the tobacco ash. She put the water pipe back on the sill. Marwan came inside to rinse the glasses and throw pillows back into storage. Routine. Camellia and Marwan moved like dancers in a minuet, cordial but distant.

At last he shut up the house. Outside, the afternoon sun struck a corner of the patch of wildflowers, where Marwan had uprooted the forget-me-not, where the weeds had already sprung back to obliterate the path.

Glowering, Camellia slid into the back seat of Ahmed's cab, beside Samir.

****

She smelled Sidon before she saw it. Fertile plain. Groves misting the air with citrus and honeysuckle. A salt backwash drifting from the sea. Roadside stands with pyramids of potatoes and cauliflower.

The road led past two Palestinian refugee camps.

The camps — Mieh Mieh and Ein el Hilweh — squatted like beggars on the outskirts of town. Inexplicably, Marwan bypassed Ein el Hilweh, which she had thought to be their destination. It was Lebanon's largest refugee camp, Marwan had said. Its 25,000 residents were drawn mostly from northern Palestine.

"Now what's he doing?" Camellia craned her neck to see past Ahmed's head.

"Maybe he takes us to the waterfront." Samir was serene as usual. "Or maybe some other place."

"Aren't you too young to be fatalistic?"

Ahmed had slowed to a maddening crawl. He trailed Marwan through a maze of alleys that twisted past skewed buildings with tilted facades and hidden entryways. Antennae sprouted from rooftops like split ends. Polished minarets made peaks in the skyline.

Water swooshed from a balcony swept clean by a maid. At ground level, men in slippers played backgammon and smoked waterpipes in cafes from which soft music wailed.

An iron grille barred entry to the Granada Cinema below deserted-looking second-story tenements.

Ahmed peered up at the empty windows. Insider's knowledge or familiarity or perhaps simple deduction inspired him to make an observation. Samir translated: "Refugees live *there*, too."

The waterfront. Sun peeled turquoise paint from the shacks. A grizzled man sat mending a fishnet. There were flecks of silver in his beard, thin as the net filaments. Beside him, a man of a younger generation smoked. The air reeked with the smell of the day's catch.

The beach. Ahmed braked behind Marwan. He flicked his cigarette into the sand.

Angela and Violet piled out of Marwan's car like candy poured from Tayta's jar. Violet shaded her eyes with her hands, the better to survey the landscape. Against the inexorable wash of the waves sounded her little squeals of delight and the cry of curlews.

Marwan paid Ahmed, and Camellia silently berated herself for having forgotten this practical detail. She should have been ready with the money herself.

"Marwan knows so many fascinating things!" Violet cried. "Look here." She stubbed her toe into the sand, stirring up spiny fragments.

"The murex. Sidon's fabled shell." She held one aloft. It was a long shell, bulbous and spiked, with an oval mouth and a tail. "Murex snails secrete a yellowish fluid. The ancients boiled them to create a dye. Purple — of all colors!"

"The color of cardinals and kings," Marwan said.

"Yes — " Angela picked up the story " — and many western Mediterranean towns were settled by Phoenicians seeking new supplies of murex for their vats. The ancient cities were constantly besieged."

Camellia stood with her hands clenched in the pockets of her jeans. "How ridiculous — to kill for a snail."

"Oh, Camellia! You're such a stick in the mud. Or in the sand, I should say." Violet giggled at her own wit. "Look!" she squealed. The Castle by the Sea had caught her eye.

It commanded Angela's attention as well.

The Castle sat crumbling in the late-day sun. Tourists, antlike, poked among its fortifications. They patted the rusted cannon. They pointed at the pink pillars, pillaged from Roman ruins, wedged like cross-pieces between the stones.

"Built by Crusaders" — Violet continued breathlessly — "who swarmed down from Acre hoping to retake Moslem positions. Oh ... Oh... See how the sun hits it — just so!"

"It's only a ruin," Camellia said, ignoring how much she had looked forward to seeing it.

"There's a tunnel here somewhere." Marwan spoke with a measure of regret, it seemed to Camellia. "It leads to the ruins of a Turkish prison." He spoke tersely to Samir, in Arabic. They set off down the beach.

"Damn! Wait!" Camellia set off after them. "Ow!" Some-thing sharp had fallen into her leather loafer, lodging between her toes. She kicked off one of the shoes. The sand was grainy and cool. She shook the shoe and a ridged shell fell out. A murex fragment.

"Wait!" Carrying her shoe, Camellia hopped after them. "I'm cut!"

"You'll live," Marwan called back over his shoulder. "Wait for me!"

"Don't you think I should come, too?"

But Marwan, a hundred yards down the beach, didn't look back.

Camellia stopped hopping. A man passed by, limping. He picked his teeth with a sliver of bark. Behind him, salt-crusted fishing boats bobbed near shore.

"He knows so many fascinating things," Violet repeated.

Angela was watching him, too.

"A Renaissance man," she said. Admiration warmed her voice. "Did you know that the Sidonians invented blown glass? I always thought it was the British! One stamped his work: 'Ennion made it: let the buyer remember.' We don't mind dying, if others remember our names." She chuckled.

Violet was wading in the wavelets.

Angela had her shoes off and was curling her toes in the sand. Her hair was loose. The sun caught its angles.

"Land ho!" cried Violet. "Shall we explore the Castle?"

"Damn the Castle." The dance of the waves, the shimmering horizon — Camellia saw them through the blur of tears. "Damn Ennion. And damn Marwan!"

Impulsive, Angela caught Camellia in a hug. "There, there," she said. "This day must seem as if it's going to last forever." Only with great effort, Camellia knew, Angela refrained from giving advice. Adding, with more sensitivity than Camellia had given her credit for: "I know we must be a liability to you here — Violet and I. If it weren't for this thing with Khalil — " She pulled back; she gave a little sigh. "I haven't had this much fun since your father and I got lost in the maze at Hampton Court! And I'm so sure you'll find Khalil! Or, at least, Marwan will."

The salt spray exerted a cooling effect on the afternoon, foreshadowing the waning of the day. Camellia grabbed a handful of sand and threw it at the ebbing tide.

"ALLAAAHU AKBAR...."

Mellifluous, disembodied, the voice inspired the momentary hush obeisance brings. The waterfront fell silent. Indeed, much of Lebanon was silent, and the entire Moslem world, hushed, stilled, as Moslems everywhere knelt, facing Mecca, called to prayer by the *muezzin*, attuned to the rhythm of sun and moon.

Angela swallowed, looking puzzled and watchful.

Camellia squared her shoulders. "Go on — go to the castle with Violet," she urged. "I'll wait for Marwan — I'll find a cafe — " She gave a vague wave of her hand. "I'm not in the mood to explore."

She turned her back to the sea and looked toward town, toward grape arbors clinging to the sides of homes, homes with their arcades of pointed arches and unfinished upper-story walls, roofs purposely made flat for summer sleeping. On balconies, lacy mullion and bits of stained glass embellished the keyhole windows.

What must it be like to live in one of those houses, to enjoy an obscured view from a window whose primary function was to thwart the view of strangers passing by....

In the cafe she ordered tea and sat mesmerized by the mackerel glint of the receding sun. A scratched Om Khalthoum recording ... the garrulity of old men. For the first time, Camellia listened. She appreciated Om Khalthoum's depth, soul, richness. It wasn't pain she expressed. It was the thrill of longing, the sorrow of unspeakable pleasure.

Repeat. Repeat. Repeat. That was the word the audience shouted back at Om Khalthoum. The audience was part of the song. Om Khalthoum acquiesced. She repeated until she drove them almost out of their minds. It was one of her best songs. The music lasted hours. "*Alf Leilah wa Leilah.*" A thousand nights and a night.

Barking dogs. Trudging footsteps. Children called home to dinner.

Marwan's unmistakable bass:

"They will talk to you. But not here. At the camp."

****

The sunset came dazzling as a venomous snake, casting an amethyst glare on the dusty streets of Ein el Hilweh.

Beads of sweat massed on Camellia's forehead and trickled between her breasts. She was trudging behind Marwan. Angela, Violet and Samir were trudging behind her, through the guarded perimeter and into the camp.

Ill-defined body odors and cooking smells permeated the inner courtyard, shot through with the scent of coffee. The heat of ovens briefly recaptured the waning day's warmth. Pottery and ovens. Sort of like Pueblo Indians, Camellia thought. Plain houses, thick walls, with touches of color in rugs, garments; ribbons twisted through hair; intricate designs painted on jugs or etched into copper. Strange, the commonalty of ovens, of hearths, of certain material goods to all oppressed peoples.

Children's voices echoed as their mothers baked bread or opened oven doors to check the *seeneyeh*, stew cooked in a tray. Outside, women in embroidered dresses or tattered shifts walked with a wide-hipped rhythm. Toddlers trailed them. Some of the women balanced great packages on their heads. The old women all wore black. Gray wash hung on lines, lines like gallows, on streets strangely empty of men.

Ein el Hilweh — a classic Palestinian refugee camp. Permanent. Temporary. Tawdry. Efficient. Looking almost like other sultry Lebanese villages, frozen in time, bustling with the life of the street. Shops, schools. There was even a cemetery. The major distinction was the denial of permanence. The inhabitants were ready, at a moment's notice, to dismantle their prefabricated shelters, to abandon their windowless stone huts and go home.

Marwan seemed to know where he was going.

A U.N. relief truck made a U-turn and left spreading dust.

"The PLO is like any other bureaucracy," he said, "rife with petty rules and inflexibilities. I'm sure the people on the beach could have helped us perfectly well. But, no, we must talk with Ramadan Zawq. And Ramadan Zawq is at headquarters, here."

Angela was subdued. Even Violet was strangely quiet.

Vacant-eyed women in billowing dresses disappeared through doorways without doors into homes where windows were gaping holes without glass. Shadows fluttered against concrete, outlines of figures stirring coffee or whisking away cobwebs. The children were as dense-packed as the dust.

Camellia averted her eyes. You could see right into the cell-like interiors. There, a man with one good eye dandled a baby on his knee. There were two wives. The man kept looking from one to the other.

Elsewhere men too old to fight or keep wives rubbed rheumy eyes with gnarled fingers and murmured in gravelly voices.

"Why did they insist we come here?" Camellia's voice faltered. "What does it have to do with us?"

(She had asked the same question of Dr. Elias once; he had answered casually: "A disaster of missed opportunities and misapplied history ... U.S. Middle East policy will never be more than that." He had said nothing about children.)

But Marwan was looking at a woman.

She stood chest-deep in a sea of children — brown-eyed girls in pigtails and boys with their mouths open.

Camellia, feeling fingers on the silky fabric of her blouse, looked down to see what Khalil would have called "urchin." The children were clustered around her. Emboldened when no one shooed them away, they pressed closer.

Marwan, greeting the woman, introduced her. Perfect cupid's bow lips, a pointed nose and heavy-lidded eyes made her the most beautiful ugly woman Camellia had ever seen. She ought to patent that look of hauteur.

She shook hands efficiently. Her high heels stamped the dirt as she elbowed past the children to Angela and Violet. Her name was Sherifa. This was all they ascertained before she took them to Ramadan Zawq.

His drab room reflected the general decor of the Beirut refugee camp: beige and gray, dull and chipped, with three-legged chairs, and desks with missing drawers. Even the framed poster of Yasir Arafat hung off center.

Ramadan Zawq looked like a fitting representative of the PLO: He smoked nervously. His facial hair was more than a week's growth, less than a beard. He looked everywhere but directly into their eyes. He was being polite, of course. Especially when women were involved. A genteel man would not stare boldly. He did not know that, to Americans, shifting eyes conveyed deception.

Sherifa introduced Marwan, Camellia, Angela, Violet and Samir. She remembered names.

After ritual greetings were exchanged in Arabic, Marwan began to speak — eloquently, Camellia hoped — on her behalf. Before he got three sentences out, Sherifa interrupted him.

Alert, Sherifa awaited his translation.

"She says, 'John Foster Dulles said the Palestinians will forget Palestine. Time has proved the falseness of that theory.'"

"We're not diplomats and these aren't peace talks." Camellia swallowed, hard. She had never imagined, even remotely, a situation where being an American would be a liability.

"My fiance is Lebanese — " she tried. But here the situation gets sticky. Which Lebanese? It mattered. How to convince them Khalil had retained his ethnic identity, but remained aloof from the political mainstream? Dr. Elias would have called such an attitude a "developed sense of pan-Arabism." But that description more accurately fitted Marwan than Khalil.

Camellia sighed. It would be easier, she thought, to deal with Ramadan Zawq, the supposed terrorist, than with Sherifa, the bureaucrat.

"Khalil was born in Beirut," she began again. "I met him in Ann Arbor." Surely that was neutral territory. "He graduated, you see, from the University of Michigan ... an engineer ... he wanted to come home ... we came together ... to — "

Zawq became interested. "I went to school in the States, to Stanford."

Camellia laughed, more from tension than camaraderie. "It amazes me how many of you Arabs are the products of the American educational system."

Marwan looked at her. "And for that reason, we will always know you better than you know us."

"Mountains. The sea." Zawq's tone was dreamy. "California is like Palestine. Did you know that the early Zionists, in choosing a Jewish homeland, almost chose California?"

"Of course, then, the biblical claim would have been a bit shaky," Marwan said dryly.

Zawq responded: "Not if you consider the Anglo-European claim of Manifest Destiny."

Camellia tried to regain control of the conversation. "Look, I'm not here to help or hurt your cause. I just want — "

"You are worried about your Khalil. But what of our people?" Sherifa's English was hostile and correct. Red spots throbbed above the hollow of her cheeks. She was not to be ignored.

"Israel rains terror on our villages, on our miserable camps. It stands condemned by every country in the world. Except yours," she finished triumphantly.

"*Ma'alesh*, ya Sherifa." Absently, Zawq flicked ash into the dust. "Americans don't understand the 'land of the fathers'."

Sherifa's body registered incredulity, negation. She whispered: "What of their children? Their dead?"

Marwan interjected gently, "They have not yet lived on the land long enough; the land of America has not yet acquired *baraka*."

This inspired a torrent of Arabic and escalating argument. But only one word stuck in Camellia's mind.

Baraka. Camellia repeated the word under her breath. Spiritual energy. Things can acquire baraka; things used lovingly, personalized, broken in, passed down. Baraka takes time. The land — of course. Baraka can pass from person to person; from teacher to taught; from healer to healed. From the bones of one's ancestors to the land of one's birth.

Marwan has it, she thought suddenly. Baraka.

Sherifa shook her head, looking only somewhat mollified. A girl snuggled up against her, and Sherifa smoothed the girl's wispy braid with claw-like pats. When she looked at Camellia, her eyes grew hard and she reverted to English.

"This girl, like the others, will marry. She will live a soft Beirut life, plant daffodils on her balcony ... Few will stay, to wither, to wait...."

"Dash! I pushed the wrong button!"

It was Violet, who had decided to introduce the children to American technology. She had set off a chain reaction in her automatic translator.

"I am a foreigner. I do not speak your language.

"I have lost my money.

"I have lost my car.

"The price is too high."

Violet punched one key, then another. Still the relentless monotone continued —

"Where is the restroom? Is it upstairs? Is it downstairs?

"Bring me sugar, please.

"I have insect bites.

"Do you have cough syrup?"

A pause. Then the machine began to repeat the entire sequence again — this time in nasal Arabic.

The children giggled as the meaning of sentence after sentence registered. Violet rolled her eyes good-naturedly. The Arab adults looked astonished.

"*Ya habibti.*" Disdainful, Sherifa continued stroking the child. "That's what we get for exposing you to Americans."

Disheartened, Camellia drew a breath of air. It was heavy with loam, sweet citrus and salt. Damn, she thought. Khalil — quick sighted and personable — would have known how to turn this situation to advantage. He always got what he wanted.

"Political kidnappings — " she began.

"They are common in Beirut, I hear." Sherifa had lost interest. Beirut was not central to her cause.

Zawq patted his shirt pocket, feeling for his pack of cigarettes and looking annoyed when he found it empty.

Camellia knew the interview was over when Marwan excused himself. His colleague, Dr. Fawaz, at Ein el Hilweh's clinic was coping with an outbreak of cholera. He needed to consult with Marwan.

Samir went with him, too.

Violet stayed, laughing, with the children. Sherifa lingered, as well. She stood alert, ready to intervene should any further threat to the children's cultural integrity manifest itself.

"Let me show you the camp."

Someone brought Zawq a new pack. In an elegant motion, he shook several cigarettes halfway out and waved the pack like a wand, holding the cigarettes within everyone's reach. Only after being unanimously refused did he light one for himself.

He led the dwindling party — Camellia and Angela — through the camp's gray-white-beige interior. Past heated kitchens and clustered bodies. Tents and prefabricated homes gave way to browns and scattered greens on the outskirts of camp. A toad hopped through the underbrush. The bare skeletal limbs of trees melted into the evening sky like dark flesh. Soldiers or policemen or guerrillas, Camellia didn't know which, ringed the perimeter.

"Scorched earth." Zawq finished something he was saying to Angela. His emphatic diction penetrated Camellia's mental haze. "It is the policy of the Israelis — of Moshe Dayan. What they cannot take, they flatten and burn."

"How distressing," said Angela.

"Last year in south Lebanon the casualties equaled a Maalot every month. You've heard of Maalot." It was a statement, not a question.

"Have I?" Angela asked. "Maalot? Is it medicine?"

"A historic massacre. Great numbers of Jews were slaughtered at Maalot," said Camellia, who had heard the arguments before. "The Arabs have an equivalent: Deir Yasin."

"Camellia, look! Crimson anemones!"

Angela galloped to a patch of bloom. She plucked a flower and cradled it in her hand.

"Marwan told me the Lebanese call them the 'Wounds of Na'aman.' They spring from Adonis' blood and Aphrodite's tears."

"Don't wander, Mother. Those guys aren't Buckingham Palace-types."

It turned out they were officers of the Lebanese army.

Zawq was apparently oblivious of Angela's shortened attention span, of her scattered sensibilities. He had warmed up. He was almost vivacious. "Last year, before Israel returned the city of Kuneitra, it dynamited or bulldozed every hospital, school, home...."

Angela strayed into the grove. Zawq's voice became a bark.

"No! Stop! Get back!"

She stood among the trees, arm outstretched, body bent, pliant and graceful as a dancer's. Angela, at home among flora, looking like a statue in a plaza, reached toward something shiny, some glittering metal, a sphere with jagged edges and sharp alloy wings. "Little baseball-sized things," the red-lipped widow had said in Beirut, describing the occasion of her widowhood, "with serrated edges that spin. They lie on the ground until someone picks them up ... *that's* when they explode." She had shrugged at her misfortune. "Usually it is the children who find them...."

"Angela!" Camellia shouted involuntarily. "It's a bomb!"

"Is it?" Angela's voice was tinny. Somewhat awed. As if she'd heard a voice from the past. One that escaped recognition.

Zawq had his arms around her. Carefully, he led her away from the underbrush. They moved in a ludicrous backward tango. Zawq in his combat fatigues covered with an outrageous furry vest, Angela looking terribly fragile in her ruffled skirt and gold huaraches... Camellia resisted the onset of hysterical laughter, which arrived with the thought: Where is the camera when I need it?

Slowly, Zawq drew Angela into the clearing.

Adrenalin surged, then drained, and Camellia, shaky with relief, leaned against a tree. Violet came running. There was the thud and shuffle of feet as refugees gathered. They stood noiseless behind the trees, like a chorus, or like spirits, drawn by disaster's silent whistle: old men, women, children ... all with a sixth sense sharpened and attuned....

The Lebanese army officers who rimmed the camp had snapped to attention. They gesticulated. They shouted. Their apparent leader sputtered futilely, like a check-mated king. A dozen rooks took aim.

When the bomb exploded, its fragments whirled dust; the clawing metal tore and seared as scorched, tufted earth danced in ghostly fragments: pitted, scarred, like deep graves newly dug.

****

It was almost 10 p.m. when they met up with the Tour.

The twang of Midwestern accents in the seaside hotel's dining room confirmed that neither urban guerrilla warfare nor sniper fire had kept Holy Land Visits Inc. from its appointed schedule.

Angela didn't know exactly which hotel was the Tour's choice of lodging for the night. But, consulting her itinerary, she insisted that the Tour was indeed in Sidon.

Had, in fact, been there for hours. Sidon was as far north as Christianity had been taken personally by its messiah; Sidon was the northernmost point where Jesus preached.

"They'll be just in from Byblos," Angela said confidently.

Sight of a gray double-decker bus easily ended the search. It was parked in front of one of Sidon's several resorts. Marwan parked his burnt-orange beetle beside it. He had not wanted to leave Ein el Hilweh. With the outbreak of cholera under control, he and Dr. Fawaz had many things to discuss. He had handed Camellia the keys to the VW, planning to take a taxi back.

Angela would not hear of it. "After all you've done, at least you must eat dinner." She pressed his hand. Reluctantly, but looking pleased, he acquiesced.

She bore him on her arm to the hotel door.

Camellia and Samir trudged behind.

"I'm famished," said Violet, bringing up the rear.

They found the party in a small banquet hall off the dining room. The Tour consisted of two dozen or so Protestants and their leader, the Rev. Mike Millet. Plus a Lebanese-Armenian guide, Jaffar Khorshandian. Everyone was just finishing dessert: *harisseh* with almonds.

"Mmmmm..." Angela sniffed. "Smells heavenly."

"Angela! Violet! We've been worried! Where have you... Byblos was out of this world... Come join us, Sisters!" A welcoming chorus rose like a hymn from the gathering.

"Off having adventures of our own!" Undaunted, as if having arrived with a mixed entourage were the most normal thing in the world, Angela took the room like a general. Sensing unstoppable force if not genuine authority, the maitre d' immediately saw to the setting of five more places.

Angela introduced Camellia and Samir. "And this is Marwan." Warmly. "*Dr. Marwan*," she amended.

Camellia sighed, envying Angela's tranquillity. At ease, among amiable acquaintances if not friends, Angela threw off strife and travail. If she still actively suffered from the minor chagrin, indeed the major inconvenience, of having gotten herself almost killed, it didn't show.

"So this is your son-in-law?" A white-haired lady wearing shell earrings leaned toward Angela. Her tone was somewhat conspiratorial. She pointed her fork delicately toward Marwan.

Angela gave a little sigh. "No."

The service began with European precision. First course: fish.

"What sort of fish?" Angela inquired, still enamored of smells. "Flounder? Mackerel?" Then, gourmet's curiosity giving way to scientist's inquiry: "What sort of fish live in Mediterranean waters?"

"Sea bass. Perch." Marwan ticked off several species. He sat beside Angela. He, too, was a gourmet. "My mother makes a marvelous *samak bi tahini*. Fish in sesame sauce. I think she uses haddock — "

"She must give me the recipe," Angela said. Then, thoughtfully, "This isn't haddock or bass."

"Let's ask." Violet's persistence on a given question could be measured according to its triviality.

"*Garcon!*" Violet cried three times.

The young man, arriving tableside, at first looked somewhat mystified as Violet employed pigeon English and hacking swimming motions, trying to get her point across. Under her energetic prompting, his amazement deepened. Finally a look of consternation crossed his insouciant, set face.

But when Violet reached for the automatic translator, for the machine, for technology as a way to end the impasse — Camellia intervened.

"Please, Violet — not now — that blatting will only unnerve him further — "

By then, thankfully, Marwan had translated the question into Arabic.

"Lebanese fish! Lebanese fish!" Hands raised to stave off further inquiry, or God knows what, the waiter fled to the kitchen.

"There's your answer, Muzz!" Giving a little squeal, Violet tossed her napkin triumphantly onto the table. "You're eating Lebanese fish!"

The other members of the Tour tittered, wiping *harisseh* from their lips with linen napkins. The blue-haired ladies chortled. They were joined in laughter by the one or two husbands who had managed to defy American-male mortality standards. (Perhaps their sense of humor had positively affected their lifespans; they sat noisily guffawing.) Three skinny teen-agers, clustered like daffodils, hid their braces behind cupped hands. All drew together in the odd intimacy of Americans abroad. They shared the half-embarrassed delight with which Americans view that which seems quaint but is merely indigenous. The banquet room could have been a church hall, they an audience for a National Geographic special, an epic on naked natives in some rare pocket of the earth. It remained only to smile gratefully when the lights came up. The violence into which they had inadvertently strayed served only to intensify their sudden kinship.

The waiter returned, bowing, bringing the late-comers their dessert, letting go of each plate as if it burned him. Glancing warily at Violet. Exiting efficiently.

Marwan grumbled at his obsequiousness. "An unadmirable but pronounced trait of the Lebanese — my countrymen," he observed to Angela. "You will find Lebanese servants in every country with a promising GNP. In Egypt, in Saudi Arabia, in Kuwait. Eager to serve. Eager for opportunity. Eager for the dollar. Eager to pimp."

To Camellia's astonishment, Angela did not look shocked. She didn't even blink.

Camellia was too hungry to eat. No doubt if she were in bed she'd be too tired to sleep. She was almost too tired to think. She picked at her *harisseh* without appetite. It hurt, missing Khalil. It hurt worse, being unable to clearly recall his face. His face! How to reconstruct it? The patrician line of his nose. The black intensity of his eyelashes. The swell of his lips. The smell of him. Memory blurred them. All that bound her to him was memory. An intensity of feeling. Passion. Love. Missing him. A vague but painful sense of urgency. Of mission. Equal parts longing and determination, deadened now by the knowledge that her own exhausting, foolish, futile foray in Lebanon had led her not one step closer to Khalil. Surely no one here could be of any help.

Here she was in Sidon and Khalil might still be in Beirut.

Had she learned nothing of the world, his culture? In fact, did not Abu Mousa stand a better chance of rescuing Khalil, simply by staying put? He was working behind the scenes, enlisting the help of the powerful, the well connected, waiting for word. Why, Abu Mousa might accomplish more simply by "being there." Abu Mousa had not plunged headlong, heedless, into a course of rash action. Abu Mousa had taken measured steps, designed to bring about Khalil's return. Guaranteeing, if nothing else, that Abu Mousa himself would "be there" alive and intact, if at some future point his presence were essential. Which was more than she could say about herself.

Would she *never* learn such art?

"Eat something, Camellia," said Angela. "The news in Beirut is ghastly."

"Is there a relationship? Between being well fed and disaster in the capital?"

"I'm finishing my plate," Violet pointed out.

"Thank heavens we're going to Baalbek tomorrow. Baalbek, I hear, is safe," said a lady from Lansing.

"Yes," murmured Jaffar Khorshandian, the guide. Lugubrious, he licked his fingers. "I must drive many miles out of my way, avoiding Beirut." He said this with an injured air.

The group was agog with rumor. The men settled back in their chairs; one lit a cigar. What would have been sports talk in America was war talk here.

In Beirut, rooftop snipers were shooting at any moving target — man, woman or child. The days since the massacre unfolded as predictably as the *muezzin's* call to prayer. This was the sequence: Mortars rain down on shoppers. Militias appear from nowhere. Street vendors pack and flee. Owners of small shops abandon them. Shoppers run for cover, parents shielding the vital organs of their children, young women folding their arms, supporting their breasts. All against a backdrop of breaking glass and spinning rubble. Chaos, then clean-up, a pattern repeated throughout the city.

"Holding a sector" came to mean "taking over a neighborhood." Street fighters clashed in the suburbs: Shiyaih, Dikwaneh and Ain Rumaneh.

Camellia's heart beat like the good wing of an injured bird. Could Khalil still be in Beirut? And what of Abu Mousa, Om Mousa and Tayta?

No one knew particulars.

"They say government authority has collapsed." The man with the cigar spoke with the detached interest of a hometown spectator in an out-of-town team.

"Life goes on." The Rev. Millet, seasoned by years of travel, had developed an air of continental resignation. Now, in Lebanon in the spring of 1975, it could be exploited. What other way was there to view the imminent collapse of Lebanon but philosophically? "Beirutis hold to their routines, moving in ever smaller circles, avoiding the 'bad' streets, detouring at the intersections where *other* people are shot." He traced a circle in the air, jabbing its center for dramatic effect.

The "Ain Rumaneh incident," as it was now called, had been a minor massacre by Middle East standards. But it appeared to have sparked a civil war.

Camellia thought: And I always believed other people were stupid. Leaders who, for example, profess to love peace, but bankrupt national treasuries arming themselves for war. And yet the populace tolerates their double-talk. I am no more far- sighted than they.

The scent of cumin and paprika wafted from the half-eaten food, reminding her of another meal. Beirut. So many clues! Lunch with Khalil and Marwan. She had been fascinated and enthralled. Both Khalil and the Beirut panorama intoxicated her. Even the lovers' spats were novel and gratifying. She had never before cared for anyone enough to fight with him. Water-skiers making lacy patterns in the Mediterranean, creating surf near the Hotel St. Georges. Heady stuff. She had hardly glanced at the nearby Hotel Phoenicia, though Marwan had pointed it out. It was open for business ... its first two stories boarded up.

Angela was still urging her to eat. "Yes, Mother." Mechanically, she forced a few forkfuls into her mouth. Angela was doing well. It doubtless took untold amounts of self-discipline for Angela to resist giving motherly, unsolicited advice. But Angela never wanted to be a nag.

The talk strayed to specifics of fighting: the implements, the shooters, the score.

"Why, they're firing automatic rifles right from the balconies."

"I saw a picture of a fighter in jungle camouflage — an ostrich-feather boa draped across his shoulders!"

"I hear half a dozen people have been killed."

"Half a dozen? No!" interjected Khorshandian the driver and guide. "Sixty at least."

Marwan said nothing. Khalil had provoked him to passion in Beirut. Goading him, trying to extract a commitment from him, Khalil had argued for the preservation of the status quo, which, in Lebanon, worked to the advantage of Christians. Marwan disagreed — passionately. "We must dismantle the archaic political system with its built-in factionalism — yes, even if the president no longer comes from the ranks of the Maronites," he had cried. "We must dethrone the *zu'ama*. We must cut the Gemayels, Franjiehs, Jumblatts — all the warring clans — down to size. We must wrest power from the monks and the imams. Banish them to monastery and mosque."

Now he sat subdued, listening to the Americans.

The lady with shell earrings had finished eating her *harisseh*. She exclaimed: "There's no fighting in Sidon! I think we should stay put."

"And miss Baalbek? The pagan temples?" The man with the cigar extinguished it in his water glass.

The Rev. Millet was blase. "We're as safe in Baalbek as here. The fighting is in the capital. There may be scattered clashes in Tripoli or Tyre — or Sidon, for that matter. But hardly likely in Baalbek. Dr. Marwan?" He looked to Marwan for corroboration.

Marwan considered. "Perhaps you will face a Syrian checkpoint on the Beirut-Damascus Highway. And, of course, you must take care not to stray too deeply into the hashish-growing territory of the valley. But I see no reason to cancel the trip if it is a valued part of your itinerary."

More debate. Some frightened tittering. A fervent objection or two. Then the majority ruled.

At first light the Tour would proceed to Baalbek.

And tomorrow, in Beirut, the bronzed bathers of the Hotel St. Georges would still be lying in the sun.

****

Sidon's shoreline arced into northern infinity, stretching into mists of fog. The sun had vanished brilliantly. Only pinks and purples remained. A chill wind swept from sea to shore. The palm fronds rattled and shook. City noises gave way to crepuscular buzzes and wing scrapings.

Birds, fast like Phantom jets, made a blurred V in the flinty sky. Low-flying clouds basked in moonlight.

Bobbing offshore, the boats looked naked. Nets dangled, empty. The fishermen were abed this night. Normally they took to the sea when sky and water melted into black. Today's news from the capital dissuaded them. After all, the memories of shooting and death were fresh. A former government official, Camille Chamoun, had attempted to wrest away their livelihood. Chamoun, with his corrupt plans to mechanize the fishing industry; with his corrupt foreign partner, the Proteine Company. The fishermen had rioted, and the plans had been scrapped.

A scampering sandpiper effortlessly dodged the glassy tongue of the waves.

Wanting solitude, Camellia had left Angela and Violet to prepare for tomorrow. They were reading up on Baalbek's ruins. She had left them behind in the lobby, chattering, visiting with their blue-haired ladies. Camellia would stroll along the beach, perhaps climb the crumbling turrets of the Castle by the Sea.

Still she could hear the old city. Static crackled on short-wave radios tuned to Beirut. Muted voices drifted from cafes. Somewhere, an engine sputtered.

Her feet crunched on murex fragments in the grainy sand.

The sea breeze moved like a rasp over the city.

The Castle by the Sea seemed to be waiting. It dominated the promontory, isolated, like aloof, deposed royalty. It straddled a spit of land bounded on three sides by slashing sea. Its narrow connecting causeway sloped, then dropped steeply, to where the waves thrashed against the sharp rocks below. Buffeted by the wind, Camellia clutched at her mohair sweater, extended an arm for balance, and headed down the causeway.

"*La'. La'.*" Two attendants sprang from behind a kiosk. They spoke in Arabic, quick and scolding. To her surprise, Camellia understood almost everything they said. The Castle was closed. She must vacate the peninsula.

"What do you mean it's closed? How can you close a ruin that's sat here for five centuries!"

Obstinate, they shook their heads, and the argument quickened, Arabic on their side, English on hers. The men's voices grew impassioned, as if the future of the hemisphere, or at least some significant point of latitude or longitude, hinged on their ability to keep a lone after-hours tourist outside the Castle gates.

When it became apparent they would not let her in, Camellia reached into her pockets and pulled out her money. Fortunately she had stuck several Lebanese pounds — along with her passport — into her pockets when she had changed from skirt into jeans. Apparently it was just the right amount of under-the-table payment for a favor of this magnitude. She was amazed and grateful when they took the money without question, pocketing it and opening the way, no longer threatening, suddenly suave.

She swung her legs over the moldering wall. General Patton had waved away the maps, the attendants. He said he didn't need maps or attendants to steer him to the site of an ancient battlefield. He said he could *smell* it.

Walls formed rooms which, vacant, echoed. Does a more desolate building material exist than stone? From a window she could see the saffron mists of the horizon. Close to shore, boats bobbed in sloshing water. Nets swung empty, like unfitted shrouds. The homes of Sidon were shuttered.

Movement. Behind her. Noise.

Marwan stood beyond the low wall.

The scent of orange and honeysuckle swirled in the night air.

"Why are you out — a woman alone?"

She had never heard his voice so brusque. What right did he have to be angry?

She flicked her hair out of her eyes. "I'm safe here. After all, men in this part of the world put women on pedestals. No one will lift a finger against me."

He frowned. Salt-moisture from the wet wind gathered in the furrows of his brow.

She added for good measure, "You have no right to follow me."

A smile flickered on his lips. "Your mother asked me to see what you — "

"My mother! You've been filling her head with myths. She might have been killed."

"Come back with me. You must be tired." His eyes gleamed above his triangular nose and square-cut jaw. His manner was understated and empathetic, almost gentle, the proper manner of a physician, like Marwan in Nabatiye, treating the young guerrilla. Then he grinned, shattering the mood. "You need sleep. There are monuments to see. Baalbek —"

"Do you think I have nothing to do? I'm not going!"

Infuriatingly, he smiled. "That's why I admire you. You're as determined as Aphrodite, who went to the pits of hell to rescue Adonis." He chuckled, crossing the low wall. "Unfor-tunately, Adonis didn't deserve it. He promptly went and got himself killed — by a wild boar, no less."

"How dare you compare Khalil to a pagan?"

"Who said I was talking about Khalil?" Ebullient, he took a breath; he might have been a general addressing new recruits. "While Europe withered in darkness, Arab scholars were compiling the great libraries. Al-Razi diagnosed smallpox and measles. Khawarazmi invented algebra. Biruni...."

"Postulated earth rotation 600 years before Galileo." She added angrily: "And the world still thinks of you as nomads."

Marwan compressed his lips. Sea lapped against shore, creating harsh rhythms to echo the strengthening wind. On the waterfront, lights twinkled in the black. "Did you know that once the people of Sidon set themselves ablaze — in their homes — rather than submit to a Persian king?"

She bent to scratch her legs. They itched where the salt had dried on them.

"Sidon's gardens flowered to the foothills." In the distance, the foothills flowed into mountains. "To the Phoenicians, the mountains *were* the gods. This coast was peopled north to the temple of Eshmun."

Camellia shrugged. "What's the relevance?"

"History is always relevant. When the remaining Jews left Tripoli — for Israel or Beirut, no one knows — they took with them everything of importance. Including their graves."

He turned away to watch the wind ride the waves.

"Look," he said softly. "The gulls dive like children in the froth."

The mist had thinned to swirls above the skyline.

Camellia sat straddling the cannon. "I don't know what to think of you."

"So." He took a breath. "Don't think."

Disheartened, preoccupied with her own dead-end thoughts, she shifted her weight forward, sitting hand to chin, elbow to rust.

She had not yet grown stiff when there came, from somewhere in the amaranth-scented gloom, the report of a gun. It sounded ordinary, like the "ploop" of a hoof pulled from muck.

After a startled silence, insects resumed their drone, sea-birds their cries.

Marwan said softly: "Will you hand me your handkerchief?"

Camellia opened her mouth. No sound came out.

Marwan was bleeding. He had been hit.

8

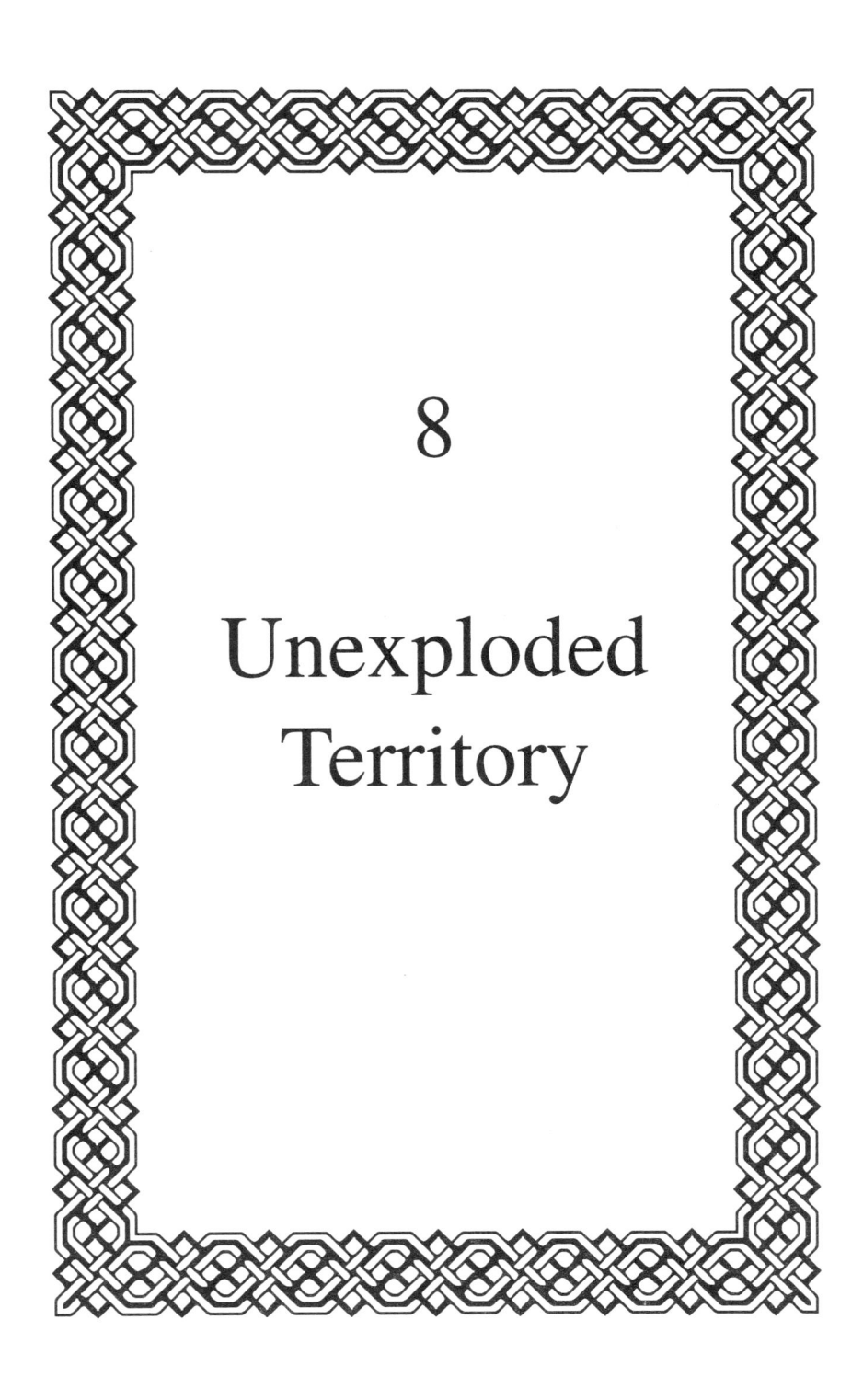

Unexploded Territory

*A*ll at once the night was filled with sound: the rush of waves and the lament of night creatures, and Camellia's voice, sounding metaphysical and thin.

"My God! You've been shot!"

My God, how dim-witted. It was all she could think of to say. So much for the belief that women are better than men in a crisis, an alleged fact she had read somewhere. Small, day-to-day predicaments supposedly drove women up the wall, compared with men — but give women a true catastrophe and they become useful, calm and utterly indispensable.

Camellia was more numb than calm. Mechanically, she brushed back her hair. "I don't have a handkerchief. All I have is my scarf. Even if it were sterile, we couldn't use it. It's prickly."

"Give it here."

Matter-of-fact, Marwan spat in the direction of the assailant. The shot seemed to have come from across the water. In that case, the gunman might never be found. A sniper could easily lose himself in Sidon. No doubt he was skulking, lost in shadows, in warren-like alleys. Or leaping roof to roof. Or padding like a cat to the foothills. "Son of a bitch."

Marwan moved away from the window. He sat cross-legged and rested his head against the stone wall. He didn't blink. She wound the scarf around his shoulder. She pulled it tight until the flow of blood nearly stopped.

"Loosen it," he said. "I don't need a tourniquet. Tourniquets are for severed arteries. This is a flesh wound."

She sensed testiness, a guarded anger, which had nothing to do with physical injury.

"Who ... who did this to you?"

"*Hiawanat*," he muttered, spitting again. He discarded the syntax of the Oxford man. His language was of the Arab. "They are animals. What do I need to know more than that?"

All at once she wanted more from him.

"Isn't it time you stopped behaving as if you were a disciple of St. Augustine? Aloof and above it all? It's your blood now, too."

"It could have been yours." He looked at her. After a moment, he continued, softly: "Do bullets have nationality or religion? Does any of it matter to the victim, once dead?" Nostrils flaring, he drew a breath. "Thank God it's my upper arm. If the bastard had hit my fingers, it would have ended my career. As a surgeon," he amended.

"I can't believe you!" Her voice cracked. Pain stood in her throat like dry food. "Are you crazy? Are you totally insane? You and everyone else is this bloody country? First Khalil is kidnapped. Then Angela is almost blown up. Now you've been wounded. Is there anything left of Lebanon except unexploded territory?"

Marwan leaned against the stone wall and drew a breath. With the coming of her anger, his dissipated. So, it seemed, had his energy. Only his eyes were expressive as he struggled to stand up.

"Help me walk."

"Here — your arm. Put it around my shoulder."

She supported his weight as best she could. Marwan wasn't tall. But he was solid, utterly compact, like a tank might look if designed by Honda.

She could smell him: blood; the salt spray of the wind; incongruous odors; sweat.

"Does it hurt?" she asked. She tried hard to put gentleness into the question. But she was guarded, too, and her voice sounded not concerned but cavalier.

Marwan reply was almost wistful. "Not nearly as much as it should."

****

"We — the Lebanese — have learned to live with death."

In Lebanon, everyone was a philosopher. This included Khorshandian, the bus driver, who was grappling with the steering wheel of the tour bus, guiding its groaning ascent into the Chouf Mountains toward Syria.

"*Wallah* they will kill each other until none of them is left."

"They," of course, were the Lebanese. In addition to philosophical depth, Khorshandian also claimed objectivity, because he was Armenian — born in Beirut of Armenian parents. He spoke repeatedly of the bigger picture, of things only he, an outsider, could see.

Five miles into the journey to Baalbek, Camellia began to wonder whether Khorshandian could see even the road ahead of him. His driving, like his philosophy, was decidedly seat-of-the-pants.

I can't believe I'm sitting here, she thought, close enough to Khorshandian to see tendrils of his hair disappearing into his collar as the bus took mile after mile of the winding road.

She shouldn't have listened to Marwan. She was here because of Marwan. The trip would take her mind off things, he had argued. Not only that, but she would be safer with the group. And Lebanon would be safer, if Camellia could keep an eye on Angela and Violet.

The logic of that was compelling. No telling what Angela and Violet might do, loose in the valley.

Grudgingly, she had agreed. Now, on the bus, she felt profoundly disconnected from the group.

At least she wouldn't miss any leads. Marwan would stay behind at Ein el Hilweh. Sherifa and Ramadan Zawq were now convinced that Camellia and her party were not spies, he said. Angela's nearly being killed apparently lent credibility to their innocence if not their mission.

Maddeningly, Marwan would only hint at the possibility of a breakthrough, or even that the Palestinians of the refugee camp might actually decide to help.

She had argued the point.

"They were hostile."

"They know you now. Therefore they trust you. It won't be long before they call you 'friend.'"

"They made me feel as if I had 'Ugly American' tattooed across my forehead. If that's friendship — "

"They met you. They listened. They cannot help but care." He wore a fresh shirt; the arm, now bandaged, showed no sign of injury. It was his left arm. Last night she had lacked the presence of mind to notice which side had taken the hit.

His tone became grim. "On the whole, the Arabs are easy to infiltrate. They are trusting. Too trusting. And emotional. They make penetration ridiculously easy for agents of the Israeli *Mossad*."

"Still — "

He put his right arm around her shoulder and gripped, hard. "You keep forgetting Lebanon is small. You can be anywhere you need to be within an hour or so. If anything turns up, I'll send Samir after you."

She pushed her Nefertiti bag deeper under her seat. It brushed against feet. Violet's feet. Violet sat directly behind.

"Give me space, will you?" Violet was petulant. Too excited to sleep, she had stayed up half the night, perusing guidebooks, memorizing pertinent facts. "I'm rereading everything on Baalbek."

Angela sat daydreaming. Her seatmate was the butterfly net, which hung out the window like a banner.

The Rev. Millet sat directly behind her. And behind him, row after row of bewildered-looking Americans: widows and widowers. A teen-ager or two. A honeymooning couple. The woman with shell earrings. Camellia was actually beginning to like them.

"Aargh!" she exclaimed under her breath. "Tours!"

The bus looked silly enough when empty, parked beneath Sidon's ornate balconies, intricate tiers and striking minarets. It looked even more ludicrous, laden with sightseers undeterred by impending civil war. One thing you could say about Americans — geopolitical controversy didn't faze them. The biggest dispute had been whether to pack a lunch or eat in the hotel.

By this morning, the faction which wanted to stay in Sidon seemed to have picked up strength. Not only were some members of the tour disinclined to visit Baalbek, but they also wanted to leave the country.

The Rev. Millet put down the revolt. There was no sense trying to leave, the willowy Episcopalian pointed out. The airport was still closed.

Regretfully, Khorshandian eyed the smooth coastal road to the capital. He sighed. Then he headed into Mount Lebanon with its narrow cliff-edged roads and hairpin curves.

"To avoid Beirut, we must shadow the river."

"Oh! The Dog River?" asked Violet, suddenly perking up. "Can we stop and see the caverns?"

"*Aasif.* Not the Dog River, but the Litani. The Litani has no caverns. It has only cool water — for all that it is strategically placed."

The Rev. Millet straightened up, shielding his eyes, straining to catch sight of the river. "The Litani is a natural boundary, they say."

Khorshandian nodded three times, signaling vigorous assent. "I am sure the Israelis will one day advance with the cry: 'north to the Litani'."

You can live to a ripe old age in America and never once talk politics, Camellia thought. Here, everyone is aware.

Violet, of course, would never be aware. She tried to change the subject.

"Baalbek!" she said with a titter, flipping through her guidebook. She exhaled grandly. "'The most colossal ruins of the Roman empire.'"

Angela tightened her grip on the butterfly net. "And to think!" she exclaimed absently. "Marwan was nearly killed by that assassin. What a relief the bullet only grazed him."

"*Wallah* the snipers have made Beirut unlivable," said Khorshandian.

The Rev. Millet shook his head. "And the news today is bad. Rockets exploding from quarter to quarter ... bombs tossed from passing cars ... More kidnappings...."

"The Phalangists may be ousted from the cabinet. *Wallah* I am happy to be Armenian. I don't care who wins."

For all that he distanced himself from things Levant, Khorshandian spoke like a true Lebanese. The emphasis was on "don't," in the "I don't care," his voice rising just slightly in pitch on the word. He drove like a true Lebanese, too — ten kilometers above the limit, twenty above safe.

The bus whizzed past homes which seemed to be scattered at random on the land like dice flung from a cup. Red-tile roofs topped snug cottages. Stone fences trailed them. Now she knew why Dr. Elias had called Lebanon "a country of paradox. Fragile yet rugged." Enthralled, his syntax had disintegrated; he could describe Lebanon only in fragments. "Zahle's intoxicating air, hanging gardens, waterfalls ... the desolation of the Anti-Lebanon ... the terrifying splendor of Byblos...."

The land she had imagined, listening to Scheherazade.

The Rev. Millet, thoughtful, tapped his forehead. She had never before noticed the scar. It cut, pencil-thin, from above one eye to the opposite temple. She wanted to ask, but didn't dare, whether he had been wounded on safari or attacked while preaching.

Like a psychiatrist who has undertaken the study of medicine to better understand his own neurosis, the Rev. Millet had become a man of God to better trace the footsteps of the son. Or at least that seemed to be the motivation for his wanderlust. He handed her a Bible opened to the Song of Songs.

His lips are as lilies, dropping liquid myrrh.
His hands are as rings of gold set with beryl:
His body is as ivory work overlaid with sapphires.
His legs are as pillars of marble, set upon the sockets of fine gold:
His aspect is like Lebanon, excellent as the cedars.

"Khalil," she said softly. She handed back the book.

The air grew thin, the slopes ever more desolate. As the bus spiraled upward, brown faded to gray. Earth became rock. Bushes clung to sand. A hawk foraged among bluffs. Soon there was only the sound of the belching muffler and the ping of Violet's chewing gum.

Then Khorshandian was leaning on the brakes, racing on the downgrade past more cottages and farms, and terraces like tentacles.

The Bekaa Valley was round and lush and fertile as a summer stew: alive with greens, yellows, rusts.

Khorshandian braked beneath an olive tree.

Violet elbowed her way out of the bus. Angela followed, net in hand; then Camellia, stretching her legs, sniffing the mountain air.

"Deir Al Baidar," Khorshandian announced, as though at least some of the credit for its pastoral beauty belonged to him. He stood beside the bus and lit up a cigarette. "Last stop before the Beirut-Damascus Highway."

He seemed indifferent to the vista of the Bekaa: Noah's plain, "where planting and harvesting had resumed after the flood," the Rev. Millet explained, "in a land abundant with trees, springs, herds, fish and grain."

She hurried to stand in the shade of pines, well out of range of Khorshandian's cigarette smoke and the Rev. Millet's continuing revelations. The pines afforded a damp shade, and she stood shivering. When a mustachioed farmer and his dimpled wife came toting a jug of lemonade, Camellia rejoined Angela and Violet in the sun.

"I'm thirsty as a horse." When it was her turn to drink, Violet took a swig of lemonade and swallowed appreciatively.

The farmer couple stood beaming — wheat-colored *fellaheen*, plump as the figs they passed around along with the cask.

"I just love Arab hospitality." Angela licked the sticky essence from her fingers, eyes crinkling as she smiled. "I just love the Arabs! It's such a shame to see everyone killing everyone else."

"Oh, Muzz!" Violet giggled. "You should have been a sahib's wife. You were born to shoulder the white man's burden."

The figs were velvety and rich, just as Khalil had said they would be. Camellia swallowed one whole and felt the cloying sweetness of the pulp slithering down her throat. The urge to quarrel was inexplicable and overwhelming.

"Do you see anyone killing anyone? We're in *Deir Al Baidar*. These are farmers."

Violet took up the challenge. "Marwan says it's all tied together. Refugees streaming north from Fatahland. Misery in the camps. Street fighting and the formation of an underground economy in Beirut. Farmers growing hashish in the valley."

Angela interjected, "Remarkable, the way that man draws parallels. Marwan — "

"To hell with Marwan! It's none of his business."

"I thought you were begging him to help," Violet said.

"I wasn't begging. Besides — " Camellia was unable to organize an explanation. "He's — "

"You know what your problem is?" Violet asked. "You're too cool. In control. Inhibited. You ought to let it all hang out."

"Oh?"

"All that anxiety bottled up inside.... Why don't you yell and kick and scream? It's healthy. Do you know what happens when I keep things bottled up inside?"

"Old people turn their hearing aids back on?"

Violet let out a whoop that was more exuberant than anguished. Her voice echoed across the valley.

The farmer couple took a step backward. Khorshandian dropped his cigarette.

"You idiot!" Camellia said. "I wouldn't be surprised if the Syrians started shelling."

Violet was implacable. "Maybe if more people shouted, fewer people would shell."

Which was so nonsensical that it made perfect sense.

Maybe I am too cool, Camellia thought. Maybe she paid a price for remaining in control. But she couldn't let go. Not yet. The sense of waiting was too strong. Of impending action. Control would be essential. Who could know what inner resources she would be forced to tap?

At last the bus resumed its jolting journey. At the highway checkpoint, Syrian soldiers peered suspiciously at Angela's butterfly net. After a minute or two they allowed the group to pass.

Khorshandian drove on, now in the shadow of Mount Hermon's frozen summit, where the fish fossils lay — 75 million of them, preserved with their backs arched upwards and mouths agape.

"Proof of the flood," the Rev. Millet said.

Camellia muttered: "As if anyone needs proof."

Baalbek's ruins were glorious. Granite glowed pink in the April sun, offering proof of grandeur and history and man's insignificance in space and time.

Camellia stood atop the grand staircase, craning her neck and squinting, dwarfed by the panoramic splendor that was everywhere. Porticoes and columns. Fountains and courtyards. Magnificent, dilapidated walls.

"Get a load of those pillars," Violet said.

There were vast temples, courts and colonnades. Steps carved from hundred-ton blocks. Altars and secret priestly cellas. Pillars fashioned of Aswan's rose granite. Pagan magnificence! The Romans had transformed Baalbek from a caravan crossing to a sanctuary of the gods. But if the silence shrieked "Athens" or "ancient Rome," other sounds whispered "Lebanon." The cries of child-hawkers. The snort of camels carrying tourists. The gossip of townswomen. The rustling wind.

Violet, enthralled with the riotous display, the gargoyles and architraves, was lost in heathen fantasy.

"Did you know that the blocks of the trilithon weigh more than a thousand tons each? No one knows who moved them or how."

Moving forward without waiting for an answer, she spotted statuary. Jupiter with whip and lighting bolt. "Do you suppose they still seek out virgins?"

"Doesn't everyone?" Camellia ran her fingers along a sun-warmed bas-relief etching.

"I'm steering clear of the altar of sacrifice — just in case. Hey — look at Muzz!"

In the hexagonal courtyard, Angela was scanning the azure sky and billowy clouds. She had spotted a butterfly.

"A *Gonepteryx* cleopatra!" she cried. "A Mediterranean Brimstone!" Her voice floated upward as she slashed at the panicked creature.

The Brimstone hovered near the altar, rocked by washes of net-stirred air. Then it flew toward the sun.

"Oh, dash! It had the most lovely orange flush on its forewings! Oh! Has it lit again?" She disappeared into the portico-studded esplanade in pursuit.

"See you." Violet followed. "I'm off to the Temple of Bacchus."

Camellia gave a little sigh.

The other members of the Tour gathered around the Lebanese guides, listening, enraptured, to the roll call of extinct civilizations. Then they moved forward, turning a corner here, entering an alleyway there, absorbed by the ruins as if by osmosis.

Soon there were only the sounds of patent leather slapping against ancient stone and rocks dropping as men kicked idly at shattered columns littering the courtyard. Giggles echoed and died into silence.

Alone, Camellia strolled through the courtyard with its fountains, rubble and darkened niches. She peered at the vast ornamentation. She perused, uncomprehending, the Greek inscriptions. Still, she was weirdly disengaged, as if caught in a dream too pedestrian to bring her awake.

She gazed absently at the busts of Victory and Mars. Intricate carved cupids. Eagles, winged genii and satyrs picking grapes. She knelt beside the basin in the courtyard of the acropolis. What must it have felt like, to be a virgin, to be washed? She moved hurriedly away. She took the chiseled steps of the monumental staircase three at a time. Picked her way through the rubble, the strewn capitals, the bits of triangular pediment and fragments of sculptured cornice awaiting restoration ... past the enormous blocks of granite that had never been set in place.

And wondered, for the first time, what she was doing here. Not just here in Baalbek. But in Lebanon.

Why was she here? In Lebanon? Pursuing a man perhaps she only thought she knew?

Though fear had never been part of the game, suddenly she couldn't shake the feeling of alarm. She had never believed anything except that Khalil was alive. That, momentarily, his captors would release him. That she could somehow engineer his release.

Now, everything was open to doubt.

They could have killed Khalil within minutes, hours. Days had passed. No word.

And if he were alive, if they released him — would the Khalil they returned to her be the same man snatched three days ago from the Green Line in Beirut?

Was she the same woman?

"You'll resume your *programme* of sightseeing," Marwan had predicted. With sudden intuitiveness, Camellia knew Marwan was right. That was exactly what Khalil would expect her to do.

And, with equal certainty, she knew she would be unable to carry it off. To take up with Khalil again, as if nothing significant had happened.

Walking aimlessly, paying little attention to her path or destination, she found herself standing in the shadow of the pillars. The six pillars of Baalbek, symbols of decayed grandeur. Mementos of sacred debauchery. Their entablature, now marred with gaping holes, carried only the fragments of once-grand sculpture. Such stupefying detail! Lions. Ovums. Pearls. Palmettes. The pillars. They had withstood the invading hordes, the Ommayads and the Mongols. They had survived earthquakes.

She reached out to touch them. The pink granite was warm. It was — alive.

Beyond the ruins, the Bekaa Valley stretched away: timeless, wheat-colored, like the barefoot farmers who threshed with horse-drawn threshers. Unshorn sheep pranced on the plain, fat as bushes. A steppe eagle hung on the wind.

An incoming taxi swirled dust.

Khalil?

She closed her eyes against the brilliance of the sun-baked plain, the land of northern Palestine, of figs and wine.

She hugged the column. It was too large. Her arms could not complete the circle.

"Exalting, isn't it?" the Rev. Millet asked.

She jumped at the sound of his voice.

"Look at the distant peaks, topped with spring ice. The Arabs give them names, like poetry: *Sannine. Makmel. Kahr el Qadib.*"

He sat down on the base of a shorn column. As usual, he didn't wait for an answer. "When Constantine put a stop to paganism," he continued, "these temples became churches. Later the conquering Arabs built mosques. Perhaps one day," he added dreamily, "new churches — "

"Why does new faith always trample on the old?" she cried.

A leaf spiraled to earth. Passages of clouds obscured the sun. The pillars poked into dim sky. Their granite sank into patterns of purple. Baalbek seemed impenetrable, full of shadows, pulsing with sanctified terror.

She moved to sit, chin in hand, near a bas-relief of maenads. The artist had trapped them in a moment of flux, wind-whipped veils fluttering.

Aggressive, she traced their outline with her finger. "And to lay the foundations of those churches, the Christians pillaged the monuments, didn't they? And first chance the Moslems got, they dismantled the holy of holies. Didn't they?"

"Faith!" he cried out — but not in answer to her question.

Muffled sounds — vague cries, the clatter of footsteps — rose from the courtyard. The Rev. Millet's response was instant. He recognized strife, whether of mind or flesh. Already, he was running toward the source of alarmed voices. An altercation? An accident? Had Angela, swiping blandly at butterflies ... ?

Dodging archaeological debris, Camellia ran, too. When she reached the top of the staircase, she paused.

Angela's voice arrested her. A lilting soprano:

"Geronimo! A Two-tailed Pasha! Higher! Higher! That's it ... now strike!"

Damn these steep, tiny steps!

The Rev. Millet was already halfway down. Camellia took the steps three at a time.

There — the courtyard. Half a dozen people clustered at the altar of sacrifice. Treacherous steps! Angela in the middle of it all. More steps. Now *she*, Camellia, was halfway. But why the urgency?

The Rev. Millet kept running.

Camellia laughed aloud in relief, slowing her descent. What foolishness! No one seemed particularly panicked or incensed. Violet, smiling, waving her arms. And Samir ... Samir?

What was he doing here?

He was perched atop the crumbling altar wall, one knee lodged in a crevice, a sneakered foot resting on an outcropping of rock.

He wielded the net as if it were a scimitar and he, Harun al-Rashid. With a deft swoop, he snared the Pasha.

"Samir?" she hollered.

He jerked his head, saw her, grinned in recognition.

"Khalil — !" he cried — still grinning — and Camellia knew instantly that she had erred.

He held the net aloft in triumph, but already he had begun to wobble. His grin became a grimace. He stuck out a leg. Balance escaped him.

"*Ism'allah!*" someone gasped.

When astonishing things happen, time grows warped. Simultaneously, it races along like the bright lights of delirium; drags like the slow days of convalescence. Samir's fall was a blur. His expression of disbelief could have been caught in a painting.

Peripherally, other details registered, such as Angela's face, upturned like a freckled seed-bed ... the wild flapping of the imprisoned butterfly ... the cascade of dislodged granite.

"Jupiter! He broke his neck!" Violet cried.

And time returned to normal.

Samir, curled up at the altar base, gripping his leg, was conscious.

Angela rushed to cradle his head.

The Lebanese guides, ineffectual, tried to chase everyone away.

Violet ran shrieking for help.

Earthbound, forgotten but alive, the Two-tailed Pasha lay ensnared in the net as the sun glinted silver on its turquoise-and-burgundy wings.

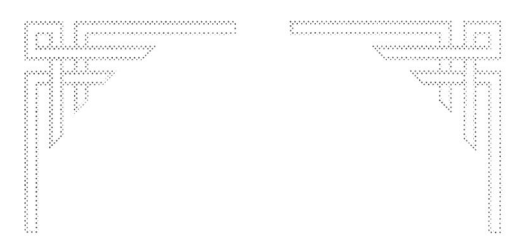

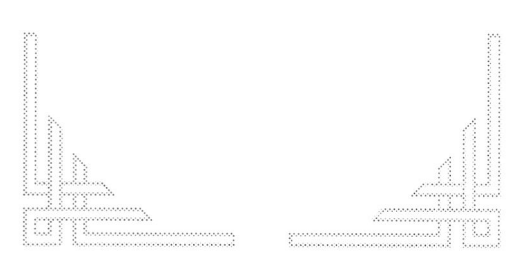

9

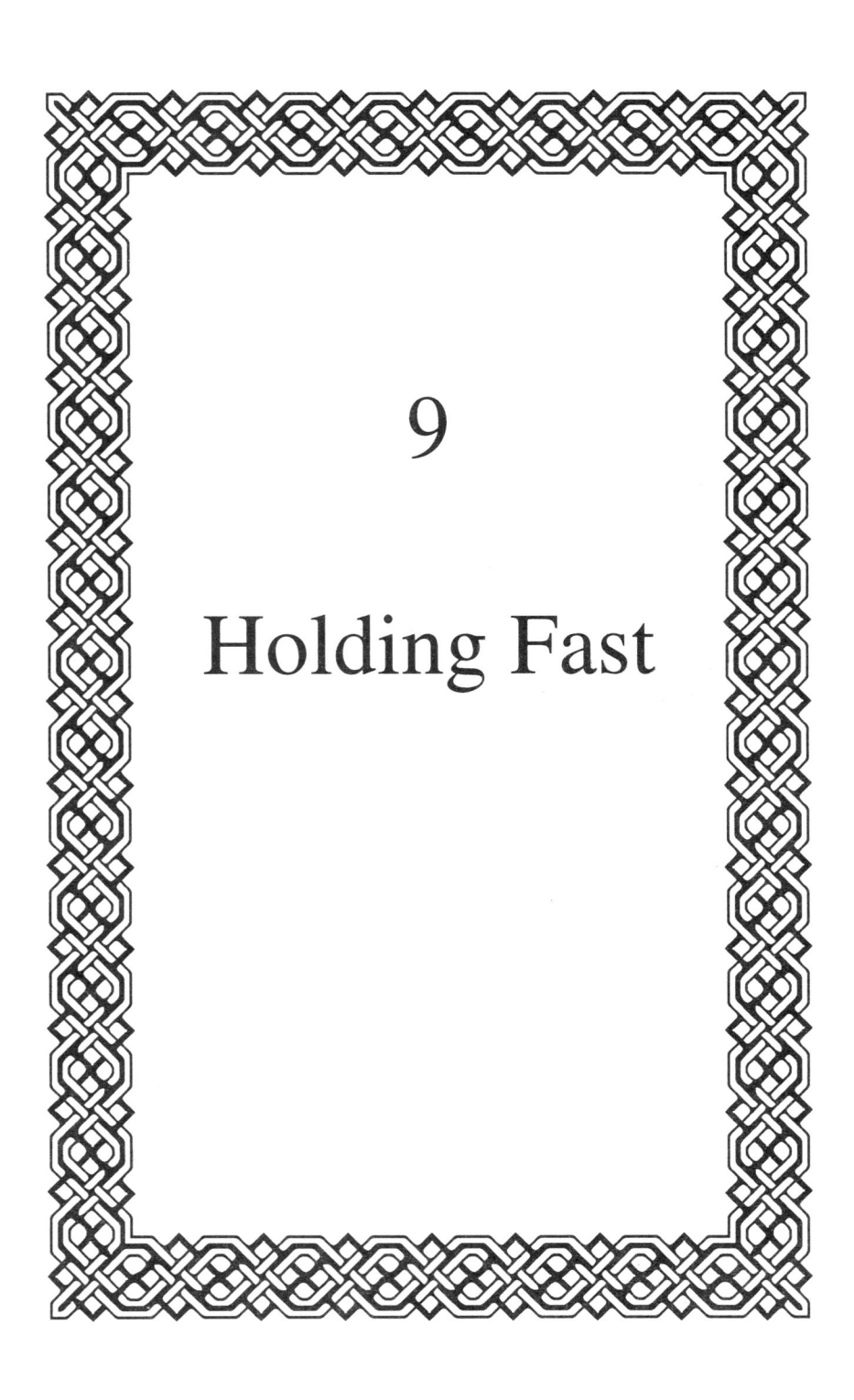

Holding Fast

*A*fter Samir was carried to the home of the local doctor, who bound his leg in a temporary splint, Angela and Violet quit the Tour for good. An affectionate exchange of good-bys ... handshakes with the Rev. Millet.... Tears and hugs for the ladies who had become their friends.... A jaunty salute from Khorshandian....Then Angela stowed her butterfly gear in the trunk of the cab to make ready for the return trip. It was Ahmed, of course, who had driven Samir to Baalbek. Now everyone piled back into the black Mercedes: destination Sidon.

The weather was a relentless drizzle, like nothing Camellia had seen in Lebanon. Ahmed, hunched over the wheel, boxed the gearshift and tattooed the horn. Window wipers squeaked.

Rain blurred the distances. The mountains, a suffocating mass of greenery, swam in ghostly purple. And inside the damp cab, everyone sat in what seemed a microcosm of dreary Lebanon.

Up front, Angela cradled her lovely winged specimen. In back, side by side, Camellia and Violet supported Samir's leg.

The painkillers were strong. Samir was already asleep.

"I hope Khorshandian doesn't wreck the bus." Camellia sat next to the window. A steady stream of mud spewed past, some of it hitting the glass.

With her premier worry alleviated, she could afford to think about other people's travails.

Angela, who also reacted to strain by voicing doubts, said, "I hope Ahmed knows the way. Samir will be too woozy to help with directions."

Ahmed, oblivious, smoked as he drove.

Violet was unaffected by weather or strain. "Head west toward the Mediterranean. I don't see how we could possibly miss it."

Violet, of course, was still in a snit over having been denied the choicest part of the tour. The Tour was traveling north to visit the sole remaining site of Lebanon's fabled cedars: Bisharre. She and Angela had missed Bisharre their first day in Lebanon — the day they had arrived at the flat.

When it came time for the Tour to depart from Baalbek, everyone spoke so wistfully of the cedars, the Rev. Millet had allowed consideration of a second visit. After all, street fighting still raged in Beirut. Visiting the National Museum was out of the question.

Khorshandian had evaded responsibility. "Americans cannot do anything without debating the pros and the cons," he observed. Magnanimously, he allowed the Tour members to argue and vote. It was unanimous: They would return to Bisharre, home of the cedars, and burial cavern of Kahlil Gibran. Angela, in a justification that had seemed to make perfect sense at the time, offered: "Gibran is, after all, the world's most widely read poet, excepting Shakespeare."

Naturally Violet felt deprived.

"Really, there is no choice," Khorshandian had said once everyone agreed. He had held up a newspaper as if it were an edict. In Beirut, the aftermath of the massacre was being played out. The papers published a photo of the bullet-sieved bus: Exhibit A of the "Ain Rumaneh incident," where so many men had died. The bus sagged on its tires. Bullets had shattered glass and rent the aluminum sides. Eerily, the headlights were still intact.

Still the fighting raged. Phalangists faced ouster from the cabinet. Palestinians, martyrs of the moment, and therefore avengers of the moment, smashed neighborhoods with rocket-propelled grenades. In the streets, armed civilians relieved policemen of their guns.

Radio stations canceled news of traffic jams to warn against a more immediate peril: kidnappings. And murder.

Storefronts shattered under the fists of fighters who preferred larceny to combat.

Militiamen wore hoods.

Israeli jet pilots flew in, broke the sound barrier, and left.

Anxious and elated, Camellia tensed her shoulders. She stretched her legs, straightening them until they dug into Ahmed's seat in front of her.

"Stop wiggling!" Violet said.

Samir's eyelids fluttered.

"The way we banged on that doctor's door!" Angela exclaimed, remembering. She reached back to dab at Samir's forehead with a Kleenex. "He must have thought the civil war had come to Baalbek!"

"Did you notice how readily he let us in?" Camellia asked. "Right in the middle of his parlor?"

"And Arab children are a delight! So helpful. Did you see his oldest boy draping the bandages? Then they spread them with goo, some sort of quick-drying plaster warmed over a lamp...."

Violet rolled her eyes. "You two are falling in love. With a country."

"Was it Dr. Elias who told me — 'the Arabs are an easy people to love'?"

"I think," Angela said dreamily, "Lebanon would be a nice place to retire to."

"Retire?" Violet asked.

"There's something incredibly appealing about a culture that respects the aged," Angela said.

"Do what you like," said Violet. "Just make sure you sign over power of attorney and leave me your car keys."

Camellia was leaning against the window, watching mud. Violet nudged her.

"What are you going to do?"

"Convince Khalil to take me to Switzerland."

Ahmed, every time he lit up a cigarette, would first offer one to Angela, Camellia, and Violet. He did this whether it was his first cigarette or his twentieth. No matter that they consistently refused. This time, when he jabbed the pack at Camellia, she accepted.

It was unfiltered. The air, already stuffy, became rank with exhaled smoke.

The road was a slick silty ribbon. A truck stood mired in the ooze. Ahmed slowed, muttered something, then accelerated, scowling. Deepening as he concentrated, the lines of his forehead were like gashes above his pitted cheeks.

Angela and Violet, having exhausted the topic of where Angela might spend her golden years — and forgotten the topic of where Camellia would settle — sat back to endure the immediate journey.

Swallowing the last breath of smoke, Camellia flung the cigarette out the window. Tayta's worry beads, at the bottom of the Nefertiti bag, were close at hand.

Ya Tayta! she thought, rolling the glistening mother-of-pearl between her fingers. Such peace in the rhythm, the muted clacking of the orb. *Baraka!* If only Tayta's *baraka* could infuse her — Camellia. Then maybe she would know the way to straighten out her life.

Wisdom. Charm. Contentment. These were the elements of baraka acquired by Tayta. I could wrap myself up in black, Camellia thought, and be old and wrinkled, content and loving, dispensing wisdom to the tribe. She tried to imagine Khalil grown old: laughing, crossing his thin legs, blowing cigarette smoke in her face. She couldn't.

It was dusk. Sidon's dusk.

"I'm going to miss it," she murmured. "Sunset on the Mediterranean — "

The play of fuchsia and mauve against gray sky ... the glint of sun on minarets ... the festive twinkle of lights at downtown cafes ... the descent of the sun into watery cavern ... the emergence of the net of stars.

The refugee camps.... They lay like unclaimed corpses at the edge of the city.

The road became flat. It curved into the thickening groves near town. The trees misted the night air with citrus ...

Sidon with its sea-scent and minarets ...

And perhaps Khalil.

****

The offshore wind was brackish and hot. It tossed the sea grass. It blew tendrils of Samir's hair into her eyes.

They walked side-by-side along the beach. At least Angela and Violet walked. Camellia and Ahmed hobbled, Samir limping between them, clinging to them.

"Ho!" Marwan cried. "Over here."

He was sitting cross-legged, watching the sea. He had been waiting.

"*Sah*. You made it." He stood up.

His voice was unnaturally hearty. Mocking. Distant.

"Where is Khalil?" Camellia asked.

"Another casualty?" Marwan reached for Samir.

Camellia slackened her grip on Samir's upper arm. Though Ahmed had taken most of the weight, still Samir was heavy. Her arm was utterly devoid of feeling or strength.

"You're heavier than you look, kid," she said.

Samir was small, well muscled. And extremely sensitive. It seemed to distress him — the thought of having caused her discomfort. He watched her as she rubbed her arm.

"Don't worry!" Marwan said. "You just need to get the blood running again."

"You seem to have a way of telling me what I need."

Marwan had already eased the burden of Samir away from Camellia, sliding Samir's arm away from her, edging her away.

"I've got him. Let go," he told Ahmed.

He pinned Samir's wrist and encircled Samir's slim waist with his other arm, lending support, until Ahmed's help was no longer needed, either.

They hadn't walked far before Camellia exclaimed: "You were so mysterious about the location of the Palestinians in Sidon. A hidden staircase, you said.... Here are the steps, in plain sight."

They were obscured only by foliage. They plummeted to unseen depths, buried in brambles in the sea-orchard, within walking distance of the beach. The Castle by the Sea was visible. Within yards of this place, Camellia had cut her foot on a murex shell. But that was yesterday. It seemed ages ago. The nick had not yet had time to heal. It was like a paper cut between her toes. Sand and sea water irritated it.

Marwan glanced at Samir who blinked like a drowsy cherub with thick eyelashes.

"What did you do?" Marwan glanced at Camellia. "Kill the messenger?"

"I would never harm a messenger bearing joyful news."

"You'll never guess what happened." Violet's voice was a trilling soprano.

"Muzz had spotted a butterfly and — "

As Violet's recounting continued, Marwan threw open the iron grille that barred entry to the steps. He paused at the threshold.

When Violet finished, he turned to Camellia.

"Are you through with Ahmed? Maybe he wants to go."

"Of course." She should have thought of that. "There's no sense waiting for tomorrow to settle up." She handed Ahmed the remainder of her Lebanese pounds without counting. Adding quickly, "Thanks, Ahmed. For everything."

Ahmed had been watching, nonplused, like a grandfather witnessing new behaviors in his offspring, behaviors he can neither change nor fully fathom. Now he said, in Arabic, translated by Marwan: "I will spend the night in Sidon. Should you need me tomorrow, I will be ready."

"So many things to settle ... I suppose we'll have to call Om Mousa and Abu Mousa, if there's an open telephone line ... "

Angela, fishing in her purse, came up with some gifts for Ahmed: three packs of Winstons, a disposable lighter and a pocket treasury with color photographs, *Insects of the World*. Later, drawing from her trunk, she would refill her purse. One of the reasons Angela liked to overpack was that she always liked to be well stocked with gifts.

"I can almost *sense* Khalil," Violet said.

Marwan's footsteps had begun to echo.

Camellia hurried after him, acutely conscious of her appearance: damp blue jeans, sweaty skin. She tried to smooth her hair. She blinked, adjusting to the dimness.

The steps were wider, coarser than the dainty chiseled ones at Baalbek.

"It rained all the way." Her voice was eerily resonant. "But here it's heavy and close ... "

"It's the gathering storm," Marwan said. "It won't break."

"Where are we? In a fallout shelter? A cavern? Something modern ... earth-bermed?"

"Ruins," Marwan said. His tone was clipped. He was awkward with her, like a marsupial whose offspring keep wandering away. He adjusted Samir's wrist to give him better balance. "A Turkish prison. Abandoned. Refugees lived here once. Now the guerrillas..."

She seemed to have lost power to discern. Refracted light shadowed walls deflecting sound. She heard laughter — or was it a pneumonic cough? And the Arabic banter of friends — or was it an interrogator's question? Was the steady "tock" that of a typist, or a news wire, or some sort of dull torture? Even the smells were wrong. She seemed to be heading away from the shore, but the sea-scent was stronger here, a faint aroma unwashed by wind: the smell of sweat after dark.

"Watch the last step. It's crumbling. We don't need another accident. I don't need another patient."

Camellia gave a little gasp. "Another patient? Is Khalil hurt?"

"Khalil is fine."

She sidestepped just in time to keep Marwan from treading on her toe. Wondering why she felt guilty, she asked: "Well, how's your arm?"

"So-and-so."

Abruptly, he stopped before a lighted doorway.

"Khalil?" She clasped her hands together. "Is he here? Really here? Please — Marwan — can you distract Angela and Violet? Just for a moment. Just for — "

Marwan looked at her. Momentarily, his eyes gleamed. Fondness? Envy? Derision?

He turned away, back toward Samir, and, bumping and shuffling, continued down the corridor until he crossed the threshold of a different cell.

****

Khalil sat on a stool. He was relaxed, like a tiger between kills.

A high, tiny window admitted night air.

"Hello, my love." He was smoking Rothmans.

"Khalil! My God! You're thin ... pale ... "

The planes of his face ... the high cheekbones ... black eyebrows like upswept wings. Khalil!

She bounded into his arms, almost knocking him off the stool. She didn't care. "Who'd you have to bribe to get those fancy cigarettes? Mmmmm...."

She kissed the hollows of his cheeks. His face was dirty. Blue thumbprint bruises. She made a quick assessment: He was thin but OK. She buried her face against his bony chest.

He hugged her with one arm. The other held his cigarette aloft. He looked like a spent lover — aloof and unrepentant.

"You're safe!" she murmured again.

Kissing her on the forehead, he subtly disengaged himself. "Of course I'm safe."

"You're free!"

"By the help of your friends." Now she heard the edge in his voice.

"Everyone was kind! Do you disapprove? What else was I to do?"

"With their help," he repeated. His eyes glimmered above his tight jaw. "Who have you been with? What have you been doing?"

"What women in love do." She stared at him. "Looking for you. What's wrong?"

"Nothing." He stubbed his cigarette out on the stone floor. "Nothing will be wrong. Once we return to Beirut."

"Beirut? I thought maybe Ann Arbor ... Europe ... Or if you insist on staying in the Arab world, then Cairo — "

My God, she thought. I'm beginning to sound like Angela.

Kneeling, she flung her arms around him again. The biggest bruise was at his temple; she kissed it softly.

"Let's not make any decisions. Are you really free? Let's stay here — in Sidon, for awhile. We can walk on the beach. Lie in the sun. Pick murex shells out of the sand...."

He inspected his fingers. There was a hangnail. He bit it off. "I suppose they have shown you papers. Evidence to convict me of God knows what."

"Papers? Why would they show me papers? No one has...." Her voice trailed off. "The nights were cold without you. Tell me —"

"It will be interesting." A voice intruded, feminine and brittle. "To hear what he will tell you."

Sherifa. From the corner of her eye, Camellia saw her, standing apart from the door, stiff-spined, with the hard, willowy grace and single-minded expression of the fanatic or athlete.

Camellia stood up awkwardly.

"Though it hardly matters what his public story is. The Maronites would pimp for the devil if he'd give them Beirut." Sherifa tossed her hair from her eyes with a contemptuous flick of her finger. She sauntered closer to Khalil. "Tell me: what is it like to kiss Israeli feet?"

Rigid, gaunt, Khalil lifted his head. "Is any price too high a price for peace?"

"Peace without rights is not peace!"

Camellia looked from one to the other. "What are you two talking about?" she asked. "What are you trying to prove?"

Neither answered. Then they began to speak — but not to Camellia.

Sherifa's words tumbled out accusingly. Khalil countered with measured phrases. Camellia recognized familiar words in the clash of Arabic. Names. Nationalities. Political parties. Dates. Anniversaries of war. The cornerstones of any Middle Eastern argument.

At last Sherifa broke into English. "Partition will never work. It is the inspiration of idiots."

"Partition?" There had to be a way for Camellia to enter the conversation.

Almost reluctantly, they remembered her. Khalil's eyes looked blue-gray in the filtered light.

"The package — " Camellia tried again.

"It was quite comprehensive." Sherifa answered for him. "Your fiance and his friends left nothing to chance. More than papers: Maps. Budgets. Even an artist's rendering of a new capitol building," she said smugly.

Camellia tried to absorb details. But at this point even catching the drift took great effort.

"Are you linking Khalil with — "

She couldn't finish the question. She couldn't ask: with foreign governments? With the CIA?

"With anyone he thinks would deliver what he asked: Beirut for the Christians."

Khalil responded in Arabic. But Sherifa overrode him in English.

"We have long known that Israel wants Lebanon partitioned." Sherifa raised her hands palms upward; her sculptured nails glittered. "After all, what better justifies a Jewish state than a Christian state next door? Especially if that state is inherently weak?" She shrugged in aggrieved resignation. "But for the architect of this Zionist plot to come from the Arab world? *Ya* my brother," she finished emphatically, nodding to Khalil. "You are not worthy of being called Arab."

Camellia blinked. Heightened awareness did strange things. It diverted one's attention to small but fascinating items. The run in Sherifa's stocking. The red eyes of the spider on the wall. Crescents of sweat beneath Khalil's arms blotting his shirt.

"You — " she began stumblingly. "I — I don't doubt that someone, somewhere, is pushing some scheme called partition. But — Khalil? A man you abducted off a street corner in Beirut? You're making him a scapegoat."

"It is more than a scheme." Sherifa, not easily sidetracked, was still talking about partition. "It is a complete plan. The Shi'ites would be given the valley ... the Druse the mountains ... He — Khalil — had dotted the i's, as you say in America. Every last detail, down to the expulsion of the Palestinians." Then, after a pause, "Khalil has spoken quite freely of this."

Camellia drew a breath. "What makes you think the Israelis are behind it? What makes you think they even care?"

Sherifa smiled. "Why don't you answer her, Mr. Phalangist?"

"The Phalangists...." Camellia cut in. Again, it took great concentration just to repeat key words. What little concentration she managed to gather was shattered by cold dismay of growing comprehension. The angriest her father had ever gotten with her was when she had discovered a leak under the sink. She had quickly closed the closet door, put the leak out of her mind, and left the mess to be dealt with by her mother. Because of water left to stand, the floor had rotted. Never again had she given in to the temptation to dodge a problem.

With renewed energy, she asked: "Is that why you approached Marwan? Did you approach others who were uncommitted, influential? Did you need their support?"

"He will tell you nothing." Sherifa's laugh was abrupt as the sound of wind chimes, bitten off. She edged toward the corridor. "He will satisfy you with excuses. Perhaps an Arab proverb. I have already heard several. _The falcon never struggles when he is caught._"

She did not look back over her shoulder. The tap of her heels faded and died.

Khalil said immediately, "It is not what it seems."

"It?"

Still seated on the stool, he swiveled to face the wall. He lit another cigarette.

"Then how much is true?"

Rings of smoke coiled like adders to the window.

He still wouldn't look at her. But he smiled. "On a scale of one to ten?"

She scratched her head; nothing had prepared her for this. She had anticipated relief. Reunion. Joy. Questions. Maybe gentle admonitions.

But this? He was holding fast to the silence as stubbornly as she was holding fast to their love.

Weariness fogged her brain and slowed her speech. What welled up in her heart felt like violation and betrayal. She furrowed her forehead in concentration. But in the end she could cast the question only in political, not personal, terms. She couldn't ask, Why did you do this to me?

"Would you let Israel take Lebanon — north to the Litani?"

He didn't answer.

"For whom did you work?" Her tone grew heated. But the words strung themselves together in an odd way, strangely formal. She twisted her fingers together but the purse straps got in the way; creature of habit, she still carried the Nefertiti bag everywhere. Inside it, silk shirts cushioned worry beads. "How much of what happened is your responsibility?"

He sat, hands in pockets, legs crossed at the ankles. His eyes were opaque, unblinking. There was a word for the set of his face: insouciant.

He had already ground the second cigarette into the stone.

He lifted his palms in a Levantine gesture of innocence. "You assume something has happened. What has happened?" he asked with inarguable authority and, shrugging, turned back to face the wall.

****

She bounded up the stairs. Outside, in the night sky, there was salt in the wind. Salt on her face. Wind dashed away tears.

On the beach, the water broke in passionate swirls. Even the ocean was different here, the Arab ocean: sensuous and swelling. It was like Arabic music in which nothing distinct is heard, only embellishment and ornamentation, and endless octaves wound around melodies; euphoric shadings. The artist achieves *taksim*, the trance from which all genuine artistic effort springs; without it the artist is a fraud. The ocean — what a powerful *taksim* its creation must have inspired!

She ran, panting, looking over her shoulder, slowing like a fox barking to baying hounds. She still would only half-admit: She wanted Khalil to follow her. To stop her. To argue. To do anything but be silent, to put himself beyond her reach.

She ran toward the causeway to the Castle by the Sea. Her shoes thudded in packed sand.

The surf frothed like a rabid tongue. Crimped and latticed clouds hung like lanterns strung along dead lakes. Moonlight created a dappling effect on the ruins. The air seemed glazed with the hint of the onrushing storm.

She, an old hand, bribed the guards efficiently, with finesse. She ran away from them before their ritual words of protest died on the wind.

She climbed over the low wall and stood, catching her breath.

And was astonished when someone climbed in after her.

"You seem to have adapted quite well to local customs. Bribery, unfortunately, being one of them."

"It's really no different from a tip." She turned, expecting Khalil. "Oh." Her voice fell.

It was Marwan.

She made no attempt to project warmth. "You missed your calling. You should have been a *mufti* with a cane, patrolling the *souqs*, rapping people on the knuckles for not saying their prayers."

"You shouldn't be alone." The voice was heavy. Gruff. Contrite.

"I'm not alone. Not any more."

He spoke quickly, anticipating being contradicted: "I am happy for you. Really ... *Bism'allah*. I can't say it in English."

He moved away from her to stand at the window. The moon outlined him, giving him an evanescent aura. In silhouette, the small bulge of his shoulder bandage showed.

A light drizzle. Droplets trickling down her neck. She squeezed closer to the wall.

"At last. The rain," he said.

"Does your arm hurt?"

"The pain does not overpower me."

His eyes lingered on the thrashing waves. "Look at the sea," he murmured. His voice was full of bewilderment and desire. He could have been a Crusader, ammunition spent, but hope still fresh. "So beautiful. And yet ... this is the very spot where French corvettes carted off the richest of Sidon's treasures ... the very beach from which young Palestinians launched suicide missions to sure death...."

"Why do you have to make everything sound so profound and universal? People are motivated by self-interest." She dug her foot into the sand.

He smiled, amused, seeming to enjoy contemplating what he would say.

But before he could press some inarguable philosophical point, she asked: "Is Khalil free to go?"

When he didn't answer soon enough: "Has Ramadan Zawq released him?" She rubbed a speck of sand from her eye.

"They will release him. But only because that is the best way to humiliate him."

Marwan bit his lower lip, then smiled. "We Arabs value some things more than ... our own individual lives. Americans don't understand that."

"You know as much about Americans as I know about — about camels."

Infuriatingly, he laughed. "I was 21 before I saw a camel." He added, "Much older when I first encountered an American."

She turned on her heel. "I came here to be alone." She called back over her shoulder: "So long."

"Americans. Always running."

She stood pigeon-toed in the sand. Dissatisfied in some indefinable, fundamental way.

"Tell me — what would you have done? Would you have endorsed Khalil's proposition? Given him what he asked? Supported the partitioning of Lebanon?"

He didn't answer.

"Are you afraid of truth?"

He stood, immobile as a stone pillar, watching her.

"Maybe Lebanon — " he began at last. "Maybe it exists only in our minds. Partition ... Look. We have it now. Christians, Moslems, Maronites, Shi'ites, Druse — all of them. They have divvied up Beirut. As if land were negotiable, a commodity to be bought or seized."

Suddenly it seemed urgent that she defend Khalil. "The Maronites wanted more. What's wrong with that?"

"Khalil? Did he want more?"

The question lingered. Marwan was always a step ahead of her. But she answered him as truthfully as she could: "Like everyone else, he wished for the joys only the future can bring."

Marwan was unpersuaded. "For Lebanon as it is," he said, "the future can hold only destruction and sorrow. So we look at life, and take from it what we can."

There was nothing more to say.

The silence carried an odd presaging quality — a quality Camellia, tingling with unpleasantness, slowly recognized. It was like tension between two people who dislike each other but suddenly realize an attraction. It was like the edginess sharp intuition can bring when the subject intuited causes pain.

It was the moment between release of firepower and vibration of stone, of earth, of walls. Of things that resisted and withstood. The moment before the terrible, tangible sibilance of jets screaming barely overhead.

"Down," she yelled. Experience gave her authority. She flung herself into the sand. Illogically, she thought: So that's why they made us read Henry James and Edith Wharton in high school. So we wouldn't be shocked when irony occurs. Then, more hysterically: "They've come to kill us."

She lay sloped, cradling her face protectively with her hands. She listened for the distant whine and crash. The sea-grass tickled her nose.

Marwan dropped down to his knees. "If they'd come to kill us, we'd be dead," he said dryly.

Low noises. Reverberations, distant and scattered.

Then she felt nothing but the whipping wind and Marwan's hungry kiss, redolent of the sea and sweat. His beard was scratchy and soft; his lips held the intoxicating earthy coolness of coming rain. The embrace was brief, heady, intense as a gathering spirit. Then he pulled back, averting his eyes.

It had begun to rain. He shielded her from the downpour with his jacket, pungent with leather-smell.

The jets had come and gone.

"Marwan ... "

She wiped her eyes with the back of her hands until she could no longer tell whether tears or rainwater ran in rivulets down her face. She shook the sand from her hair.

"Here's to your ... your *baraka*."

The wind hit her with a salty slap as she ran. Away from the empty fishing boats. Back to the beach and the Turkish ruins.

Back to Khalil.

****

Morning broke, a vast panoply of sky and sun. Outflung spikes of color burst like anemones on a coral reef. The Mediterranean frothed where fish broke the surface. Breezes tickled the sea-grass. The sand glittered with green and purple shell-specks.

Fishing nets gleamed like dew-dripped webs against the pink stone of the Castle by the Sea.

When the *muezzin* erupted with the half-sung rhythms of the call to prayer, the city was further mesmerized, held in momentary mystic thrall, prodded gently from somnolence.

Camellia inhaled the scent of wild cyclamen and gave a little sigh.

The *adhan* wavered, dying on the wind. Then it was gone like the first day of spring.

She felt Khalil's hand on her arm.

"I'm ready." She smiled absently, glancing at him through half-closed eyes.

A woman's voice drifted from the souq; a housewife haggling over eggplants.

Khalil was in charge. He had summoned Ahmed who, as luck would have it, had kept his word and spent the night in town. Destiny, Violet opined. Camellia figured Ahmed wasn't ready to return to Beirut, where peace had not yet broken out.

Khalil, brisk, had pointed to the road to Beirut. He had given terse directions. Camellia hated to break the party up. It seemed unsettling, to depart at different times, though for the same destination.

"There is not room enough in the car," Khalil pointed out.

So Ahmed sped away, with Violet and Angela in the back seat, their belongings in the trunk.

Where were they going? To Khalil's parents' summer home. The home in the mountains Camellia had heard about. And would soon see.

Marwan had made the phone calls. Khalil had hung up in disgust. The operator was an idiot. The lines were bad. No answer in the flat. Marwan kept trying. Was there a neighbor, a friend? Anyone who could locate Om Mousa and Abu Mousa?

Marwan got through to Yasmina.

"Oh! Let me talk to her!"

It was a pleasure to hear Yasmina's agreeable voice. Om Mousa, Abu Mousa, Tayta — all were fine. Even Bahija, the maid! They had all moved to the summer house. No phone, of course. But they would be there, waiting.

And what of Kamel, her fiance, who had gone underground?

"*Wallah* he comes and goes," Yasmina said.

She rang off. "At last I get to see the summer house!"

"I could have told you they were there."

That was last night. Warmth of morning did little to improve Khalil's mood. He slid into the driver's seat of Marwan's VW and waited. Marwan had given him the keys.

It was time to go.

She slid into the seat beside him. Samir was in the back. They were waiting for Marwan.

Khalil had refused, at first, Marwan's offer of his car. But Marwan had insisted. He was going to Beirut anyway, to Barbir Hospital. To reach Khalil's parents' mountain home would require only a short detour. Besides, Marwan had hurt his arm and couldn't drive.

A crunch of footsteps, the squeak of the car door ... and then Marwan, with a breathless, "Sorry," squeezed himself into the back and settled in with his knees against Khalil's seat. "Sure you can manage the VW?" he asked, cradling Samir's leg.

Khalil squinted into the rear view mirror. "If the engine holds up; I can drive."

"Stop first at Ein el Hilweh, will you? Dr. Fawaz ... "

"Bleeding wounded?" Khalil interrupted.

"Dysentery."

Through Sidon's gritty downtown, humming with optimistic commerce ... Emaciated men tending dusty storefronts ... Dead neon ... English capital-letters obliterating graceful Arabic script.

Near Ein el Hilweh the land looked empty. Lacerated. Skeletal trees, mange-like bushes edged the settlement. No laughter emanated. The thrum of insects drifted on the wind. So did scratchy sounds of old recordings, dead musicians, replayed endlessly like passages in a holy book. Grief-stricken old women stood in the roads. Girls in blue uniforms wandered to school.

"I won't be a minute," Marwan said.

Khalil tapped the steering wheel impatiently. He stopped the drumming when Marwan emerged from the clinic and returned, accompanied by Ramadan Zawq. Sherifa came, and the three exchanged unhurried farewells beside the car.

Zawq, raffish, leaned above her window. "Why don't you stay?" he asked Camellia. He smiled, displaying pitted teeth above the stubbly beard. "You could teach English to the girls."

She smiled at the thought; then warmth flooded her face as she realized that Khalil, white-knuckled, had started the car. She couldn't answer. She could only call out thanks and good-bys over the engine's rattling vibration.

Khalil had already thrust the VW into gear and rammed through the angles of a three-point turn. Cursing, he jolted through the spun dust, relaxing only when wheels glided onto paved road, the straight road to Beirut.

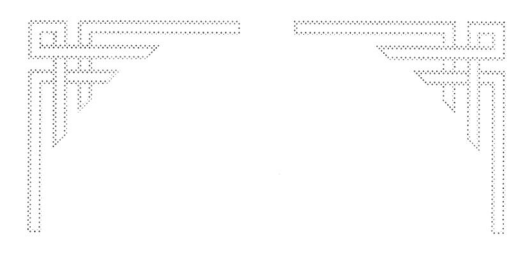

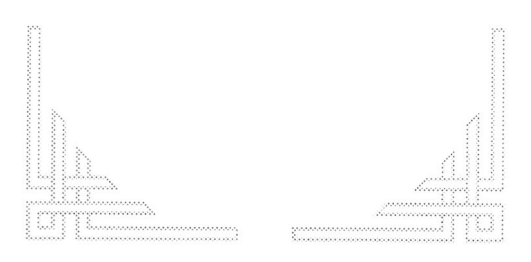

10

Garden of the Mad

While the heart weeps at what it has lost, the spirit laughs at what it has found.

Arab proverb

The road stripped north along the coast, slicing between Mount Lebanon and the sea. Camellia watched the opening gash.

The mountains had chased them all the way from Sidon. Fruit trees and olives clung to the slopes. Patches of wildflowers plummeted from the summit like spring fashions.

Camellia sighed, watching the snow-swept pines shimmering in the north.

"Do you remember?" She patted Khalil's hand, which lay on the gearshift. "You always said Lebanon was beautiful in the spring."

He nodded slightly.

"Too bad the cedars couldn't survive," she continued dreamily. Grandly: "Deforestation is a symbol of the fall of empires."

Khalil stared at the road ahead, his profile elegant against the sea. "You are hopelessly romantic."

Marwan sat in the back seat, supporting Samir's leg.

Camellia skewed herself to face him.

"The Pharaohs knew the value of the cedars, didn't they, Marwan? By using the sap, they preserved mummies."

Marwan glanced at Samir's closed eyes. Then he nodded. "Every time an Egyptian died, the Lebanese made money."

Camellia laughed in delight.

"The beauty of Lebanon!" she exclaimed. "The sheen of the eastward mountains in the sun — "

Satisfaction softened Marwan's bearded face as he gazed at unpolished rock.

"*Hane'en lemen lahu marqad anzeh fe Lubnan,*" he quoted in guttural rhythm.

Camellia understood just enough to laugh incredulously. "A Lebanese goat's bed? That can't be right. Such a beautiful statement couldn't be ludicrous."

"That is what I get for trying to teach you Arabic," Khalil said irritably. "Mangled poetry."

Painstakingly, she tried to translate. "*Anzeh* means goat ... *marqad* means bed...."

"'Lucky the person who owns a goat's bed in Lebanon.'" Khalil put the words swiftly together.

Marwan shook his head. "Literal translation won't work. The goat's *marqad* isn't *exactly* her bed: it's the patch of earth just large enough to cradle her in sleep. We feel ... we *feel* about our land — even a tiny piece...."

Camellia, flush with recognition, interrupted: "Kahlil Gibran! It sounds so like him." She glanced at Khalil, silhouetted against the grey glitter of the sea. "'Love is the lover's eyes,'" she began, "and the spirit's wine, and the heart's....'"

"'Nourishment.'" Marwan picked up the verse. Gruffly: "'Love is a rose. Its heart opens at dawn and the virgin kisses the blossom and places it upon her breast....'"

Khalil loosened his tie. "Cloying," he said. "No wonder Gibran died penniless."

Camellia rolled down the window, feeling suddenly stuffy. "His books sell millions in America."

"But not *here*. And he did not speak of *marqad anzeh*. That was Mikhail Naimy."

Camellia turned to Marwan for confirmation. "Naimy?"

"Gibran's best friend."

"And a much better writer," Khalil countered. "Although, Gibran did say one thing worth remembering." He glanced at the rear view mirror. "'You have your Lebanon, I have mine.'"

Camellia looked from Khalil to Marwan.

"I think I've finally found my Lebanon," she said. "I think I finally understand. Remember, Marwan, when you told me that, to the Phoenicians, the mountains are the gods? American slopes are bigger. Greener. But these..."

"Mount Lebanon." Marwan made it an endearment. His jaw tightened and he continued: "Before the Bible, Lebanon was Eden. Mount Lebanon rises from Palestine to touch Syria and Turkey. In places it is delicate and bare; in others, thickly forested and rugged. The Litani feeds Jezzine's umbrella pines. But elsewhere, naked rocks preside at peaks undressed by sudden driving rains, so desolate the birds can't reach them...."

Camellia sighed, remembering the line in Jeremiah, and the Rev. Millet's hushed tone, reciting it: "'Will the snow of Lebanon ever fall from the rock of the wilderness?'"

Khalil glowered. An oncoming Mercedes truck roared past, honking, pitching dust.

Marwan was still in the mountains. "Look at that barren slope." He pointed to the north. "Too steep for the goats. Yet an olive grows ... virtually without soil. Young. Yet so determined to live."

"You can say the same of nettles," Khalil said.

Ignoring him, Marwan continued. "And look how close to the sea. A writer once called these slopes 'drowned mountains.' Homes hang, suspended on cliffs; roads are virtually chiseled out of rock. Then, in Beirut, Mount Lebanon eases back...."

Khalil had been waiting: Beirut was *his*. "Beirut is one-third the size of Ann Arbor, Camellia, with ten times as many people. Now that's urban density."

Marwan checked Samir's leg, elevating it slightly. Then he pointed to the mountains grown lush with trees.

"See the clustered villas with their porticoes and Italian marble, Camellia? Summer homes for the affluent. We're about 20 kilometers from the city, wouldn't you say, Khalil?"

Khalil grunted assent.

Camellia settled back in the smudged seat and contemplated the land. "At last I can say I've seen the Lebanon of Fayrouz."

"Fayrouz — now there is an idea." Khalil punched a cassette into the tape deck and mashed at the unfamiliar buttons, snarling the tape in mid-song. It screeched twice before flowing into the melody of love. Khalil exhaled.

Lightly, Camellia pinched Khalil's cheek. "You're like the mad king soothed by Mozart."

"Oh?" He glanced at her from the corner of his eye.

Marwan had been listening; wistfulness misted his eyes. Off-tune, he translated, his deep voice blotting out the melody:

O love, over there on top of the mountain
We have a tent, waiting for us to visit in an amorous night
Stars shower its slopes with kisses, as clouds kneel at its rims
O love, we have a tent, a vase and two white roses
And together we shall be at the edge of the sky.

Khalil raised the volume.

"I thought only nomads lived in tents," Camellia said brightly.

"Arabs never outgrow them," Marwan answered. "Though many Lebanese prefer villas."

"My father's home is 40 years old," Khalil said. "Sturdy. Comfortable — hardly a villa."

Without warning, he veered onto a side road that arced into the mountain.

The sharp turn jostled Samir, who yelped.

"Careful," said Camellia. "You'll wake him."

"Sorry," Khalil said curtly. "If this were a Mercedes...."

"The VW will make it." Marwan kept his fingers firmly on Samir's leg. "She just needs a steady hand."

"Where are we?" Groggy, Samir raised his head.

"Almost there." Khalil forced the VW into a near-vertical climb; engine whining, it zigzagged past back-yard apple trees and tiny terraced fields where plump grapes dangled from vines. The slope grew too steep for all but a few junipers and pines — and the occasional cedar: majestic as kings.

"If you squint, you can see it." Khalil pointed to a clearing barely visible through the trees. "House of my birth."

Camellia shivered. "It's chilly. Like Michigan."

Khalil rounded a corner, spiraling the VW upward, and momentarily the house disappeared.

"There!" he said as the house came into view.

A cordon of cedars pressed protectively around the walls of burnished pink stone and showered the roof with soft needles.

"An enchanted forest! I feel like Snow White!"

Another curve put them at the clearing. Khalil stomped the brake, stalling the engine. "Just don't go looking for a prince."

"Khalil! You're safe!" Violet flew out of the house, dark curls flying.

Angela came flying behind. "Camellia! Khalil! And poor dear Samir! Oh! Be careful!"

Marwan eased Samir onto a blanket to create a litter, which Khalil, striding around the car, grasped at one end. Abu Mousa, who came running from the house, took the other end. Marwan stood cradling Samir's head. Grunting, they tested Samir's weight, adjusting blanket to limbs.

Om Mousa stopped in the doorway just long enough to see Khalil safe. Her face registered quick joy. Then she hurried away.

By the time they carried Samir to the front room, she had spread the day bed with sheets.

Tayta stood holding a quilt.

Camellia, dimly aware of activity and chatter, stood absorbing the scent and feel of mountain and home. The wind's whisper invested the airy stone cottage with quickness and life. Everyone exclaimed over Samir. Tayta covered him. Om Mousa revived him with sips of water.

When he was settled and comfortable, Om Mousa turned to Khalil. It was as if she had never seen him before. Repeated kisses ... hugs ... torrents of phrases and words. She spoke in the lavish poetic language Arab mothers use to address their babies: *Ya habibi. Ya a'ne. Ya rouhi.* My darling. My eyes. My soul.

Tayta did the same. Then the embraces spread like ripples on a pond to include Camellia. And Marwan, warmed and welcomed without encumbrance. Khalil introduced him, at length. Presumably the introduction outlined family connections and identified religion, summed up the landmarks of a life — all the indicators that would give Abu Mousa, Om Mousa, and Tayta the criteria by which to judge him.

When they spoke, they told him they were grateful for his help. Rituals of word and touch. A heady outpouring of emotion: spontaneous, unbridled by thought.

Violet, for once, was speechless.

Angela was euphoric, slightly taken aback. She gave Camellia a quick kiss, hugged Khalil, and shook Marwan's hand. "Oh, isn't it wonderful?" Then she launched into a charming stream of incoherences, concluding:

" — and with Khalil rescued in time for April nuptials!"

"Oh, Muzz!" Violet regained her voice. "Always looking for a happy ending."

Camellia settled down beside Khalil's grandmother.

"Tayta..." she murmured. Tayta's intelligent eyes shone puzzled beneath her head cover.

Where to begin?

Sheepish, Camellia reached into her Nefertiti bag.

"I borrowed these. I'm sure you missed them. Somehow I believed them infused with — with your *baraka*."

Tayta did not respond to the sound of Arabic. Maybe it didn't sound Arabic, the way Camellia said it. It was a deep and guttural word.

"You see, now I understand the concept. At least, I *think* I do. It's not grace. Not charisma. Baraka."

How much did Tayta understand?

"There's no other word like it. I guess the closest we have to it is the American Indian word: medicine. A great, indwelling force, a spiritual energy.... Baraka. I'm happy I learned it." The mother-of-pearl glittered. She handed the string of worry beads back to Tayta.

Tayta looked suddenly wistful. Momentarily, she kneaded the beads between her fingers. Then she returned the string to Camellia, pressing it back into Camellia's hand. An accompanying murmur of Arabic came like the steady rustle of a breeze.

"Are you sure?" Camellia asked. "But they're yours."

Tayta grew insistent, almost agitated. Camellia, bewildered, could only guess at the words, though the depth of emotion was unmistakable.

Marwan had been watching. Unobtrusively, he translated:

"There is nothing she owns she would not give to Khalil. Or to you." Then he smiled, raising his hands expressively, accurately interpreting the old woman's body language as well. "What are beads?"

Camellia's fingers tightened around the mother of pearl. She grinned, partly out of foolishness, partly in awe. Lacking knowledge of Arabic, she couldn't engage in ritual, couldn't respond.

"What do I say?" she asked Marwan.

"You don't have to say a thing."

Angela, hovering, tapped Camellia on the shoulder.

"What about Samir? Is he all right?"

Camellia emerged from the moment. Tayta would understand. It was time to be practical. "A compound fracture," she said. "Mild shock. Marwan says he'll be fine."

"A healing dose of Aziza's brew may help." The kitchen was only a few steps away. Angela dipped a cup of steaming broth from a kettle. Her voice came from afar. "I don't know what this is," she called out. "It has parsley, rice — God knows what else."

She brought the cup for Om Mousa to serve.

Om Mousa, damp-faced, took it gratefully. She held the cup to Samir's lips.

Khalil sniffed appreciatively. "Chicken soup."

"Well, yes, but...." Angela shrugged, breezy and ready for a change of subject, as always when she had misunderstood something. "Your mother's a wizard, you know, Khalil. The potions, the teas she makes! And I just love her given name: Aziza. You should use it always, Aziza. You see, Camellia? She understands. We don't need language."

Violet giggled. "Muzz speaks veerrry sloowwly. When that doesn't work, she shouts. As if Khalil's mother were simply hard of hearing."

Om Mousa, uncomprehending, supported Samir's head.

Samir swallowed more broth.

"Whatever. Anyway, it works." Angela clasped her abdomen. "My stomach was killing me. Montezuma's revenge — what is it in this part of the world? Mohammed's revenge? I'll tell you, when Aziza made me a pot of — can you believe it? — chamomile tea, she gave it some outlandish name..."

"*Baboonich?*" Camellia asked.

"Harvested, plucked off the mountain, then boiled with sugar and water."

Violet moaned theatrically. "How do you spell relief? B - A - B - O - O - N — ."

"S - H - U - S - H !" spelled Camellia. All the baraka in the world wouldn't be enough to give her the patience to deal with Violet.

"But, Camellia, she served it in a glass." Angela had long ago learned to tune out the squabbling of the girls. She furrowed her forehead. " — a *glass* glass. It scorched my fingertips."

"That's how the Arabs drink tea."

"How odd!"

Khalil smiled disarmingly. "When I returned to Beirut from my first trip to London, I bought my mother a china service. But I have never been able to persuade her to use it."

"Maybe she wants to see what she's drinking," Marwan offered.

Samir was striving to be alert. But his head kept lolling as the effect of fresh doses of pain-killers took hold.

Om Mousa plumped the pillows around him, watching him sink into sleep. Momentarily, she relaxed. But when the room began to buzz with conversation, she grew tense, and Camellia knew she was remembering her responsibilities: the guests to be fed, the dinner to be served. Bahija was not here, after all. Her family had taken her to Damascus.

"*Ijlesi*." From somewhere, Camellia found the courage to use words she could easily recognize but had never before tried to pronounce. She put her hand on Om Mousa's shoulder. "*Ana bahadder al-tawleh*." She stuttered and was unable to finish. "Oh, hell. I'll have to say it in English: Let me set the table. You've done enough. Sit with your sons."

Om Mousa seemed to understand.

Khalil was sitting between her and Tayta.

Marwan spoke in Arabic with Abu Mousa.

Angela watered a wilted pothos.

Violet lost herself in a Sweet Valley High romance.

It was quiet in the kitchen.

The scent of cedar wafted through the windows, riding the hot kitchen air and mingling with fragrance of crushed spices. Om Mousa, anticipating Khalil, had prepared a feast: stuffed grape leaves, rice, grilled steak, okra and tomatoes.

Camellia smiled to herself. Faced with cataclysm, people still observed the little rituals, the schedules of socializing, of cleaning and organizing, baking and eating. Nuclear holocaust could occur, and survivors would cling to routine. Small habits were the hardest to break.

She opened the oven and found chicken roasted with *sumac*. She transferred the *waraq dawali* to a plate, taking care not to rip the tender leaves. She heaped *laban* into a bowl. She garnished the platter of rice with the toasted *snobar*.

Everything was done.

The pot of sweetened water was ready for heating. She found some cinnamon bark and crushed it, letting it filter through her fingers into the pot.

Later she would measure out the tea leaves.

Outside, the wind rustled in the pines.

Om Mousa spoke in a murmur to Khalil. Her voice was like a zephyr: placating, endearing.

Tayta's voice broke in: querulous and quick. Uncompromising. Scorching as a khamsin blown in from the Sahara.

Khalil responded at intervals, defensively.

I'll be damned, Camellia thought. The old lady's giving him hell.

"The wisdom of the old and the brashness of the young," Dr. Elias had said, "this is what ensures the survival of the tribe."

She smiled, and at the same time bit her lip to keep tears from welling. From where did sadness spring? She inhaled deeply: the fertile, aromatic smell of the woods, of bracken and wet moss. It teemed with the scent of crawling things, unsubtle decaying things. Into this flourishing primitive environment Om Mousa had injected some order: she had brought with her the potted zinnias, the tea roses from Beirut. They sat on the windowsill, silky and delicate, like parakeets.

Camellia sighed and turned to the stove, where the tea-water had come to a boil.

At dinner, everyone sat on the floor, the Americans awkwardly, the Arabs at ease. Summer homes had scant furniture, but there were plenty of large dusty pillows to lean on. There was nothing to do but drink Amstel beer and pick at the food. A common language eluded them.

Camellia ate a piece of roasted chicken, purple and pungent with *sumac*. Then she wiped her fingers and drank another beer. What the hell, she thought. "Every rainstorm starts with a few drops." She asked a question, breaking the silence.

"How did you get out of Beirut?" She gestured eloquently, leaning toward Khalil's parents, acting like a caricature of herself, as if exaggerated movements would help them understand.

They answered swiftly, speaking at once, happy to be engaged in conversation. Marwan, translating, described their final harrowing hours in the city. Tayta added an occasional word for emphasis.

Shortly after Camellia's and Samir's departure, Ain Rumaneh had become a serious combat zone. Bahija, the Moroccan maid, had fled with her sisters to Syria, a less dicey country. Abu Mousa, Om Mousa and Tayta stayed huddled in the basement — this was after Angela and Violet had departed, ostensibly for the airport.

By nightfall, the army had evacuated the neighborhood — using armored vehicles as if they were city buses.

Gathering their belongings, Abu Mousa, Om Mousa and Tayta climbed aboard. And just in time. The evacuation ended abruptly, they later learned. Private militias commandeered the tanks. Private militias confiscated tanks from the army.

Riding by tank to the outskirts of the city ... from there, hailing a cab, they traveled from Beirut to the mountains.

All this relayed matter-of-fact, with little regret, no perceptible sense of grievance. Camellia wondered if Abu Mousa thought about the red Mercedes, whose hulk had never been recovered. It couldn't have been repaired. And, anyway, cars weren't useful in a crossfire. But men miss their cars, and Camellia wondered why he didn't mention the loss.

"Before the 'Ain Rumaneh incident,'" said Marwan, "fighting would break out, then slacken. People would draw lines, chalk up scores, almost as if it were a game."

After the Ain Rumaneh massacre, the rules changed. Now streets were blackened and surreal. Fighters ran, crouching, from building to building. Men in sombreros or stetsons, berets, *kaffiyehs* or hoods restlessly congregated, rifles slung across their shoulders. Barefoot women pleaded for help. And always, shooting emanated from rooftops, indiscriminate. Marksmen (who were they?) squatted on balconies, embracing their automatic rifles, fresh clips taped ready for reloading. Everyone was a target.

"I saw a road sign, posted by the traffic department. It said, 'Sniper,'" Marwan finished softly. He toyed absently with his spoon. "It won't be easy, getting back to Barbir Hospital. I'll let you off at the airport, Angela. If you and Violet can be ready by morning. Assuming the planes are flying."

"But we can't leave Camellia here alone. The fighting ..." Unable to organize an objection, Angela nibbled at a grape leaf.

"Be realistic, Mother. What else can you do?"

"Well, everyone could come with *us*." Angela's sweeping gesture encompassed Khalil's family: her future in-laws. "We'll petition the U.S. Embassy for political asylum!"

"Khalil's family can't just uproot."

"Why not? For a visit," Angela suggested. "For the wedding. Ann Arbor is lovely in June."

"But this is April. Anyway, it's out of the question. We ..." Camellia faltered, dimly aware that if she left Lebanon, she would leave Khalil.

Incredulous: "Surely you don't intend to stay?"

"Why not?" Khalil had put down his bread. "We are safe, despite the warnings of alarmists. Camellia! We could have a mountain ceremony ... music ... feasting ... we could do it now. A wedding to remember ... forever." His voice seemed an octave too high. "You always wanted rings on your fingers and a belly dancer at your wedding."

Marwan wiped a trace of *laban* from his beard. "Angela and Violet simply must leave. Lebanon is on the verge of civil war."

"I've never seen a war." Violet adjusted the bracelet she had bought somewhere along the way. It was gold, shaped like a snake, and she wore it on her upper arm. "Except on television."

"You will not see one here." Confident, Khalil swallowed a stuffed grape leaf. "The Palestinians have fought themselves into oblivion. The army will finish them off."

"I've had it with you." Camellia slammed her fork to the table, losing her resolve to avoid a quarrel. "You've been kidnapped. We've ... you've ... what does it take to make you aware?"

Khalil shrugged. He looked at her. Softly: "Nothing will affect us. Nothing will change."

"It already has."

Angela's hands fluttered like stray nymphalids on a bush. "You're still getting married, aren't you?"

"I ... " Camellia said. "We ... "

Khalil's face was white.

She added in a rush, speaking only to him: "Your family always wanted you to marry a Maronite. Not an American."

"I chose you."

"Not an American?" Angela was aghast. She had never been chauvinistic, but overseas travel has a strange side-effect: it turns even the most mild patriot into a fanatical flag-waver. "Your father would spin in his grave. Aziza — is this true?"

Om Mousa stood, teapot in hand, poised to pour. When she heard Khalil's translation, her expression became a look of dismay. Her words were hurried but firm. Her tone said they were inarguable.

"'My son loves Camellia.'

"'She saved his life,'" Khalil continued, vindicated. "'Of course she must marry him.'" He shrugged ingenuously, palms up. "Her words. Not mine."

"I said I need ... time."

"You risked your life for me. You went to unfamiliar places. To dangerous places." It was the first time he had acknowledged her effort. "You dealt with — with all sorts of people," he continued, glancing at Marwan. "Now you want time?"

Violet patted Khalil's hand consolingly. "It must be a terrible shock. Camellia's usually dull as a dromedary, I know. Now she's a changeling. But don't worry. She'll get over it."

Camellia bit her tongue. She looked at the faces, at the expressions of dear ones and new friends, hoping to see a glimmer of comprehension, a sign someone understood.

Khalil inclined his head.

His parents sat quietly, patient but puzzled.

Violet sat fascinated, sensitive to escalating tension; she muttered: "Better than *All My Children!*"

Angela bit down; her teeth caught the tines of the fork. "Dash!" she said.

Tayta nodded in sympathy.

For some strangely infuriating reason, Marwan looked amused.

Angela sighed in capitulation.

Marwan, decisive, crossed his arms pragmatically. "You can't very well get married tonight."

"Why not?" Khalil asked.

Camellia stood up. "I'm going to pack."

Tayta raised a gnarled hand.

She was listening — tilting her head, focusing her eyes to the right, off into the distance, as if she were attuned to the pulse of the mountain.

Camellia sensed rather than heard reverberations. They were not quite audible. Vibrations intensified, like a descending swarm, and Camellia recognized the thump of goat-skin drums. Louder. And other sounds: the tribal ululations of women, yearning and vocal, insensate with passion that was part pleasure, part anguish.

Violet shivered.

"My god, Geronimo!" Angela exclaimed. She trotted to the window and peered anxiously outside. "Have you tribes in Lebanon?"

The drums throbbed in primitive concert. Honking added to the clamor as cars, in procession, wound up and around the mountain. Their headlights set the stone walls of the cottage aglow.

Khalil smiled bitterly. "A wedding," he said.

Then the headlamps vanished, leaving only the pink flush of the sunset, a vivid violet against deep green.

****

Angela's trunk weighted the room like the blocks of Baalbek's trilithon.

Camellia pried open the lid and began to stuff in her clothes. The mohair sweater. The things Om Mousa had salvaged from the flat. The things that were indisputably hers.

He gave a little sigh. The green frothy dress still hung in Khalil's closet in Beirut. I think you're crazy to give him up," Violet said.

Crisply: "He'll forget me."

"But how on earth will you ever forget him?" Breathlessly: "He's one of a kind." Violet lay on the bed, staring at the ceiling. "Although, come to think of it, Ramadan Zawq was awfully cute, too. In a *Soldier of Fortune* kind of way."

"Since when do you read *Soldier of Fortune*?"

Ignoring them, Angela said wistfully: "But you were so much in love."

"That's the hell of it. I still care about him." Camellia buried her sandals beneath one of Angela's hats. "But I've got my feet on dry land, while Khalil is sailing around on some Phoenician ship. He can't put into port long enough to enjoy the charm ... the *baraka* of his people. To him, I'm just a compass indicating 'West.'"

"Maybe he's just macho," Angela suggested. "Maybe he'll outgrow it."

"Oh, Mother. What about his harebrained scheme to partition Lebanon?"

"I thought *that* part made sense. Why shouldn't Beirut belong to the Christians? After all, they've always lived there."

Camellia exhaled in exasperation. "So do Moslems. Kurds, Armenians, Palestinians ... "

Angela fluttered her hands. "I thought we were talking about a man — not a country."

Violet nodded. "If Scarlett had objected to Rhett's politics, Margaret Mitchell never would have written *Gone With The Wind*."

"Hunh?" asked Angela.

"Scarlett had her faults. But at least she knew the value of the land. Anyway, Lebanon is different." Camellia wrestled down the lid. It popped back open. "Khalil is different. He wasn't straight with me. I still don't know who he was working for. I don't think he'll ever say. What would you have done, Mother, if Dad hadn't told you everything?"

"I never expected him to. There are things I still don't know about his early days in Europe...."

Violet sat on the lid. Camellia snapped the latches shut.

"I expect ... " her voice trailed off. Then, stronger: "I want honesty. Passion. I always wanted to be the woman Beethoven wrote Fuer Elise for...."

She dropped wearily on the bed next to Angela. She rested her head against the gentle sanctuary of Angela's small, soft bosom and murmured: "I love Lebanon too much to ever live in it halfway."

Awkwardly, Angela patted her head. Her voice grew maternal. "You're such an unforgiving generation," she said.

****

A soft knock at the door startled them all. Standing there, almost apologetically it seemed, was a middle-aged man, obviously American. He said it was urgent that he speak with Camellia Kessler.

He told her he was from the American embassy and wished to talk to her about Professor Jerry Hurst of American University. She took him to an adjoining room, followed by Khalil. Without understanding why, she asked Dr. Marwan to join them.

Inside the visitor introduced himself as Lucas Robbins, Beirut station chief of the Central Intelligence Agency. He showed them credentials to underscore the introduction.

"I have bad news, I am afraid," he began. "Professor Hurst was abducted two hours after you and he had lunch. Forty-eight hours later his body was found in the trunk of a partially burned car. He had been beaten. He was garroted. Can you tell me what the meeting was about?"

Fear she had never known threatened Camellia with a garrote of its own, followed at once with a rush of guilt that forced from her a small cry of pain.

"I ... Khalil was ..." she began. Khalil stood there ashen and trembling, a pathetic figure she had never dreamed she'd see. It was rock-like Marwan who moved close to cup her elbow in his hand.

"Professor Hurst told her he would try to find out who had abducted Khalil," Dr.

Marwan spoke into the silence. "She never heard from him again. Now we know why."

"You are marked." The CIA man looked directly at Camellia. "The embassy will give you protection until tomorrow when you must be on that plane with your mother and sister. Losing Hurst was a personal loss to me. What a waste," he said with a withering glance at Khalil. Without waiting for a reply, he bowed ever so slightly and turned on his heel, to go as quickly as he had come.

Sobbing, Camellia broke away and ran to her room to finish packing. Angela and Violet knew from her face it was no time for questions, they only knew something terrible had happened.

****

"Are you ready?" Khalil asked.

His gaze was probing and equivocal. He wore strain like an altered suit. He had lost weight. His bone structure was a gaunt blueprint. His cheekbones poked out like chicken wings.

She had expected arrogance. Indignation. Off-handedness. But vulnerability —
So much harder to resist.

She plopped down onto a dusty pillow.

Tayta sat like a buffer between them. Marwan had gone out. The house seemed empty.

"Look — don't worry about my things in Beirut. I haven't left behind anything of consequence."

"How can you leave?" He bit his upper lip. "If I had known you would reject politics..."

She opened her mouth to argue but felt Tayta's hand on her arm.

She closed her eyes, just for an instant. "How could you not have known?" she murmured. Then: "You never worked as an engineer. You weren't even looking for work, were you?"

"I hate engineering! Road-building! Concrete slabs and ignorant Pakistani laborers — did you expect me to devote my life to that?"

"You chose civil engineering. Why?"

"The government chose it for me. I was on scholarship, remember."

"You never told me how you felt about engineering. Or, for that matter, how you felt about me."

"No more secrets," he said softly.

The cool pronouncement must have cost him. Momentarily, she wavered. How easy it would be, to let passion ignite and swell, to hear him say, "None of it matters," his reassurances washing over her like the Sidonian surf. Did she love him? Or did beauty seduce her: his white skin, delicate as the creamy skin Tayta kept hidden from the sun, black lashes framing liquid eyes the color of a wizard's smoke?

He extended graceful fingers awaiting her touch.

"I love you. Enough to die for you."

"Enough to live for me?" Camellia, clumsy, stood up.

Challenging: "You are running away."

She edged toward the door. The forest lay beyond the cottage. The conjuring sun transfixed the landscape; shafts of rose light filtered through branches.

Abu Mousa, sitting cross-legged beneath a tree, smoked a water pipe. He looked dusty but, for once, happy. He wore loose trousers and a fez.

He passed the stem of the *nargeila* to Marwan.

Camellia looked back at Khalil. "I wish I could think of something wise and appropriate to say ... "

Now Tayta's firm but gentle hand was on Khalil's arm, and Camellia knew he would not follow her.

She took the path that spiraled upward through the trees, her rubber soles thudding softly on the earth, over rocks, on flat ground, upward, so high the wedding beats and cries advanced in a shimmer of sound, an oasis of sound ...

The path narrowed to a faint trail where the trees converged and the light grew strangled. How massive they were! A hundred feet high. A thousand years old. How insignificant she was beside them. From memory, half-forgotten lines of Persian poetry —

"And that inverted Bowl they call the Sky,
Whereunder crawling cooped we live and die —"

She stopped, suddenly, panting, smelling the damp moss, loam and salt; and stood awash with the euphoria of the utopist's vision, of discovery. She had entered, however fleetingly, the Lebanon of Kahlil Gibran. He saw dreams in the trees, hope in the rocks, solitude in the flowers.

More poetry, from half-forgotten classes, not Persian, but as romantic as the Rubiyat —

"Silent as the sleeve-worn stone
Of casement ledges where the moss has grown — "

She heard someone humming. A male voice. She recognized the tune: a Fayrouz melody. The song they had heard earlier today. Khalil? Did she love him?

The voice — raspy, off-key — battered rather than sang the melody. The effect was fascinating against the background throb of the primordial drums.

Marwan.

He broke off, seeing her.

"You shouldn't wander alone."

"I came looking for 'the edge of the sky'."

"I understand from your mother that camellias require slightly acid soil."

"Yes, but once they take root, nothing can kill them."

She smiled up at him. Only yesterday, Marwan's concern and protectiveness would have been an irritation if not a threat. Strange, how today she did not resent him. She was beginning to understand him, his thousand complex and dynamic attitudes and behaviors, his welling tribal consciousness, deeply rooted commitments ... and other things which she would probably never fully understand but could only accept.

"White roses — "

"You're shivering." Wind-whipped curls framed the rugged face, rescued from lack of symmetry by affectionate expression, engaging smile. "Take my jacket."

Oddly disappointed, she slung it around her shoulders like a cloak. It smelled of smoke from the *nargeila*.

"I guess roses don't grow here."

"Nothing grows here but oaks and pines."

"Not even the crimson anemone? The flower you told Angela about? The 'wounds of Na'aman?'"

"But remember — the lovers spent only half the year in love. The other half, they lived in utter deprivation."

She gave a little sigh. "Beirut was an idyll. I'll never recapture it."

"Then you — "

"I needed to believe in my Valentino."

"You're young," he said quickly. "Here, even saplings grow in rock."

"I don't feel young." She ran her hand along the veiny bark. A lizard darted away. The sky was barely visible though the web of trees as dusk hovered between darkness and light. The stars seemed close. "When will the killing stop?"

He gave a sigh that, had she not been looking, she would have mistaken for a sound of pleasure. "They say of Lebanon, 'God gave the Garden of Eden to those who are mad.'"

Thoughtfully, she drew the jacket tightly around her, letting its soft leather warm her. "Will you go back to Beaufort? Will you stay there, always?"

"Always ... But I won't give up my work in Beirut."

"It must be nice to know where you'll be — always." An idea had begun to form in her mind. "On your way south — will you drop me off in Sidon?"

"Sidon? But Sidon is ... "

"I know. I can teach at the refugee camp. It would be sort of like Peace Corps work. Temporary but fulfilling."

His eyes were luminous and speculative in the dusk. "You're needed elsewhere." He added softly, "South of the Litani. My mother's cottage — it's empty — "

"I'd scandalize the *fellaheen* — living alone."

He stood straighter. "You could ... "

She placed her fingers on his lips, effectively stopping the suggestion. "I've outgrown my Valentino. But I'm not ready for Omar Sharif."

Marwan brushed her fingertips with his lips.

The wind whispered through the cedars, fresh and ageless, dewy, the new and verdant replacing everything crisped, everything sere.

The trees melted into black.

"It is said time rides on the winds of the desert," he whispered. "We can let it bring us to our tent."

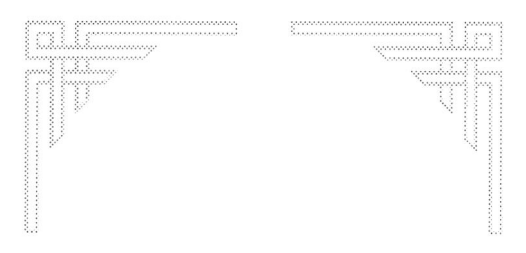

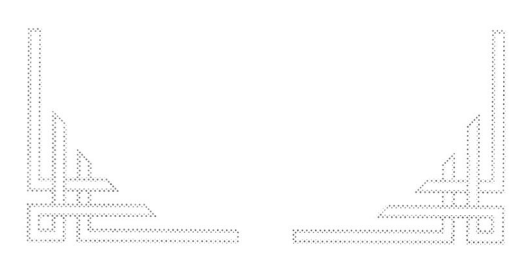

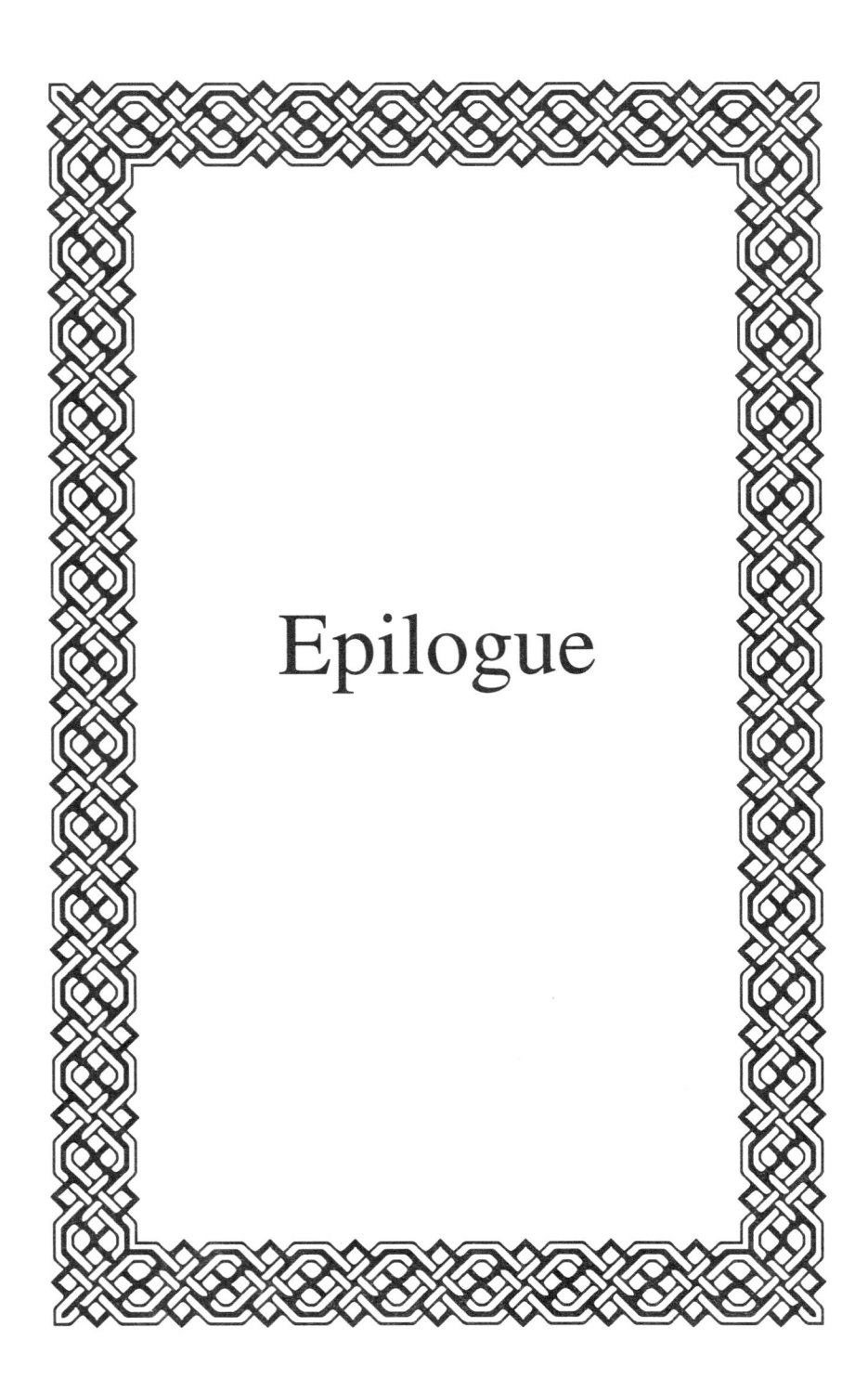

Epilogue

A once-beautiful city now lies in rubble. Twenty years of fighting have devastated it. Its people, who once survived tidal wave and earthquake, repelled Crusaders, resisted the Moslem *jihad*, endured the Ottomans and freed themselves of the colonial French, have fallen victim to themselves — the fate of all who cling to fatal visions.

But what a land that city ruled! From Jounieh's sparkling coast to the forbidding peaks of the Anti-Lebanon, this land, tucked into an eastern corner of the Mediterranean, had attracted the enlightened, the hedonistic, the chic. But it had also given refuge to the hermitic, the persecuted, the vanquished. The Christian Maronites who had blunted Mohammed's sword on Mount Lebanon could never accept, in the capital, Moslem rule. Nor could their Crusader-battering counterparts but resent the subsequent Christian leadership. Indeed, Lebanon's national covenant promoted such hotly defended divisions. When, in 1970, the Palestinians fled, humiliated, from Jordan and swelled Lebanon's refugee population in the south, they shared space with Lebanon's inhospitable Druze — whose religion neither sought nor allowed converts. Elsewhere in Lebanon, Sunnis, Alawites and other obscure minorities smoldered under resentments unique to them. Only the Greek Orthodox seemed to remain neutral.

The beautiful city paid. When Israel decimated south Lebanon's cities and Palestinian shelters, it gave the flaccid Lebanese army another chance to be impotent. It also inspired the private militias — under private command — to rearm and regroup. (Each new killing justified the next: in a particularly heinous episode of sectarian violence, Bashir Gemayel and his men wiped out a political rival: Tony Franjieh, 36. Franjieh's wife, their 3-year-old daughter, the maid, the chauffeur and the family dog were also killed.) Vengeance killings, snipings, car-bombs, kidnappings and assassinations became as common to Beirut as power outages and water shortages after Israeli air raids.

Complicating an already turbulent political scene, Israel had grown restive militarily, pounding the south and swelling Beirut with swarms of rootless Palestinians, by now thrice-refugeed. In 1975, Lebanon was, according to chronicler Jonathan C. Randal, "a land shot through with the accumulated paranoia of so many minorities."

But what a city it had been! Host to deposed monarchs, haven for spies, splinter groups, jet setters and journalists, Beirut was unique politically and socially, its laissez faire economic prosperity mystifying even the economists (the country had no natural resource but its people and the beauty of the land.) The elite population sipped chilled *arak* on sultry afternoons and slipped as easily into English and French as they did into designer fashions. In the dusty *souqs*, shopkeepers could determine nationalities with a swift, unerring glance. Ultimately, however, the people — by fighting political reform, embracing their archaic confessional system with its built-in factionalism, and making internecine hatred a national pastime — wrote the script for ruin. Like their free-wheeling Phoenician ancestors, they failed to develop a political consensus, to forge a national identity.

Bashir Gemayel once proclaimed (before becoming president-elect of Lebanon and thus having a measure of diplomacy thrust on him): "We will not rest until every true Lebanese has killed at least one Palestinian."

He was killed by a bomb blast before he could assume office.

His Moslem rivals were no less bellicose: Druze patriarch Kamal Jumblatt once spoke unguardedly — before *his* assassination — of his desire to "drink blood from Maronite skulls."

No one knows just what the Palestinian refugees who lived (and later died) in such camps as Sabra, Shatilla and Tel Zaatar would have said were they permitted the luxury of organized speech.

By revering tribal loyalties, by allowing *imam* and *zu'ama* to wield unconscionable amounts of power, the Lebanese achieved a state of anarchy described in *an-Nahar* by Ghassan Tueini: "The government does not exist, and whatever part of it exists has no authority, and whoever has authority is not the government." One bloody event led to the next. A West German filmmaker — shooting a Beirut script — had to turn away the numerous young Lebanese boys who offered to bring him, for the scenes requiring corpses, the real thing.

During the early '70s — the time of the kidnap-assassination of U.S. ambassador Francis Meloy and two other men at the crossing between East and West Beirut — U.S. foreign policy remained one of misread signals and missed opportunities. (Meloy's killers have never been found.) "We tried to keep all the balls in the air to distract attention," asserted an American diplomat at the time. "If we told the truth and said things were going to hell, they would only have gone to hell even faster."

In a more innocent era, bikini-clad Lebanese girls met U.S. marines on the beach during their 1958 landing. Not quite 25 years later, pro-Iranian Islamic fundamentalists exploded a U.S. bunker and the peace-keeping marines who slept inside.

Inevitably, Beirut had become an urban battleground — not just for its citizens but also for imported fanatics espousing unresolved causes.

Unfortunately, the tragedies failed to produce subsequent enlightenment: five years after Meloy's assassination, French ambassador Louis Delamare fell victim in the same neighborhood.

Seemingly random, apparently unrelated events set the global stage for Lebanon's civil war: Anwar Sadat made his historic trip to Jerusalem (a sally resulting in the collapse of proposed Geneva talks and Sadat's own later assassination.) At the same time, the Israelis — witnessing Palestinian genocide — proudly unveiled the jet fighter Kfir, or "Lion Cub," which could fly at twice the speed of sound and outperform even the Soviet M16-23. Elsewhere the last U.S. helicopters left Saigon and Richard Nixon sacrificed himself to Watergate.

And Lebanon? Lebanon was always beautiful in spring. But, in the spring of 1975, the Christian Phalangist massacre of Palestinians sparked a civil war. Biographer Randal returned to Beirut late that spring "during the early stages of what the Lebanese still refused to admit was a civil war ... [and] never had I seen an entire society collapse so thoroughly and so quickly."

Lebanon still struggles to recover, to recapture its spring. Winter comes and goes. The ice of Mount Lebanon melts to reveal — like Mount Hermon's fossil fish, preserved with mouths agape — the rubble of the city.

The night wore on. She did not sleep. She sat by the window. No thought made sense juxtaposed with any other thought. Why was her mind filled with static? Every few minutes she leaned over the counterpane to scan the surroundings.

The moon glittered on broken shards in the street where they lay as if the buildings had vomited glass.

Once, a car whipped around the corner, made a panic stop, screeched through a U-turn and pulled away.

The night was remarkable by its absence of sound. There was nothing to hear. No nocturnal wing-rubs of insects. No furtive scuffle of running feet. No abrupt shutting of a window.

Where was Khalil?